Praise for *Martyrs of the New Millennium*

"In this important and timely book, Robert Royal has not only completed the work begun in his magisterial work, *The Catholic Martyrs of the Twentieth Century*, but has also addressed a terrible gap in the world's and the Church's attention—the intense persecution of the Church in the first quarter of the twenty-first century. The lack of knowledge, and even lack of interest, in the persecution of Christians within the Church will not be excusable after reading Royal's book. It should be on the desk of every bishop in the Western world."

—Fr. Benedict Kiely, Founder, Nasarean.org

"Today, in many parts of the world, Christians are the most cruelly persecuted community of faith. Particularly in countries with a Christian tradition, Christians are socially discriminated against, professionally disadvantaged, and even legally persecuted and imprisoned because of their commitment to the unconditional dignity of man as an image of God. Therefore, the careful documentation of the modern global persecution of Christians that Robert Royal presents here is not just historical information. Rather, he shows the truth of faith in Christ, which is revealed in His disciples' courageous confession of Him right up to the final consequences of following the mocked, tortured, and crucified Son of God."

—Cardinal Gerhard Müller, Former Prefect of the Congregation for the Doctrine of the Faith

"With this compelling and moving book, Robert Royal continues his noble work as a witness to the witnesses: the martyrs who lived their Christian faith to the limits of love by following Christ through death into eternal life and imperishable glory. *The Martyrs of the New Millennium* is essential historical reading and rich spiritual fare."

—**George Weigel, Distinguished Senior Fellow,**
Ethics and Public Policy Center

"Many hoped that the collapse of the Soviet Union meant the end of communism and its victims. Robert Royal knows better and chronicles the ongoing sacrifices and deaths of those who dare to profess the faith in North Korea, Vietnam, Laos, and Cuba, as well as in Nicaragua and Venezuela. His focus on Communist China is both up-to-date and indispensable. *The Martyrs of the New Millennium* is a powerful reminder of communism's crimes—and the power of spiritual witness."

—**Elizabeth Spalding, Chairman,**
Victims of Communism Memorial Foundation

The Martyrs of the
New Millennium

Also by Robert Royal
from Sophia Institute Press:

Columbus and the Crisis of the West

Robert Royal

THE MARTYRS
OF THE NEW
MILLENNIUM

The Global Persecution of Christians in
the Twenty-First Century

SOPHIA INSTITUTE PRESS
Manchester, New Hampshire

Sophia Institute Press
Box 5284, Manchester, NH 03108
1-800-888-9344
www.SophiaInstitute.com

Sophia Institute Press® is a registered trademark of Sophia Institute.

hardcover ISBN 979-8-88911-504-5
ebook ISBN 979-8-88911-505-2

Library of Congress Control Number: 2025932289

First printing

Contents

Foreword

In late October 2024, Aid to the Church in Need (ACN) issued the report *Persecuted and Forgotten*, which examined the martyrdom and harassment of Catholics and other Christians over a two-year period (2022–2024) in eighteen countries of special concern. It was a time when the international community was preoccupied with recovering from the COVID pandemic and facing the outbreak of war in Ukraine and in Israel. It was also a period in which Christians were being ever more frequently subjected to prejudice, persecution, and violence, with virtually no notice by the world at large.

The figures are sobering. Among other findings, ACN discovered the following:

- ❖ In *Syria*, the Christian community was more than 1.5 million before the civil war started in 2011, *today Christians could be as few as 250,000.*
- ❖ In *Burkina Faso*, more than *two million people – about 10 percent of the country's population – have been displaced* because of the ongoing Islamist insurgency.
- ❖ The Burmese military stands accused of having *destroyed more than 200 places of worship,* including *85 churches.*

❖ In *China*, it is estimated that people imprisoned by the Chinese Communist Party ranges from *the low thousands to over 10,000*.

❖ In *Eritrea*, as of June 2024, *around 400 Christians are imprisoned — without trial — just because of their faith.*

❖ In *India*, *720 attacks or other incidents of persecution against Christians* were reported in 2023, up from 599 the year previous.

❖ In *Iran*, cases of Christians detained … rose from *59 in 2021 to 166 in 2023.*

❖ In *Iraq*, the Christian population declined sharply during the brutal regime of Daesh, currently consists of fewer than 200,000 *people* out of a population of more than 41,000,000; roughly 0.46 *percent*.

❖ *Nigeria* is ranked eighth in the 2024 Global Terrorism Index. Militant Fulani insurgents in the Middle Belt regularly committed massacres and other violent atrocities, *with a disproportionate number of attacks against Christians.*

❖ In *North Korea*, anyone identified as a Christian or even showing interest in Christianity or the Bible will almost certainly be considered *an enemy of the state.*

❖ In *Pakistan*, research found that *2,120 individuals had been accused of blasphemy between 1987 and 2022.*

❖ In *Saudi Arabia*, converting from Islam to Christianity is strictly prohibited and *converts can face honor killings.*[1]

---

[1] "Persecuted and Forgotten? 2024 Edition," Aid to the Church in Need, accessed December 19, 2024, https://acnuk.org/pf-edition -2024/?srsltid=AfmBOoq9GOkK3w1u4N7AYFgGn1X4kvuv CaWREe9SuPo2EC6rhjV8U_kN.

These are just a few of the reasons ACN believed it necessary to make a fuller study of Christian martyrdom and persecution in the twenty-first century. The Catholic Church is calling for the honoring of such Christian victims during the 2025 Jubilee Year. And it is right to make the record of such injustices a more prominent part of the Church's understanding of what's going on in the world. But it deserves greater attention in other contexts as well. What is happening to Christian believers today is not of interest solely to other Christians. It's essential to non-Christians and even nonbelievers who want to understand the world today—because Christian martyrdom and persecution is real and widespread. To ignore it is to fail to understand a quite shocking truth about our time.

We are happy that Dr. Robert Royal, whose landmark earlier volume *The Catholic Martyrs of the Twentieth Century* appeared as part of the 2000 Jubilee celebrations at the Vatican, was able to produce this new account of Christian suffering and martyrdom in the first quarter of the twenty-first century.

It would be easy to be overwhelmed by the sheer volume of material collected here. But this is a book to read slowly and absorb deeply. Many Christians around the world expose themselves daily to physical and social harm just by the fact of being Christian believers. They deserve our attention and support. And it's worth every effort we can make to provide them with protection from the many ways in which they are persecuted and killed by malefactors of all kinds in the modern world.

—George J. Marlin
Chairman, Aid to the Church in Need, USA

Introduction

*Therefore, since we are surrounded by so great a
cloud of witnesses, let us also lay aside every weight,
and sin which clings so closely, and let us run with
perseverance the race that is set before us.*

—Hebrews 12:1

On Easter Sunday, April 21, 2019, suicide bombers attacked St. Anthony's and St. Sebastian's, two Catholic churches in Colombo, the capital of Sri Lanka, leaving 171 dead and many more wounded. National Thowheeth Jama'ath, an ISIS-related radical Islamic group in Sri Lanka, carried out the attacks, which also included—on the same day—the bombings of a Protestant church and three luxury hotels, with hundreds of additional casualties. The perpetrators clearly intended to strike at basically "Western" religious and tourist groups and considered themselves "martyrs" for their willingness to give up their lives in an effort to rid Sri Lanka of non-Muslims. Five years later, 50,000 Sir Lankan Catholics petitioned the Colombo

Archdiocese to ask the Vatican's Dicastery for the Causes of Saints officially to declare the 171 dead to be martyrs.[2]

Though it has gone largely unnoticed amid so much other violence and mayhem, the modern world continues to produce a remarkably large crop of Christian martyrs. Some have even argued that there were more believers killed because of their Christian faith in the twentieth century than in all previous centuries combined.[3] It would be hard to prove that claim definitively because of the fragmentary knowledge we have of the early Christian martyrs and the deliberate coverups of evidence by repressive regimes throughout history, even where we might think—as in more recent cases—reliable sources of information should be readily available. Still, it's arguably so, given the large-scale persecution of all types of religious believers and dissidents under the various totalitarian systems that arose in the century just past. And it's one of the reasons why three recent popes—St. John Paul II, Benedict XVI, and Francis—have named martyrs at a much faster pace than happened in the past.

Much of that history is documented in my earlier book, *The Catholic Martyrs of the Twentieth Century: A Comprehensive World History*.[4] And the present book is something of a sequel to that

---

[2] Walter Sánchez Silva, "More Than 50,000 Sign Petition to Recognize 171 Killed in Sri Lanka Attack as Martyrs," Catholic News Agency, April 23, 2024, https://www.catholicnewsagency.com /news/257477/more-than-50000-sign-petition-to-recognize-171 -killed-in-sri-lanka-attack-as-martyrs.

[3] I.Media, "There Are More Christian Martyrs Now Than in All the Previous Centuries," Aleteia, August 30, 2020, https://aleteia.org /2020/08/30/there-are-more-christian-martyrs-now-than-in-all-the -previous-centuries.

[4] Robert Royal, *The Catholic Martyrs of the Twentieth Century: A Comprehensive World History* (New York: Crossroad, 2000).

account in two main ways. First, it includes some of the twentieth-century cases that were unknown in 2000, when the earlier book appeared. In that category, there are also figures who died for the faith in the last century but who have been formally declared *martyrs* or saints by the Church only in this century. Second, these pages focus primarily on the continuing saga of religious persecution and death in the first quarter of the twenty-first century. It must be stipulated, at the outset, that only the Church can confer the titles of martyrs or saint on anyone. So, while there are many people included here who may ultimately receive those honors, this book tries to give a fairly representative picture of people who appear to have died for the faith, often in years too recent for the formal processes to have been finished.

Some readers of my earlier volume objected that it focused too much on victims of communism while paying less attention to those produced by right-wing authoritarians and the "security state." But that was inevitable since the numbers of Christian deaths—and death of all kinds—under communism in the twentieth century simply dwarfed all other causes. Such totalitarian repression has not disappeared. In its 2024 World Watch List, Open Doors, an organization that has tracked Christian persecution and martyrdom since the 1950s, puts Communist North Korea in the number-one spot in the world for religious persecution, with China, Laos, Vietnam, and Cuba—all communist regimes in one form or another—also high on the list.[5]

But martyrdom is not so much to be read through partisan political lenses as through deeper philosophical and theological dimensions operative in many kinds of regimes in the modern

---

[5] Open Doors, World Watch List 2024, https://www.opendoors.org/en-US/research-reports/wwl-documentation/.

world. Whether they were systems of the "Left," as in the Soviet Union and its clients, or of the "Right," as in German Nazism and Italian Fascism, modern ideological states typically claim jurisdiction over all of human life.[6] And they are, therefore, intolerant by their very nature of alternative sources of meaning and authority, none more so than religious communities such as Christian churches that regard God as Sovereign and Judge over every earthly ruler and political order.

In a strange way, one of the most fervent religious movements on earth in the twenty-first century—militant Islam—has taken a similar stance against Christians in many parts of the world. Most Muslims are, of course, nonviolent and, since the founding of the faith, have often enough lived peacefully alongside other monotheistic religions in various places. And many Muslims in the twenty-first century have themselves been victims of Islamists who disagree with the kind of Islam they practice or think they have compromised with non-Muslim elements. Yet Salman Rushdie, the celebrated Indian Muslim novelist, who was physically attacked after an Iranian *fatwa* was issued against him for allegedly blaspheming the Prophet in one of his books, is right in saying that, "after having overcome fascism, Nazism, and Stalinism, the world now faces a new totalitarian global threat: Islamism." As the chapters that follow will show, militant Islamism is the most widespread threat to Christians in particular in a variety of countries today.

---

[6] These older ways of referring to political factions stem from the French Revolution but have become less useful than they once were. Today, for example, is Communist China a regime of the "Left" because communism was once regarded as a progressive movement? Or is it of the "Right" because it allows for a certain economic freedom, even as it affirms Chinese nationality and collective purposes, as did National Socialism and fascism?

And the threats against Christians in the twenty-first century do not stop with these obvious cases. There are more subtle contexts as well. In the postmodern, "free," Western world, too, religion has also come to occupy an unusual position. On the one hand, it's regarded by many people in influential cultural and political positions as a pale holdover from the adolescence of the human race, surviving precariously because of emotional attachments that are ultimately destined — so goes the narrative — to disappear with the spread of education, science, and technology. On the other hand, religion presents a radical challenge to the technological paradigm and the reign of political "experts," along with a claim to "follow the science," even in moral and policy matters, where value-free scientific inquiry has virtually nothing to say.

So, even in advanced "democratic" societies, there's a certain dynamic by which religious believers are tolerated when their religion is weak, but when it's not weak, they are often oppressed, sometimes bordering on persecuted, though not (yet) martyred. Indeed, one of the main reasons people in the developed world hear very little about Christians being martyred is that the usual news outlets and international bodies are not much interested in this horrifying phenomenon. Despite appearances, religion in the developed world is in a somewhat similar position, if on a slower and less organized track, than it was in the totalitarian regimes, whenever it directly challenges worldly power.

Christianity is especially vulnerable because, since the Enlightenment, the modernist-postmodernist paradigm is basically oriented toward replacing Christianity's cultural and social dominance — and, not incidentally, along with it, the Jewish tradition, from which Christianity emerged. Expressions of Christian belief in the public square, therefore, are routinely discouraged in ways that, in the West, would be regarded as biased and excluding if applied to "marginal" religions such as Islam, Hinduism, and indigenous peoples' practices. The double standard works because appeals to being "inclusive" must play down the traditionally dominant faiths of the West—again, Christianity and Judaism—while raising up the faiths or even the mere cultural practices of the others, who have been turned into an ideological "Other" with which to chastise the West.

That this obvious fact is rarely recognized does not make it any less true. This is just one of several reasons why it is important to pay proper attention to contemporary Christian martyrs. First, it's only right that innocent Christians who suffered unjust deaths in recent decades be recorded and honored. This type of historical justice is important for Christians, of course, but also for a proper appreciation about the history of our times. Anyone who wants to have a full and fair idea of the world today must know of the outrages against Christians, just as they must know about the Jewish Shoah, the Chinese persecution of the Muslim Uighurs, the repression of Buddhist Tibetans, and many other such realities. Ongoing Christian martyrdom—despite the lack of recognition in most current journalism and academic work—is a fact of modern world history.

It's also worth making clear what Christian martyrdom means in comparison with things that might look similar. People die for all sorts of causes, bad as well as good. In recent times, people have died for—when they were not killed by—the German Reich, the world communist movement, authoritarian regimes, and dictators of various personal and political hues. And the list goes on. A case very much in point is the Sir Lankan massacre mentioned earlier; the Islamic suicide bombers considered themselves and are regarded by their fellow radicals as martyrs who killed themselves in carrying out a religious duty to kill non-Muslims. The use of the word *martyrs* in this context—not all Islamic communities, by any means, would agree to that usage in so starkly murderous an operation—shows that there may be confusion about the term worth keeping constantly in mind in Western understanding. Christianity does not permit suicide, even for the noblest causes, and a Christian who deliberately kills himself in order to kill others is committing a sin, not a heroic act of faith.

The early Christian martyrs, for instance, did not "kill themselves," as one prominent American magazine claimed in 2024. After an ex-U.S. Air Force officer committed self-immolation in front of the Israeli embassy in protest against the war in Gaza, *Time* magazine attempted to contextualize the act—apologizing for it really—as an extreme political protest. And perhaps with the Muslim use of the term *martyr* also in the background, the magazine made a false historical claim: "Self-immolation was also seen as a sacrificial act committed by Christian devotees *who chose to be burned alive* when they were being persecuted for their religion by the Roman emperor Diocletian around 300 A.D."[7] Though, in any large group of people, you can always find exceptions to any generalization, that was simply a false suggestion, seemingly trying to render all faiths equally prone to self-immolation. Early Christians didn't seek death, let alone burn themselves, for the faith.

A Christian martyr is a person who is willing primarily to *die*, not to kill himself or others, for the faith. And that attitude is deeply rooted in Christian history because Jesus Himself, as Catholics believe, *died to save the world*. By contrast, though not every

---

[7] Solcyré Burga and Simmone Shah, "The History of Self-Immolation as Political Protest," *Time*, February 26, 2024, https://time.com/6835364/self-immolation-history-israel-hamas-war/.

Muslim thinker would agree that suicide bombings to build up the faith are ethically licit under sharia law, Islam grew by the sword. And it's a sheer fact that, unlike in the twentieth century, when secular totalitarianisms were the primary engines of murder, many Christian martyrs in the twenty-first century are killed by Islamic militants. Indeed, the 2024 World Watch List of countries where Christians are persecuted estimated that 340 million Christians are potential targets for persecution and that 4,998 Christians died that year for their faith. North Korea was the leading persecutor, but almost all the top fifty were majority-Muslim nations. The desire for good ecumenical relations—which are worth pursuing if done in truth and sincerity—should not be allowed to obscure that fact. Nor should it obscure the fact that it is happening today; the killing of Christians by Islamic radicals, either directly or by suicide bombings, even in formerly Christian European nations, serves as a warning.

An event that is emblematic of the barely contained tensions between Islam and Christianity and the asymmetries in their divergent understandings of martyrdom occurred, ironically, because of an academic lecture given by a pope, Benedict XVI, at his old university in Regensburg on September 12, 2006.[8] Joseph Ratzinger had been elected pope just a little over a year earlier, and during a trip to his native Germany, he wished to affirm some things that had marked his entire life as one of the most preeminent modern Catholic thinkers. His lecture was titled "Faith, Reason, and the University—Memories and Reflections." And besides the personal

---

[8] The full text with an illuminating commentary about the pope's intentions in the lecture and the reactions to it may be found in James V. Schall, S.J., *The Regensburg Lecture* (South Bend, IN: St. Augustine's Press, 2007).

element, Benedict wished to reaffirm that two of the constituent elements of properly Catholic thought were faith and reason—and the liberty of conscience that derives from being created as intelligent, free beings by God. Implied in those assertions was that the Church—and especially European intellectual circles—had forgotten such principles and could justify neither the pursuit of truth in the academy nor the freedom proclaimed by liberal democratic societies unless they recover both.

All this Benedict had repeatedly argued in various ways throughout his career as a professor and then as a Church official. But amid the arguments about the need for the Christian world to return to the fullness of its understanding about faith and reason, he gave an obscure example that, as an academic, he may have thought simply illustrated his point. Or perhaps it was also directed at a problem within Islam as well, particularly with the attacks on New York and Washington, D.C., on September 11, 2001, and the subsequent increase in radical Muslim militancy in its aftermath.

He referred to a conversation in 1391 between the Byzantine emperor Manuel II and a "Persian gentleman" who was a Muslim. The Greek had quoted from the Quran: "There is no compulsion in religion." Benedict went on with further assertions by the emperor along with a commentary of his own:

> "Show me just what Mohammed brought that was new, and there you will find things only evil and inhuman, such as his command to spread by the sword the faith he preached." The emperor, after having expressed himself so forcefully, goes on to explain in detail the reasons why spreading the faith through violence is something unreasonable. Violence is incompatible with the nature of God and the nature of the soul. "God," he says, "is not pleased by blood—and not

acting reasonably (σὺν λόγω) is contrary to God's nature. Faith is born of the soul, not the body. Whoever would lead someone to faith needs the ability to speak well and to reason properly, without violence and threats.... To convince a reasonable soul, one does not need a strong arm, or weapons of any kind, or any other means of threatening a person with death.[9]

This is a reasonable enough point, though, given Islamic militancy at the moment, it was not universally taken as such.

Bloody consequences soon followed that confirmed the very distinction Benedict was trying to make. Protests erupted among Muslims in many parts of the world. And in Mogadishu, the capital of Somalia, Sr. Leonella Sgorbati paid the ultimate price. A Consolata Missionary who had worked for thirty years in both Kenya and Somalia as a nurse and had trained nurses to care for the local populations, she was far from being on the military or even intellectual battlelines between Islam and Christianity. But as has occurred countless times in Christian history, that was not sufficient to keep her from falling foul of violent forces.

In a local Somali mosque, a radical sheikh had been urging his followers to hunt down Christians in retribution for the pope's "insult to the Prophet." On September 17, 2006—five days after the pope's lecture in Regensburg—the sixty-five-year-old sister was shot by a Muslim as she crossed the street between her hospital and her convent. A Muslim who was serving as her bodyguard was also killed, as were several other Christians in the area. According to her fellow sisters, in the ambulance on the way to the hospital, she died repeating, "I forgive."

---

[9] Schall, *The Regensburg Lecture*, 133–134.

Seven years later, a diocesan investigation concluded that a process for beatification might begin, and Pope Francis declared that she had been slain *in odium fidei* (in hatred of the faith), the central finding needed for a formal declaration of martyrdom and her canonization. She was not the first and will certainly not be the last to die at the hands of Muslim militants. If anything, it's far more likely that in the twenty-first century such martyrs will become more common.

The Christian Spirituality of Martyrdom

Martyrdom is so wrongly misunderstood in the modern world that, before turning to modern cases. it's worth exploring the *spirituality of martyrdom*, especially how central the willingness to go so far as to die for the Faith has been—and is—to Catholicism. Jesus Christ was, in a sense, the first Christian martyr, and it has always been understood, especially in the early Church, that those who would "follow Him" had to be willing to give up their lives for His truth. Indeed, so strong was this sense among the first Christians that a great modern scholar has remarked: "The stories of the acts of the martyrs were to become the first books of spirituality alongside the scriptures, the first such being the Acts of the Apostles, which depicts St. Stephen's martyrdom as an imitation of Christ's Passion."[10] St. Stephen was a deacon, of Greek background, to judge by his name, and the "protomartyr" because he is the first martyr we know of from authoritative sources. With the exception of St. John the Evangelist and Judas, the original apostles died as martyrs, along with St. Paul, who was beheaded in Rome.

---

[10] Servais Pinckaers, O.P., *The Spirituality of Martyrdom: To the Limits of Love*, trans. Patrick M. Clark and Annie Hounsokou (Washington, D.C.: Catholic University of America Press, 2016), 1–2.

The author quoted above remarks that it's difficult even for modern Christians to appreciate how important the example of martyrs was at the beginning of the faith because "it seems to conflict with the current trend, which favors an acceptance of pluralism among divided Christians, diverse religions, and all opinions generally."[11] This may be a justifiable live-and-let-live armistice in the politics of democratic states with multiple groups of widely varying believers. But within the borders of Catholicism, it waters down what is a central principle of the Christian life—following Jesus' example—and threatens to replace a religiously demanding vision with one that presents itself as less "dogmatic" and "traditional."

Still, the historical record over the centuries is clear. And it's no exaggeration to say, with St. Augustine, that the eighth beatitude "included and confirmed all the others. It represented humanity in all its perfection."[12] That beatitude reads, "Blessed are those who are persecuted for righteouess' sake.... Rejoice and be glad, for your reward is great in heaven" (Matt. 5:10, 12). These are Jesus' own words—a hard saying, to be sure. But millions of Christians have taken them to heart and have been willing to follow them—amid the many threats that have existed all over the world in every age. Those early stories of martyrdom, "the first books of spirituality," were distributed widely and felt deeply.

Catholicism is composed, of course, of a set of doctrines about the Trinity, the Incarnation, the Eucharist, and much more. Any form of Christianity that abandons those revealed truths puts itself on the way to dissolution. The gospel spread and eventually absorbed the mighty Roman Empire—one of the most manifest of miracles, according to St. Thomas Aquinas—by the preaching

---

[11] Pinckaers, *Spirituality of Martyrdom*, 2.

[12] Quoted in Pinckaers, *Spirituality of Martyrdom*, xi.

and teaching of those truths, the evident spiritual power that the early Christians manifested, and not least by the witness of all those who choose to *live* those truths in their daily lives in a hostile and repressive pagan culture. It would not be an exaggeration to say that, in line with the eighth beatitude, that witness unto death, despite persecution, produced not only heavenly rewards but earthly benefits as well.

Persecution of Christians may seem a mere historical accident, but that, too, is something that Jesus' own words put into a different context. As the great modern philosopher and theologian Hans Urs von Balthasar underscored, Jesus warned His flock to expect persecution—"If they persecuted me, they will persecute you" (John 15:20)—and not only from their immediate Jewish rivals or pagan opponents. In his *Moment of Christian Witness*, the great Swiss thinker argues that when Christ tells His disciples, "I send you out as sheep in the midst of wolves" (Matt. 10:16), He does not refer "simply to a possible situation, but to an inevitable one, because in the absolute decision to follow Christ one is exposed to the counter decision of 'the hate of the world.'"[13] And that is because Christ Himself is a contradiction to the world's sins and shortcomings, from which He came into the world to save us: "The willingness to lay down one's life for one's fellowmen is not a humanistic ideal dealt out to mankind in small doses. It keeps on the horizon the death of Christ ... as something by which I interpret my own life as a Christian."[14]

This was not lost on the many people over the centuries who have committed their lives to God. But it must have been a frustration to

[13] Hans Urs von Balthasar, *The Moment of Christian Witness*, trans. Richard Beckley (San Francisco: Ignatius Press, 1994), 17.
[14] Von Balthasar, *Christian Witness*, 29.

Roman authorities to see that, from the backwater of Palestine to the heart of Rome itself, violent persecution served only to confirm the believers in the new faith. Tertullian's saying—"*Semen est sanguinis christianorum*" (The blood of Christians is a seed)—has often been quoted in this context, but his larger point also bears repeating: "Kill us, torture us, condemn us, grind us to dust; your injustice is the proof that we are innocent. Therefore God suffers that we thus suffer.... The oftener we are mowed down by you, the more in number we grow.... On this account it is that we return thanks on the very spot for your sentences. As the divine and human are ever opposed to each other, when we are condemned by you, we are acquitted by the Highest."[15]

Considering the modern and postmodern context in which we all live now, it's worth explaining that by opposing the human and divine in this way, Tertullian, and no sane Christian, means that God and man, as such, are in conflict. The Christian God created man and sent His Son into the world to redeem him by dying a horrible death. But what Tertullian is getting at here is somewhat parallel to what St. Augustine said in his magisterial *City of God*. The City of Man opposes the City of God because of what each places at the center of its loves. The City of God puts God at the center and knows that all else that is good will then be added to it. The City of Man puts man at the center, fallen man, man without God, man who thinks he can save himself and—as the totalitarian slaughters of the twentieth century demonstrate beyond all doubt—when men turn their backs on God, it produces not Heaven but Hell.

Given all this, it is not simply Christian boasting to say that the very term *martyr*, as used by the followers of Christ, has no exact

---

[15] *Apology* 50.

parallel in the ancient Greco-Roman culture, in non-European religious groups, or in the various ways people have given their lives to worldly causes. The Christian difference lies in the fact that, by following Christ, either in a willingness to endure everything for the truth or in the actual sufferings of persecution and death, Christians believe they are participating in the Passion of the Savior, which means in His coming to this earth for the sake of redeeming it, saving it from its age-old evils in each of us—and in our public spaces.

Though the term has largely fallen out of use, even among modern Christians, this reflects a *spiritual combat*: the conflict not only between what we normally think of as good and evil in political, economic, cultural, and social life but a contest within each of us between good and evil spirits. As the great Russian writer Aleksandr Solzhenitsyn discovered as a prisoner in a Soviet *gulag*, "the line separating good and evil passes not through states, nor between classes, nor between political parties either—but right through every human heart."[16] Modern societies have largely dismissed the notion of spiritual combat, but the fullness of Christian vision makes no sense without it, even extending into the ultimate destiny of all souls beyond the grave.

The Modern Situation

It's complicated to relate this Christian understanding to the actual phenomenon of modern martyrdom because the idea of dying at the hands of people who practice *odium fidei* (hatred of the faith)—the classic criterion for martyrdom—assumes that the persecutors understand what is at stake. Quite often, they do not

---

[16] Aleksandr Solzhenitsyn, *The Gulag Archipelago*, pt. 4, chap. 1.

because of the mysterious spiritual realities that lie behind such clashes. The great Swiss theologian Servais Pinckaers suggests that to the question "Under what conditions may a Christian be considered a martyr?", we may be tempted to answer by referring solely to the external dimension: when one is put to death on account of faith in Christ or on account of the Christian religion. The difficulty is that the persecutor, who does not share this faith, will quite often have motives that are entirely unrelated to religion or do not correspond to the beliefs of the Christian. And how, then, are we to sort through the murkiness and complexities?[17]

He provides some criteria that we may apply, even as other factors are taken into account, by which we may still declare certain victims of violence to be martyrs: "One can be an authentic martyr for refusing to commit an injustice, for refusing to lie, for refusing to take an oath. However, the official recognition of a martyr by the Church requires that the cause be clear, [and] that it be officially established that the question of faith in Christ was directly involved."[18]

This, of course, is quite helpful at the conceptual level. But it also means that only the Catholic Church, through a careful consideration of all the details, can pronounce final judgment on a particular case. And this, in turn, entails a formal procedure with some well-established rules. To begin with, before anyone is declared a martyr, which also means a saint, a five-year waiting period must normally be observed, during which time information is gathered and carefully reviewed. Then, in the steps between beatification and canonization, one or more miracles connected to the deceased are usually required. And finally, there must be a

---

[17] Pinckaers, *Spirituality of Martyrdom*, 71.
[18] Pinckaers, *Spirituality of Martyrdom*, 72.

decision by the pope—who may also choose to waive the standard requirements—to make the formal declaration.

Popes often choose, for various reasons, when precisely to make such a declaration. It would have been seen as merely a partisan decision, for example, if Salvadoran archbishop Oscar Romero—who was murdered in 1980—had been declared a martyr and a saint in the midst of El Salvador's civil war. By 2015, when Pope Francis formally declared him a martyr and canonized him three years later, the case could be judged with far less partisan emotion.

New Categories of Martyrs

It was Pope John Paul II who, looking back over the violent history of the twentieth century all over the world and wishing to complete the record for the Jubilee Year 2000, promoted the notion of "new martyrs" (*nuovi martiri*). What he meant by the phrase was not just recent persons killed for the faith but some new types of Christian witness. As one official commentator on what he meant by this new term has rightly observed, it is a concept very "abundant and difficult to summarize."[19] But like much else about the Polish pope, who had experienced both German Nazism and Soviet communism, it responded quite strongly to the particular conditions of modern times.

The "new martyrs," of course, often present us with stories similar to those told of the ancient martyrs, of persons killed quite explicitly for the things they believed. That is what most people think of when they hear the word *martyr*. But it was John Paul's

---

[19] Vicente Carcel Orti, "Pope John Paul II's Teaching on the Martyrs of Our Century," Vatican website, https://www.vatican.va/jubilee _2000/magazine/documents/ju_mag_01031997_p-56_en.html.

intention to recognize that modern conditions also presented unprecedented threats and therefore that modern martyrs do not always fall neatly into conventional categories. To take just one example, Fr. Giuseppe "Pino" Puglisi, an anti-Mafia priest who lived in Brancaccio, a crime-infested neighborhood of Palermo, was assassinated in 1993, presumably by a mob hit man, for his efforts to protect his flock from criminals.[20] Some might regard this as merely a kind of political or social clash, but the fact that Fr. Puglisi considered what he was doing as part of his ministry as a Catholic priest cannot help but be taken into account in an overall evaluation of his life and work. This is why Pope Francis beatified him in 2013.

Similar killings have occurred in other highly Catholic nations, such as Mexico, Brazil, and Colombia, where priests have crossed drug cartels or human traffickers—and paid the price with their lives. The following pages will describe some of these complex situations.

The older form of martyrdom almost always involved organs of the state and sometimes clashes with other religions. And, therefore, there are often political considerations as to who is or is not named a martyr. St. John Paul II wanted to commemorate the horrors of Nazism by declaring Maximilian Kolbe and Edith Stein, both of whom died in Auschwitz, martyrs. It's difficult to make the case that they fit very well under the usual categories. Kolbe famously volunteered to die in place of a layman who had a family. That had never before been the cause for declaring someone a martyr. But he became a "martyr of charity" for his sacrificing himself

---

[20] Andrea Gagliarducci, "The First Martyr of the Mafia," *National Catholic Register*, May 27, 2013, https://www.ncregister.com/news/the-first-martyr-of-the-mafia.

for another person. Stein was an even more unusual candidate for designation as martyr. It may just be that the pope simply wanted a heroic woman — and a convert from Judaism — to be remembered as one of the martyrs at Auschwitz.[21] In any event, he proclaimed her a "martyr for truth."

In a similar vein, Pope Francis declared the 813 Catholics killed in 1480 by Muslim invaders in Otranto, a city in Italy's heel, to be martyrs — in 2013! It was the first year of his pontificate, and it may be that he wanted to make a statement about the Muslim slaughter of Christians since September 11, 2001, despite his later efforts at good relations with Muslims. Perhaps for the same reason, in 2023, he also added to the Roman Martyrology the 21 Coptic Orthodox Christians beheaded in Libya by ISIS in 2015.

Both pontiffs knew that such killings go on regularly in various places around the modern world, even outside of the old-style totalitarian regimes. And each made some adjustments to take into account factors that were sometimes present to a certain degree in the ancient conditions as well but were only rarely commented on explicitly in the official martyrologies.

John Paul II declared Kolbe a "martyr of charity," which opened to door to recognition of others who have died on behalf of their neighbor. And looking at modern conditions, the Polish pope even spoke of a new form of persecution, a kind of "civic death" — if anything, an even more widespread pathology, even in modern democracies:

They include various types of discrimination against believers and against the whole community of the Church. Such

---

[21] I have outlined some of the arguments, pro and con, for Stein to be considered a martyr in *The Catholic Martyrs of the Twentieth Century*, 167–191.

forms of discrimination are often practised at the same time as is recognised the right to religious liberty and to freedom of conscience, and this in the law of individual countries as well as in declarations of an international nature.[22]

This happens even in basically tolerant areas such as Europe. The Observatory on Intolerance and Discrimination against Christians in Europe, a Vienna-based organization that tracks across the European continent, documented in its 2022–2023 report that there were 792 anti-Christian hate crimes during that year, many more than in the recent past, most of them perpetrated by extremists. Further, "Christians who expressed traditional Christian worldview have faced legal discrimination."[23]

Finnish Lutheran Bishop Juhana Pohjola and Päivi Räsänen—onetime chair of the Finnish Christian Democrats and a physician who was elected to the Finnish parliament and had served as minister of the interior—are modern cases in point. Both have been charged with "hate speech," Räsänen for merely tweeting out the passage in Genesis "male and female he created them" (1:27).[24]

Though these two figures are not Catholics, it's telling that in a modern, highly secular system such as Finland's, they could be regarded as having committed a crime merely for quoting one of the earliest texts in the Bible. Further, they represent what John Paul II identified as the ecumenical nature of modern

---

[22] Orti, "Teaching on the Martyrs."

[23] "OIDAC Europe Annual Report—2022/23," Observatory on Intolerance and Discrimination against Christians in Europe, https://www.intoleranceagainstchristians.eu/publications/annual -report-2022-23.

[24] "Finland: Censorship against Scripture," Aid to the Church in Need, June 6, 2023, https://acninternational.org/religiousfreedom report/news/finland-censorship-against-scripture.

persecution and martyrdom: "Perhaps the most convincing form of ecumenism is the ecumenism of the saints and of the martyrs. The *communio sanctorum* speaks louder than the things which divide us."[25]

Four Pathways to Canonization

It's worth paying some attention to the specific ways in which a person may be declared a saint in the Catholic Church—martyrdom being one of those pathways. There are currently four. To reach the stage of beatification and, finally, canonization (declaration of sainthood) requires:

* A lifetime of "heroic virtue"
* Devotional cults supported by "constant and common attestation"
* Martyrdom (dying *in odium fidei*—via hatred of the faith—in some sense as defined by the Church)

To these three, Pope Francis added a fourth in 2017 via a *motu proprio*—*Maiorem hac dilectionem* (Greater love than this)—what he termed *oblatio vitae* ("a free offering of one's life," usually on the spur of the moment). This category seems to extend further the attention St. John Paul II paid to the nature of modern persecutions—and perhaps martyrdom. In the text announcing this new pathway, Pope Francis states that this is not necessarily martyrdom, but the five criteria he specifies for *oblatio vitae* seem to border so closely on recent declarations of individuals as martyrs by the Vatican that it would be no surprise if further developments would not include persons who fit these descriptions simply as modern martyrs:

[25] Orti, "John Paul II's Teaching on the Martyrs."

a) The free and voluntary offering of one's life, and heroic acceptance *propter caritatem* [i.e., on behalf of charity—John Paul, as mentioned earlier, had already identified what he called "martyrs of charity"] of a certain and soon-to-come death;

b) A *nexus*—i.e., close relation—between the offering of one's life and the premature death of the one who offers it;

c) The exercise, at least in ordinary degree, of the Christian virtues before the subject's offering of his or her life and, afterward, perseverance in those virtues unto death;

d) The existence of *fama sanctitatis*—i.e., the reputation for holiness—on the part of the subject, and of signs [in confirmation thereof], at least after death;

e) The necessity, for beatification, of a miracle, one that occurred after the death of the Servant of God, and by said Servant's intercession.[26]

It's telling of our current circumstances that the Church under Francis would believe it necessary to recognize—and properly honor—some of these difficult-to-judge cases that the modern world presents to us. In several respects, we know about them because of improved means of communication. (It sometimes seems that nothing happens anymore without photos or even videos recording the event on someone's cell phone.) But we also know about them because violent confrontation with people preaching or practicing the Catholic faith still occurs quite often in our day.

---

[26] "Pope Francis Creates New Category for Beatification: *Oblatio Vitae*," Vatican Radio, July 11, 2017, https://www.archivio radiovaticana.va/storico/2017/07/11/pope_francis_makes_new _beatification_category_oblatio_vitae/en-1324398; brackets in the original.

As Pope Francis has said:

Today there are more martyrs than at the beginning of the
Church's life, and martyrs are everywhere. Today's Church
is rich in martyrs, it is irrigated by their blood which is "the
seed of new Christians" (Tertullian, *Apologetic*, 50, 13) and
ensures growth and fruitfulness for the People of God. The
martyrs are not "holy men," but men and women in flesh
and blood who—as Revelation says—"washed their robes
and made them white in the blood of the Lamb" (7:14).
They are the true winners.[27]

And the fact of persecution and death is not something merely
to become angry or depressed about, he argues: "Looking at the
martyrs of yesterday and today, we can learn to live a full life,
welcoming the martyrdom of daily fidelity to the Gospel and con-
formation to Christ."[28]

The following pages are a humble effort to pay homage and do
justice to the heroic and holy lives of such men and women—many
of them martyrs whose names will never be known in this
world—and, all too often, to their untimely deaths.

---

[27] Kathleen N. Hattrup, "Martyrs Are Everywhere Today, Says
Pope Francis, and We Should Imitate Them with Our Daily Self-
Denials," Aleteia, September 25, 2019, https://aleteia.org/2019
/09/25/martyrs-are-everywhere-today-says-pope-francis-and-we
-should-imitate-them-with-our-daily-self-denials.

[28] Hattrup, "Martyrs Are Everywhere."

A NOTE ON THE TEXT: The author is quite aware of the great mass of material—indeed, the whole countries—left out of this volume, probably more so than the casual reader. But in a work of this kind, to keep it manageable and readable, painful choices have to be made. The many stories and analyses included here are representative of the many more victims, named and unnamed, who continue to suffer and die for their faith in Christ in the twenty-first century. This book was completed in mid-November 2024, and events move so quickly that it could not include material on the December overthrow of the Assad regime in Syria, with unpredictable consequences for Christians, or the sad repetition of attacks on Christmas markets in Europe. We may hope that, as further information becomes available, there will be more comprehensive and continuing treatments of individual persons, nations, and international trends. It has always been the case, however, that we must imagine the "great cloud of witnesses" (Heb. 12:1) who surround us going back into the mists of time and daily being added to. We may all hope to know one another someday—and as the great St. Thomas More put it on the way to his own martyrdom, "that we may meet in heaven together, where we shall be merry for ever and ever."

1

Latin America

I am a man: little do I last
and the night is enormous.
But I look up:
the stars write.
Unknowing I understand:
I too am written,
and at this very moment
someone spells me out.

—Octavio Paz

Mexico: "The Most Dangerous Place
to Be a Catholic Priest"

To most casual observers, Mexico seems to be one of the most religious—and predominantly Catholic—countries in the world. And
that's true. More than three-quarters of Mexicans call themselves
Catholic, with various small Protestant groups trailing far behind.
At 15 percent, nonbelievers, too, are in a distinct minority, much
smaller than is typical of most modern nations. And public spaces
in Mexico are saturated with Christian churches, processions, and

shrines—most notably, the Basilica of Our Lady of Guadalupe, just outside Mexico City. La Guadalupana, as the Virgin Mary is often called there, in the famous image produced miraculously in the early sixteenth century, was one of the most potent forces that led not only to the conversion of Mexico to Christianity but to the spread of Catholicism throughout Latin America.

In the twentieth century, however, one of the places that first produced a large crop of Catholic martyrs was—ironically—the newly "democratic" Mexican government that emerged from a bloody civil war. That government was actually a strongly socialist regime hostile to Catholicism and religion of all kinds. The 1917 constitution enshrined some basic liberal ideas, such as land reform and workers' rights, into Mexican law, but it also limited the rights of the Catholic Church as well as other religious bodies. In the hands of later, virulently anticlerical governments, those limitations expanded to include the closure of churches, the banning of public religiosity, and the persecution and assassination of Catholic priests and religious by government forces. Those abuses have been extensively chronicled in standard histories and even received notable literary treatment in Graham Greene's 1940 novel, *The Power and the Glory,* and in his travelogue, *The Lawless Roads.*

In the second half of the twentieth century, overt governmental persecution receded, but threats remained. Indeed, when Pope John Paul II first visited Mexico in 1979, shortly after his election to the papacy, and then again multiple times in the 1990s, there was speculation about what the Mexican government might do, since it was still forbidden for Catholic clerics to appear publicly in clerical garb. Nothing happened, to be sure, because the Mexican people and the rest of the world would have been outraged if something had. But Catholics and other Christian bodies could routinely still be harassed or threatened with fines and closures for alleged infractions of laws curtailing religious practices—even for the offense of the mere owning of property by churches. (Churches were often designated, by a kind of pious legal fiction, as being owned by private lay organizations.) The constitution was finally amended in 1992 to grant Mexican religious groups the rights they had previously been denied for the previous three-quarters of a century. But the Mexican government still exercises some controls over religion that are rare elsewhere—such as requiring religious meetings outside registered venues to be licensed by the government.

As governmental repression receded, however, Catholic clergy in Mexico soon came to face a new kind of threat: widespread criminality, at times with cooperation by corrupt government and police officials. In 1993, for example, just a year after the constitutional reform, Juan Jesús Posadas Ocampo, cardinal archbishop of Guadalajara, was killed at that city's airport by assassins believed to be working for the Tijuana Cartel, a violent band of drug traffickers, who mistook him for Joaquín "El Chapo" Guzmán, head of the rival Sinaloa Cartel. That, at least, was the official version of the event. But in 2000, after the Institutional Revolutionary Party (PRI)—which had ruled Mexico without interruption since 1929—was defeated for the first time in presidential elections since the revolution, facts came to light that Cardinal Posadas had been threatened by a previous president, Carlos Salinas, because the prelate was in possession of information about the collaboration of the Mexican government with human trafficking, drugs, prostitution, and other criminal enterprises. A reforming cleric with such information threatened multiple individuals and institutions within the government itself.

Though his murder remains unsolved, Cardinal Posadas's assassination was an early sign of a phenomenon that was to grow in scope and depth: the intimidation and killing of Mexican clerics as threats to a corrupt, criminal, public order. Indeed, a 2023 news analysis noted, based on verified cases, that the most dangerous place in the world to be a Catholic priest is twenty-first-century Mexico, with other countries in Latin America showing a similar pattern: "More religious leaders have been killed in Latin America in the last decade than anywhere else in the world. The number of priests killed in Mexico in the last 15 years is even higher than in Nigeria, the African country renowned for violent attacks against Christians. And the figures for Colombia and Brazil trail only slightly behind that for Mexico."[29] The causes in these countries are all too familiar: pure criminality that the clerics opposed in various ways, to be sure, but also government corruption aiding and abetting international criminal networks.

Many of these cases may fall under the category of either the "new martyrs" that Pope John Paul II formally recognized or the *oblatio vitae* that Pope Francis recognized in other instances. In the early twentieth century, martyred priests in a country such as Mexico mostly belonged to the older kind of modern martyr: clerics and laypeople killed by an aggressive, overweening atheist state that openly sought to stamp out the religion of the people—which is to say, traditional Catholicism. Those forms of persecution have largely disappeared from Latin America in the twenty-first century, but some remnants remain. (Witness the persecution of the Church in Nicaragua, where the socialist government and corrupt tyranny of the Ortega family has imprisoned bishops, intimidated clergy,

---

[29] Kelsey Zorzi and Julio Pohl Garcia Prieto, "Mexico Is Officially the World's Most Dangerous Place to Be a Priest," *The Hill*, June 14, 2023, https://thehill.com/opinion/civil-rights/4047813-mexico-is-officially-the-worlds-most-dangerous-place-to-be-a-priest/.

closed charities, prohibited priests from making hospital visits, and expelled clerics who speak out against the regime; or in Venezuela, where many of the same things happen under an authoritarian regime.) Almost all of the most recent "new martyrs" in Latin America are the product of a new dynamic: Christians—specifically as Christian witnesses carrying their faith into practice—trying to stop or thwart the lawlessness of criminals whose vast financial resources and networks among powerful political and economic actors allow them to function with impunity.

That distinction is important here because it's not only religious leaders, of course, who are victims of militant criminals. To take just the Mexican example, cartels and traffickers of various kinds routinely kill mayors and other local officials, police chiefs, entire police forces, prominent businesspeople, journalists, human rights activists, and cultural figures who may present an obstacle to their operations. Indeed, during the 2024 campaign for president, it was estimated that around 2,000 officials died in various clashes, and something on the order of 170,000 murders were recorded in the six previous years (2018-2024) of the presidency of Andrés Manuel López Obrador. Ironically, López Obrador was a president whose administration also made what, in some respects, were serious efforts to rein in criminality. Yet by the end of 2024, it was reported that the Mexican cartels are the nation's fifth-largest industry.

Still, the numbers of religious killed in Mexico and Latin American more generally are shocking. Fides, the agency of the Pontifical Mission Societies, keeps track of Catholics killed "on mission" around the world, and it recorded in its annual report that in 2005, which was only the beginning of the new wave of violence, one bishop and twenty-five priests, religious, and laypeople were murdered globally, and "the continent of America registered the highest number of Church personnel killed: 8 priests, 2 Brothers and 2 Sisters."

Only some of those killed could be roughly classified as martyrs, to be sure, even according to the expanded categories of recent popes. And like other people who try to stop injustices in modern societies, Mexican clerics may have multiple motivations for resisting the gangs. Prosecutors of the Mafia in Sicily, as noted in the introduction to the present volume, have sometimes been quite open that their work was driven by both a sense of civic responsibility and their commitment, as Christians, to justice. No doubt among the Mexican dead are religious people with similarly mixed political, moral, and religious motives. It's important to make such careful distinctions not only for Mexico but for all nations where similar conditions obtain. Still, as Bernardo Barranco, a Mexican sociologist, has rightly observed, "the rise of violence against priests reflects the role in which they place themselves: as warriors on the front lines of the struggle for human rights in the midst of drug-related violence."[30]

Even observers who try to limit the rush to declare every murdered priest a martyr recognize that, in a place like Mexico, "a pastor is committed to the single endeavor of service to God and his people. Therefore, whether a priest is killed in order to steal his car, pilfer the parish collection or punish his refusal to administer sacraments to known narco personnel, in the end, the underlying and real reason for this violence is that the singular integrity of the priests threatens the narco reality and the new social order of Mexico."[31]

---

[30] Deborah Bonello, "In Mexico's Guerrero State, Priests Are a Prime Target for Drug Gangs," *Los Angeles Times*, November 29, 2015, https://www.latimes.com/world/mexico-americas/la-fg-mexico-priests-20151129-story.html.

[31] Rafael Luévano, "Why Priests Keep Getting Murdered in Mexico," *America*, June 23, 2022, https://www.americamagazine.org/faith/2022/06/23/mexico-priest-killings-narcos-243231.

This complex of motives does not deny, by any stretch of the imagination, that some of the murdered are surely martyrs. Still, a priest killed in his rectory by a thief seeking money is, as such, not a martyr, not even a "new martyr." But wherever a Christian conscience is operative, whether in a priest or a layperson who dies while acting to affirm Christian truth and goodness, even in a secular context, we're in the realm of potential martyrdom. Only the Church, of course, has the authority to decide who is and who is not a martyr—in effect, also a saint. (Almost all the cases included in the present volume are too recent to have been declared authoritatively one way or the other.) But to pay careful attention to these cases is an important way of broadening and deepening our sense of what a Christian conscience means in the world of the twenty-first century.

And there are certainly enough of them. Mexico ranks as the most dangerous country in the world for Catholic priests because nine priests have been killed there—that we know of—during the six years of the López Obrador presidency (2018–2024). Taking a longer period, between 2007 and 2022, a mere fifteen-year span, somewhere between forty-five and fifty Catholic priests were assassinated in what reports have characterized as "narco-related violence." If nuns, seminarians, and lay pastoral workers are added, the count is even higher. Some of them were innocent bystanders, but others have been murdered because of direct or indirect opposition to drug trafficking and human trafficking. (Mexicans—religious and laypeople alike—generally know it's not a good idea to confront the traffickers directly.) Still others, faithful to their vocations, have been killed for as little reason as refusing to perform a Baptism or a wedding involving criminal families. In any event, such numbers come close to the body count for priests during the bloodiest years of Mexico's Cristero

War. On the threshold of the twenty-first century, St. John Paul II declared twenty-five of the lay and religious leaders killed in that earlier conflict to be saints and martyrs.

They have more recent confreres. In 2022, for instance, two elderly Mexican Jesuits, Javier Campos Morales and Joaquín César Mora Salazar, much beloved for their work in a poor rural community, were killed apparently for trying to shelter a tour guide being pursued by Sinaloa Cartel traffickers. Ironically, the prime suspect in their murder, José Noriel Portillo Gil, who was nicknamed *El Chueco* (the Crooked One), was himself found dead nine months later after a manhunt by Mexican authorities. His death, however, seems to have been the result not of police action but a hit by the cartel itself, which has been known to execute members who draw too much attention to their activities.[32]

The murder of priests is not always tied so closely to some immediate local conflict with criminals. In 2023, for example, Fr. Javier García Villafaña, a priest who had just been appointed to a parish in a small town in the state of Michoacán, was shot multiple times in his car, apparently in retribution against the Mexican bishops. This happened just a day after the Mexican Episcopal Conference issued a public condemnation about a failed attack on Durango archbishop Faustino Armendáriz Jiménez—during Mass at his cathedral. García Villafaña's murder necessitated yet another public statement by the Mexican bishops deploring the general state of violence: "It is a painful reminder of the serious situation we face as a society, in which the presence of organized crime and impunity continue threatening the lives and safety of

---

[32] "Report: Killer of Jesuits in Mexico Found Shot to Death," Associated Press, March 22, 2023, https://apnews.com/article/mexico-jesuits-killed-church-mexico-cartels-violence-649c768f9de04acfcece5705e802a72e.

so many."[33] As the Associated Press reported at the time, García Villafaña was the ninth priest killed in the previous four years.

Some have argued that the Catholic Church—both in and outside Mexico—should take an even more open public stance against criminality and violence. It has done so repeatedly but to little effect, given the complexities of Mexican culture and politics. In 2016, for instance, Pope Francis sent condolences to the bishops of Mexico after the bodies of two priests were discovered in a field north of Veracruz. Alejo Nabor Jiménez Juárez and José Alfredo Suárez de la Cruz had been kidnapped from Our Lady of Fátima parish in the town of Poza Rica. The reason for their abduction was not clear, but it's not hard to believe that it was because they had run afoul of cartel activity in some way. The pope did not hesitate to call their deaths an assassination, and he prayed for "for the eternal repose of these priests of Christ, victims of an inexcusable violence." The pontiff had visited Mexico earlier the same year and urged all parties to find a way to stop "the cycle of drug-trafficking and violence." After the double murder, he encouraged clergy and lay Catholics alike to continue their mission, imitating Christ despite everything—a call, in effect, for heroic witness even to the point of death.[34]

On top of the familiar forms of violence and criminality in Mexico, however, new challenges have arisen for the Church of a specifically spiritual—one might even say, demonic—nature. In the runup to the 2024 elections, for instance, the Mexican bishops had

---

[33] "Priest Killed in Mexico; 9th Slain in Country in Past 4 Years," Associated Press, May 24, 2023, https://apnews.com/article/mexico-priest-killed-04849e23cf9b1d650f1293f6b3d082e4.

[34] Elise Harris, "Pope Francis Condemns 'Inexcusable Violence' in Murder of Mexican Priests," Catholic News Agency, September 21, 2016, https://www.catholicnewsagency.com/news/34593/pope-francis-condemns-inexcusable-violence-in-murder-of-mexican-priests.

to denounce the use of the figure of Santa Muerte (Holy Death) in political campaigns.[35] Santa Muerte is a grotesque skeletal figure with vague roots in pre-Christian Mexico. Scholars have discovered evidence of death worship in some pre-Columbian rituals. That cult seemed to have all but died out under the influence of Spanish Catholicism—until it reappeared on the radar of several anthropologists in the 1940s. No doubt, it had been leading some shadowy nonpublic existence all along. It was not until the 2000s, however, that this demonic figure began to enjoy a widespread public presence in Mexico (the cult is strong among the cartels in Veracruz, where the two priests were murdered, and in Michoacán) and also in Central America and even in U.S. cities such as Los Angeles.

It's difficult for Westerners living in societies where "spiritual" beliefs of all kinds have become radically attenuated to appreciate, but Santa Muerte is a powerful presence even among the hardened members of the cartels. She is presented at times as "Our Lady" Sacred Death, almost as if it were a title of the Virgin Mary. But this is clearly a cult associated with violence in a way that no authentic representation of Mary ever has been. In the strange ways of popular modern cults, Santa Muerte has become powerful among gang members in prison and also—in the even stranger ways of "marginalized" groups in the twenty-first century—with LGBTQ+ movements. Santa Muerte seems to be a "patron saint" for all those condemned by Christianity—both Catholics and Evangelicals—or excluded by mainstream society. Various rituals have grown up around this cult that tend to mimic Catholic practices, though groups that perform such rituals typically separate

[35] David Agren, "Mexico's Bishops Denounce Use of Santa Muerte in Political Advertising," *Our Sunday Visitor*, April 26, 2024, https://www.osvnews.com/mexicos-bishops-denounce-use-of-santa-muerte-imagery-in-political-advertising/.

themselves from the Church, which has rightly condemned these rituals as something akin to demon worship.

While the invocation of Santa Muerte may just be a social fad in certain criminal quarters, in others it has taken on characteristics typical of a religion. The Michoacán cartel La Familia, for example, began life in the 1980s as a kind of mafia in a specialized sense not unknown in the origin of other mafias. In the absence of a well-functioning state government, La Familia started out as a group of vigilantes carrying out rough justice, caring for the poor, even considering its assassinations and assaults as something they carried out explicitly as a "divine right." As it grew more powerful, it allied itself for a time with other cartels, such as Los Zetas, but went on to become an independent force in its own right. Despite the religious element—and its activities in education, support for children and families, charity to peasants, and discouraging of drug use by its members—it's also a murderous drug-trafficking operation and a serious repressive force in Michoacán. It's not surprising, then, that in 2016, Pope Francis made a point of visiting the city of Morelia in Michoacán and calling on young people to be Jesus' disciples, not hit men. It's inevitable that a group like this would clash with the Catholic Church. As one FBI report revealed, in 2009, one of Santa Muerte's "high priests," Romo Guillén, "called for holy war against the Catholic Church."[36]

And there are other threats emerging as well. In its 2022 report on International Religious Freedom, the U.S. State Department commented that:

---

[36] Robert J. Bunker, "Santa Muerte: Inspired and Ritualistic Killings," *FBI Law Enforcement Bulletin*, February 5, 2013, https://leb.fbi.gov/articles/featured-articles/santa-muerte-inspired-and-ritualistic-killings.

The nongovernmental organization (NGO) Catholic Multimedia Center (CMC) reported 800 incidents of extortion and threats against priests nationwide between October 2021 and October 2022. CMC reported it accounted for approximately 850 reports yearly for the past five years. According to CMC, the number was likely underestimated because it did not include digital extortion cases, which priests said have increased since 2020. Religious leaders were often involved in politics and social activism and were thus more vulnerable to generalized violence.[37]

In the current understanding of the Catholic Church, involvement "in politics and social activism" may (or may not) have a religious dimension. Each case would have to be examined in detail. So the U.S. State Department may be partly correct when it claims, "Incidents of violence against religious leaders did not appear to be based solely on religious identity." The question is whether *solely* removes questions about religious motivation, at least as the Church sees things.

Government authorities themselves are not beyond suspicion in cases of repression, as one incident included in the State Department report, among many that were not, documents:

> The Dioceses [sic. Cf. diocese] of San Cristóbal de las Casas issued a statement calling on authorities to cease persecution, repression, and intimidation of its priests, following

---

[37] Office of International Religious Freedom, *Mexico 2022 International Religious Freedom Report*, U.S. Department of State, https://www.state.gov/wp-content/uploads/2023/05/441219-MEXICO-2022-INTERNATIONAL-RELIGIOUS-FREEDOM-REPORT.pdf.

the arrests of seven priests and church representatives. According to the dioceses [diocese], authorities accused the priests of committing violence related to their peace-building work in Indigenous communities. In the same press statement, the dioceses [diocese] said organized crime had infiltrated local police, and the judicial and political systems. Local media outlets reported that the Office of the Prosecutor sought to falsely blame priests for the disappearance of 19 persons in 2021. The disappearances were reportedly committed by a self-defense group called "*El Machete*," whose stated purpose is to defend against the actions of drug cartels and criminal groups.[38]

In the conditions of corruption caused by the wealth of the criminal cartels and their infiltration of every level of government, it's always difficult to assess such situations. But there can be no doubt about the conditions on the ground: "The CMC identified Mexico as the most violent country for priests in Latin America for the 14th consecutive year, reporting killings of more than 39 priests over the past decade. Some NGOs said criminal groups continued to single out Catholic priests and other religious leaders because of their condemnation of criminal activities and because communities viewed them as moral authority figures."[39]

As in many places in the contemporary world, as in many places in different ages of the Catholic Church, the challenge to control by religious witnesses and their moral authority in Mexico may count toward a definition of martyrdom whether the killing is carried out by a national state or by a large, organized—often international—criminal organization.

[38] Office of International Religious Freedom, *Mexico 2022*.
[39] Office of International Religious Freedom, *Mexico 2022*.

Colombia

Despite the dangerous situation it has created for priests, Mexico has not nearly been as troubled by violence as other Latin American nations have been in the closing decades of the twentieth century and the early part of the twenty-first—at least not in large institutional terms. Mexico's Cristero War ended almost a century ago, in 1929. But throughout the twentieth century, Colombia has endured several prolonged periods of political violence perpetrated by multiple actors. And it shows in the body count of religious figures. The same annual 2005 report by Fides referred to above remarks with a certain air of exasperation: "Once again this year Colombia had the highest number of victims, 4 priests and 1 woman religious. In that country where social conflict is acute the Church pays a heavy tribute for her efforts to promote social reconciliation and justice in the name of the Gospel and the victims of the long and bloody conflict included also two Catholic priests 'mistakenly' murdered by guerrillas."[40]

Colombia's national history is complicated. During the colonial period, it had been the Viceroyalty of New Granada (which meant a territory that included modern Colombia, Venezuela, Panama, Ecuador, and parts of other nearby territories). It boasted as its first president El Libertador (the Liberator) Simón Bolívar, but it suffered from internal tensions both during and after his rule. It eventually broke up into several independent states. One piece became Panama, with the urging of the United States and France, to facilitate the construction of the Panama Canal. America eventually paid Colombia $25 million in compensation after the canal was built.

[40] "The Names of Those Killed on Mission in the Year 2005," Agenzia Fides, December 30, 2005, http://www.fides.org/en/missionaries /6461-THE_NAMES_OF_THOSE_KILLED_WHILE_ON _MISSION_IN_THE_YEAR_2005.

The modern state basically did not take on a stable form until the early twentieth century, but that form has remained contested. In the 1930s, the League of Nations settled an ongoing land dispute, but by the 1940s and 1950s, a period of violence (which gave it the historical title La Violencia) arose between the two main political parties. The capital city, Bogotá, underwent massive unrest (the *Bogotazo*) that resulted in the deaths of hundreds of thousands. The Conservative Party and the Liberal Party eventually put an end to the worst violence by forming a National Front, a kind of establishment system in which the two sides agree to alternate holding power at five-year intervals.

Of course, this did not pacify everyone by a long shot. In the 1960s, various anti-government guerrilla movements arose, amounting to a virtual civil war (1964–2016). Most prominent among these revolutionaries was a Marxist group, the Armed Revolutionary Front of Colombia (FARC), which controlled a large swath of the country (sometimes waggishly called FARClandia). But there were other serious actors as well. The M-19 army succeeded in several assaults over decades. And the Ejército de Liberación Nacional (ELN, "Army of National Liberation") even combined Marxist-Leninist ideas with Christian social principles in a kind of armed liberation theology. In addition, it gained notoriety when it was headed by the famous priest, professor, and militant revolutionary Camilo Torres Restrepo, who died after a military engagement with government forces.

Though the violence in Colombia has primarily been the result of political divisions common to much of Latin America in the twentieth century, it did not spare religious figures by any means. In the violent circumstances of the last half of the twentieth century and stretching into the first quarter of the twenty-first century, it's difficult to be entirely sure of the body count. But reliable sources have estimated that between 1984 and 2017, "seventy Catholic priests, two bishops, eight nuns and three seminarians were slaughtered there, many falling victim to the nation's notorious narco-cartels."[41] Unlike Mexico, however, the narco-cartels in Colombia have largely been part of the financial support for militants — particularly the FARC.

In 2018, Fr. Dagoberto Noguera was found dead in Mamatoco, Colombia, tied up with multiple stab wounds.[42] The ultimate cause of death seems to have been strangulation. Initial police reports indicated that the priest was simply the victim of a robbery. But as investigations proceeded, it became clearer that, in fact, the motive was revenge. Fr. Noguera was a native of Ecuador but had studied in Colombia. He had been temporarily working in a parish in Brooklyn, New York, but about four years prior to his murder, he decided to move back to Colombia to retire and to help with the troubled circumstances there. By all accounts, he had been a valuable presence, providing food for the poor and seeking to reconcile people who often resorted to violence.

Ironically, he was murdered by two Venezuelans; Venezuela had been going through very difficult economic times owing to the missteps of its Marxist-inspired rulers. The UN Refugee Agency has estimated that more than six million Venezuelans have left the country (which formerly had been a relative success story, owing to its vast oil and mineral deposits) mostly for other nations in Latin America and the Caribbean, fleeing crime, repression, food scarcity, and general social chaos. Anti-government sentiment has, of course,

---

[41] "Catholic Priest Found Stabbed to Death in Brazil," *Crux*, August 26, 2017, https://cruxnow.com/global-church/2017/08/catholic -priest-found-stabbed-death-brazil.

[42] Ed Wilkinson, "Priest Who Served Brooklyn Parishes Found Murdered in Colombia," *National Catholic Reporter*, March 14, 2018, https://www.ncronline.org/priest-who-served-brooklyn-parishes -found-murdered-colombia.

been high there, which led in 2014 to the kidnapping of a military chaplain, Fr. Reinaldo Lures, by opposition forces seeking to oust the president. He died while in their hands. This cross-border chaos is, unfortunately, all too common in several troubled Latin American nations—and has even spilled over into the United States.

El Salvador

While Catholics are martyred year after year, it often takes time for them to be officially declared martyrs, as the Vatican sorts through claims and counterclaims. Especially where there's great social unrest and open violence, it can be hard to distinguish martyrdom from mere murder. It was not until 2022, for instance, that the Catholic Church canonized four Salvadoran martyrs who were killed in 1977: two priests, Fr. Rutilio Grande, S.J., and the Italian Franciscan Cosme Spessotto, and two laypeople, Manuel Solorzano and Nelson Lemus. All were killed by "death squads," as was Archbishop Oscar Romero, who died in 1980 and was declared a saint and martyr in 2018—though only after long dispute about whether he had been killed for political or "new martyr" reasons.

Ironically, Romero was something of a traditionalist; he participated in an Opus Dei retreat, for example, shortly before he died. But it was his adherence to the true "liberation theology" of Paul VI, as he put it, the Catholic protection and promotion of the people in both their material and spiritual lives, that pitted him against a violently repressive right-wing regime. In all, fourteen priests along with numerous laypeople were killed during El Salvador's violent decades, in the 1970s and 1980s. At Romero's funeral alone, between thirty and fifty people died (reports vary).

Indeed, by a strange new reverse contamination, gangs were transferred into El Salvador from the United States, where they had flourished in places such as Los Angeles.[43] And it has been the Salvadoran government under the controversial president Nayib Bukele that has taken the lead in curbing gang violence by mass incarceration. It's one indication of how religious rights are being lost in the postmodern world that reports on human rights abuses in El Salvador, in the course of Bukele's crackdown, highlight prisoners' rights, women's rights, LGBTQ+ rights, and so on but entirely ignore the ways in which religious leaders are involved in efforts at rehabilitating criminals and encouraging gang members to forgo a life of violence and crime, something that everywhere provokes violent backlash.

Argentina

Perhaps more than any other region in the world, Latin America has been marked by Catholics martyred in the twentieth century but not recognized until the twenty-first. This phenomenon has something to do, of course, with the fact that an Argentine pope was elected in 2013 with a special knowledge of many lesser-known cases. But it's not the whole explanation. The big, murderous totalitarian regimes of the twentieth century were pretty well documented by the start of the new millennium. There are good surveys of the martyrs under the Soviets and the Warsaw Pact countries,[44] the Nazis, the wholesale slaughters in the Cristero War

---

[43] Leila Miller, "They Left Gangs and Found God. But They Weren't Spared in El Salvador's Crackdown," *Los Angeles Times*, April 19, 2023. See, in particular, the account of how "LA born" gangs returned to El Salvador.

[44] See, for instance, the monumental volume by Stéphane Courtois and five other authors, *The Black Book of Communism: Crimes, Terror, Repression* (Cambridge, MA: Harvard University Press, 1999).

in Mexico and the Spanish Civil War. By contrast, there is much less available for several countries in Latin America, partly because the body counts weren't nearly as high, partly because—except in cases such as the Jesuits killed in El Salvador—the world simply didn't pay much attention to the priests and even the occasional bishop killed here and there.

In Pope Francis's own Argentina, for instance, Bishop Enrique Ángel Angelelli Carletti was assassinated on August 4, 1976, in the midst of the Guerra Sucia, the infamous "Dirty War" that ran from 1974 to 1983. During that war, a military junta ran "death squads" that sought to eliminate members of various groups thought to be promoting communism, socialism, left-wing Peronism, or international Leftism in general, including a Catholic movement known as the Montoneros. Tens of thousands were "disappeared," a term that was developed to describe political murders not only in Argentina but in other places—especially El Salvador—in Latin America. The U.S. government, which was fighting "proxy wars" against communism on several continents as the Cold War was reaching its turning point, was complicit—especially in the person of then secretary of state Henry Kissinger—in the Argentine repression.

Bishop Angelelli was closely identified with the Church of the Poor, a movement that was to mark the future Pope Francis as well. He was killed shortly after the murder of three other people in his diocese of La Rioja: two priests, Carlos de Dios Murias, an Argentine Franciscan, and Gabriel Longueville, a French missionary from Viviers; and the lay catechist Wenceslao Pedernera. They had been working out of a parish in La Rioja, trying to oppose state-sponsored human rights abuses, an effort that, in itself, could get people marked as "dangerous Leftists." The priests were kidnapped after a parish Mass, and their dead bodies were found in a field with signs of torture. De Dios Murias's eyes had been gouged out and his hands cut off. Pedernera was shot multiple times in front of his wife and three children.

Their bishop's death followed logically, though it was rare in Latin America for bishops to die in times of political unrest. The details of his murder, sadly, resemble similar events that were taking place around the same time in Eastern Europe, thereby mirroring the worst features of the communist oppression from which the Dirty War was allegedly protecting Argentines and, more generally, Americans. Bishop Angelelli had worked for many years among Catholics in the slums but probably drew the most attention from authorities for his role in organizing labor unions, which were often perceived as—and sometimes truly were—of the Left and anti-government. He also tried to get the local governor, Carlos Menem, later president of Argentina, to release a large stretch of land for use by the population. The grant was approved, then denied. The bishop put the whole area under an interdict, suspending Masses and religious functions. Pope Paul VI sent the then head of the Jesuits, Pedro Arrupe, and a local archbishop to examine the case. The pair supported the embattled bishop.

Bishop Angelelli visited Rome in 1974 and was warned by the Vatican not to return to Argentina. But he believed he could not abandon his work or his people. Indeed, his assassination occurred as he was driving back in a truck from celebrating the funeral of Frs. de Dios Murias and Longueville. Isabel Perón had just been ousted from Argentina's presidency, and the military junta was taking aggressive steps to root out opposition. Fr. Luis Pinto, who was at the wheel of the bishop's truck, later reported that they were forced off the road by two other vehicles. Fr. Pinto survived, but Bishop Angelelli died in the crash—or from an attack on his person after the truck had overturned.

A decade-long investigation ensued. Officials claimed that Fr. Pinto simply lost control of the vehicle for some reason. It was implausible—the brakes and steering were found to be functioning—but the explanation was accepted at the time. Ten years later, Argentina was a democracy again, and three suspects—air force officers José Carlos González, Luis Manzanelli, and Ricardo Román Oscar Otero—were identified as having carried out the premeditated murder. Various trials were started, halted, and restarted as laws were passed that changed the approach to investigations of abuses during the Dirty War. It was only in 2015 that Manzanelli and another man were convicted of the murder. Before then, *L'Osservatore Romano* in Rome and even an archbishop of Buenos Aires, Juan Carlos Aramburu, had accepted the official version of events. In 2016, Pope Francis named Bishop Angelelli a martyr and started the process that led to his beatification in November of that same year.

Peru

Bishops, priests, religious, and laypeople have long—from colonial times forward—been engaged in promoting peace throughout Latin America. These efforts are not, to say the least, always welcome by those who benefit from the chaos and mayhem in various countries. No violent death is to be taken lightly, of course, but in some instances, they occur in such absurd conditions that it's difficult to believe that depraved gangs will stoop to such things. One such instance occurred in 1990 but came to prominence only in 2023. Sr. María Agustina Rivas López was working at the Social Promotion Center in La Florida, Peru, teaching young women cooking and other domestic arts that they needed to live better lives in the midst of the civil disturbances then plaguing their county—and to keep them away from the Sendero Luminoso (Shining Path), a violent Maoist import seeking to overthrow the Peruvian government that declared itself "feminist" and thereby attracted many young women to its cause.

A group of armed men from that movement broke into the Social Promotion Center and rounded up half a dozen people, including Sr. Rivas. Their leader announced their sentence: "You are sentenced to death because you sow peace, promote the social condition of people, and give them sweets." Despite the ridiculousness of this gesture, they meant business. Sr. Rivas offered herself, Kolbe-like, as a ransom for the others, but the offer was refused. She knelt on the floor in prayer as the killers brutally executed all six captives. Ironically, this took place as part of the "People's War" that the Sendero Luminoso was waging in order to install what it called a "new democracy," a rather typical claim for armed Marxist guerrillas in Latin America. Sr. Rivas understood the risk she was taking in her work; thus, in accord with the recent understanding of martyrdom, Pope Francis declared that her attackers killed her *in odium fidei*, and he beatified her in 2022.

The year after the murder of Sr. Rivas and her companions, nine priests were killed by Sendero in Peru, including two Polish missionaries, Miguel Tomaszek and Zbigniew Strzalkowski—with the explanation that "this is how agents of imperialism die"—and an Italian priest, Fr. Alessandro Dordi. Almost needless to say, these priests were not agents of anything other than the gospel, let alone "imperialism," and they had chosen to put themselves in harm's way in order to minister to the Peruvian people and do what they could to lessen suffering and promote peace. They were all beatified by Pope Francis in 2015. And though their status as martyrs seems clear, and the pope used that term to describe them, the Vatican is waiting for the usual confirmation via miracles before canonizing them.

Nicaragua

The large totalitarian regimes of the previous century have mostly disappeared—though not in the case of China—but there are still elements of the communist itch to control the Church even in Latin America. Among the many instances of persecution and death in various countries (notably, Nicaragua, Cuba, and Venezuela) that have many similarities with one another, one might be taken as emblematic of the rest because it displays both a continuation of the old twentieth-century Marxism in its sometimes-new forms in the twenty-first century.

Nicaragua was one of the countries in which the several "proxy wars" in the larger Cold War took place. From 1985 to 1990 (after which subsidies from the Soviet Union ceased upon the USSR's demise), the Sandinistas—a Marxist regime headed by Daniel Ortega Saavedra—immediately began to put increased pressure on the independence of the Catholic Church. Ortega had already been active in a revolutionary movement known as the Junta of National Reconstruction. Indeed, when Pope John Paul II himself traveled to Nicaragua in 1983, as Marxist forces were already dominating in the small nation, he was subjected to loud interruptions by an organized mob during his Mass in Managua. The Sandinistas had not only installed themselves directly in front of the altar but had even wired a second sound system,[45] which they controlled, using it to try to drown out the pontiff's homily about unity in the Church and forcing him famously to cry out in Spanish, "*Silencio!*" Toward the end of the first quarter of the twenty-first century, after various ups and downs, in and out of power, Daniel Ortega was again ruling Nicaragua. He had taken

---

[45] George Weigel, *Witness to Hope: The Biography of Pope John Paul II* (New York: Cliff Street Books, 2012), 455.

power again in 2007 and not given it up, and he again trained his repression on the Catholic hierarchy, especially prominent Bishop Rolando José Álvarez Lagos.

Bishop Álvarez was placed under house arrest in 2022 after he had protested the closure of several Catholic radio stations and the Nicaraguan regime's human rights abuses. He was charged with multiple crimes: treason, conspiracy, "organizing violent groups … to carry out acts of hate against the population," "damaging the Nicaraguan government and society," and spreading "false information," among other alleged infractions.[46] Merely to list such crimes is to show how ridiculous these charges are in the case of a sixty-year-old priest and prelate who had, in reality, done little more than try to protect the Church and the Nicaraguan people from widespread attacks. But under a legal system controlled by the whole Ortega family, when he refused to leave the country—and be sent to the United States (one condition was that he sign a blank piece of paper that might later be "filled in" so as to confirm his confession of "crimes")—he was sentenced to twenty-six years in prison.

Álvarez was born in Managua, the Nicaraguan capital, and began his studies for the priesthood at several places in Central America before taking degrees in theology at the Lateran University and in philosophy at the Gregorian University, two highly regarded Catholic institutions of higher learning in Rome. In addition to these accomplishments, he went to Spain's University of Salamanca to study modern Catholic social doctrine, clearly to

---

[46] "Rolando Álvarez," United States Commission on International Religious Freedom, accessed December 5, 2024, https://www .uscirf.gov/religious-prisoners-conscience/forb-victims-database /rolando-alvarez.

prepare himself for his return to Nicaragua, where the traditional Church and her hierarchy, especially Cardinal Miguel Obando y Bravo, were contending with priests and others in the government who were promoting a heavily Marxist-laden form of liberation theology. Back home, he was tasked with running the Managua Archdiocese's youth ministry, Radio Nicaragua, and a local parish as well as other duties. In a clear recognition of his competence and influence, he was also named executive secretary of the Central American Bishops' Secretariat (2009–2011), after which he was consecrated bishop of Matagalpa.

The shape of his whole priesthood was such that it brought him inevitably into conflict with the Nicaraguan regime. There were plenty of such points of conflict, given the way the Ortegas repressed all dissent. As he detailed them on Radio Nicaragua and elsewhere, Álvarez came under ever closer personal surveillance. He was constantly followed by the police. His family felt threatened. Finally, in 2022, he announced that he was going on a hunger strike in protest against police harassment. In a video of the announcement that he sent to Aid to the Church in Need, he explained: "At one point I asked the police why they were there, and they told me it was for my own safety. But we know that in this country insecurity comes precisely from the police, they were the ones making me feel unsafe." And he added: "I will fast until such a time as the police, through the president or the vice-president of the Bishops' Conference, and only them, inform me that they will begin to respect the privacy of my family's circle."[47]

---

[47] Felipe d'Avillez, "Nicaragua: Bishop Goes on Hunger Strike to Protest Police Harassment," Aid to the Church in Need, May 24, 2022, https://www.churchinneed.org/nicaragua-bishop-goes-on -hunger-strike-to-protest-police-harassment/.

This only increased efforts to silence him: they forced the closure of the Canal Católico, the Church-run television channel, and blocked roads to prevent people from reaching his Masses or communicating with him, among other measures. A priest familiar with what Bishop Álvarez and others were trying to do characterized their work in this way: "The Gospel teaches us that we must open our doors to those who are persecuted, and this is what we did. Our churches were turned into refuges, not into opposition planning centers, as the government claims."[48] The sequel was predictable. As the *New York Times* reported it, "the most prominent voice of protest in Nicaragua" was arrested in August 2022 and placed under house arrest, while eight of his colleagues went to jail. He was "the most senior clergyman to be detained in Latin America for political views in decades."[49]

Protest erupted internationally and in the Vatican. Pope Francis made a carefully worded plea for reconciliation, but under the circumstances—Ortega did not have the votes to be reelected and had decided to hold on to power by suppressing all opposition—that proved impossible. The small diocese of Estelí, however, where Bishop Álvarez had also served, was able to issue a statement to the Ortega regime. "It is you who are creating fear and disorder in this country," read the statement issued by the Estelí clergy. "We are trying to reconcile the people who you are dividing with your actions. We state that it is possible to be brothers despite our differences."[50]

---

[48] D'Avillez, "Hunger Strike."

[49] Alfonso Flores Bermúdez, Anatoly Kurmanaev, and Yubelka Mendoza, "Nicaragua Silences Its Last Outspoken Critics: Catholic Priests," *New York Times*, updated August 24, 2022, https://www.nytimes.com/2022/08/23/world/americas/nicaragua-catholic-church-daniel-ortega.html.

[50] Flores Bermúdez, Kurmanaev, and Mendoza, "Nicaragua Silences."

The bishop was held for six months under house arrest and then imprisoned along with Bishop Isidoro Mora and about a dozen other priests. Their fates were unknown for several months as the Nicaraguan government negotiated with the Vatican—and tried to pressure the pope into allowing the Ortegas to oversee the appointment of bishops. Happily, they were all later released. By that point, several were ill from mistreatment or prior medical conditions, but they were sent safely to Rome.

It's worth naming them here. Too often, the prominent spokesman is recognized while others who run the same risks remain obscure. They are:

* Msgr. Carlos Avilés, vicar-general of the Archdiocese of Managua
* Msgr. Óscar Escoto Salgado, vicar-general of the Diocese of Matagalpa
* Fr. Ismael Reineiro Serrano Gudiel, pastor of San Miguel Arcángel parish and exorcist of the Archdiocese of Managua
* Msgr. Silvio Fonseca, pastor of Santa Faz parish and vicar of family, children, and youth of the Archdiocese of Managua
* Fr. Pablo Villafranca, pastor of Nuestra Señor de Veracruz parish in Nindirí, Archdiocese of Managua
* Fr. Héctor Treminio, pastor of Santo Cristo de Esquipulas parish, Archdiocese of Managua
* Msgr. Marcos Díaz Prado, pastor of Santo Tomás Apóstol parish of Puerto de Corinto, Diocese of León
* Fr. Mykel Monterrey, pastor of Nuestra Señora de Candelaria parish, Archdiocese of Managua
* Fr. Raúl Zamora, pastor of Jesús de la Divina Misericordia parish, Archdiocese of Managua

❖ Fr. Gerardo José Rodríguez, pastor of Purísima Concepción parish, Archdiocese of Managua

❖ Fr. Miguel Mántica, pastor of San Francisco de Asís parish, Archdiocese of Managua

❖ Fr. Jhader Hernández, pastor of Mother of the Divine Pastor parish in Nejapa, Archdiocese of Managua

❖ Fr. José Gustavo Sandino Ochoa, pastor of Nuestra Señora de los Dolores parish in Santa María de Pantasma, Diocese of Jinotega

❖ Fr. Jader Danilo Guido Acosta, parochial vicar of San Pedro Apóstol Cathedral of Matagalpa

❖ Fr. Fernando Calero, pastor of Our Lady of Fátima in Rancho Grande parish, Diocese of Matagalpa

❖ Seminarians Lester de Jesús Sáenz Centeno and Tonny Daniel Palacio Sequeira.[51]

According to a report by Aid to the Church in Need, in 2023 (including cases from the previous year) forty-six Catholic priests, four seminarians, and two bishops were being held for similar trumped-up charges in Nicaraguan prisons. Whole orders of nuns—Mother Teresa's Missionaries of Charity among them—were expelled, and Catholic schools were closed.[52] To get a sense of what such numbers mean in a small country: Nicaragua has a population of just under 7 million (fewer than New York

---

[51] Edgar Beltrán, "Bishop Álvarez Freed in Nicaragua, Exiled to Vatican," *Pillar*, January 14, 2023, https://www.pillarcatholic.com/p/bishop-alvarez-freed-in-nicaragua.

[52] Tyler Arnold, "Report: Over 130 Catholic Priests and Religious Arrested, Kidnapped, or Murdered in 2023," Catholic News Agency, January 10, 2024, https://www.catholicnewsagency.com/news/256498/report-over-130-catholic-priests-and-religious-arrested-kidnapped-or-murdered-in-2023.

City). Communist China has a population of 1.4 billion, two hundred times larger than Nicaragua's, and had around half the number of Catholic priests in detention that same year. A common worry in Latin America once was whether a government crackdown on the Church in a particular country meant that it might turn into "the next Cuba." In the 2020s, people were sometimes heard to say such repression might be turning a country into "the next Nicaragua."

Cuba

Ironically, around the time Nicaraguan police were harassing Bishop *Rolando* Álvarez, Cuban Fr. *Castor* Álvarez was being beaten by Cuban police in the eastern city of Camagüey for a similar set of charges—"public disorder"; specifically, he was protesting government policies and inaction that were squeezing the Cuban people. This event might serve as a symbol of a return of Cuba's harsh treatment of religion in the twenty-first century, which had for much of the early 2000s been a bit more tolerant than in the decades following Fidel Castro's communist revolution in 1959. Fidel had been educated in part by the Jesuits but became an atheist and—when he entered his revolutionary phase—a sharp foe of the Catholic Church.

Like all the Catholic establishments in Latin America, the Church in Cuba had had ties with both the government and the wealthy elite. But the Cuban Church in particular had an unusually good record in reaching into native and poor communities. Unlike elsewhere, in the nineteenth century, half the parishes in Cuba had pastors who were native-born priests. And the Church had carried out important missions in education, health care, and relief for the poor. But as in other places where communist regimes came to power, the Church was regarded as solely an obstacle to revolution, the "opium of the masses," and the ally of a corrupt and unequal political social structure—which certainly did exist in Cuba.

Over the next half century and more, then, the Cuban regime tightly controlled the Catholic Church and other religious bodies. The anti-religious stance softened slightly after the fall of the Soviet Union in 1991, though Communist China began to take the USSR's place in providing support for an otherwise disastrous economy. Communism had turned Cuba, once among the wealthiest and best-educated of Latin countries, into an impoverished and backward nation. But by the early years of the twenty-first century, Open Doors—the international organization that supports persecuted Christians worldwide—described the new situation like this: "While the persecution of Christians in the past included beatings, imprisonment and sometimes murder, it continues in the form of harassment, strict surveillance and discrimination, including occasional imprisonment of leaders. All believers are monitored, and all church services are infiltrated by informers."[53] For a while, Cuba even dropped off Open Doors' top-fifty persecutor nations.

This may have been partly the result of Pope Francis's outreach, his travels to the island nation, and his efforts as a Latin American to improve relations. With the death of Fidel Castro in 2016 and the assumption of power by his brother Raúl, some believed that there was a potential opening for civil society institutions

---

[53] "Christianity Once Considered a 'Disease' but Now 'Tolerated' in Cuba," World Watch Monitor, October 26, 2016, https://www .worldwatchmonitor.org/2016/10/christianity-once-considered -a-disease-but-now-tolerated-in-cuba/.

to operate at least a little more freely; this is not surprising, relatively speaking, after the harsh control of the twentieth century. But as economic and political conditions worsened, the regime resorted to the usual tactics. Beginning around 2020, pressure on Christians increased once again. By 2024, Open Doors put Cuba around the twenty-second worst in the world—about the same as notorious places such as Burkina Faso, the Central African Republic, and China.

Fr. Álvarez was beaten and arrested because he was trying to protect others—who were also arrested—who protested sharply worsening economic and health conditions. These are always precarious in communist command economies, but in 2021, they were especially bad, owing to repressive government policies and the appearance of COVID. Inflation was rampant, which squeezed an already struggling population, and medical care was simply inadequate to deal with the new virus. Electrical blackouts started to occur. Fr. Rolando Montes de Oca, a priest of the Archdiocese of Camagüey, where Fr. Álvarez was arrested, remarked, "It is a situation that takes us Cubans back to a period of crisis, which is a kind of national trauma, the special period in the years 1992, 1993 and 1994, in which there were blackouts of many hours." (The early 1990s were especially difficult in Cuba because the large subsidies that the nation received from the Soviet Union dried up with the dissolution of the USSR in 1991.) Fr. Montes de Oca added, "This that is happening in Cuba is unique, at least in the last six decades. I'm 40 years old and I had never seen something like this: all the protests and all the violent repression of the government."[54] The

---

[54] David Ramos, "Priest Beaten, Arrested amid Cuba Protests," Catholic News Agency, July 12, 2021, https://www.catholicnewsagency.com/news/248345/priest-beaten-arrested-amid-cuba-protests.

government, of course, resorted to its old tactic of characterizing these protests as anti-revolutionary acts sponsored by the United States and issued an order that "all the revolutionaries ... take to the streets to defend the revolution everywhere."[55]

Anti-government sentiment is always boiling just below the surface in Cuba—hence the constant surveillance. Besides the immediate limits on Church activity, it's difficult to get permissions and materials to build churches—an urgent need because numbers of believers continue to grow despite repression. Bibles and Christian literature are banned. As a Protestant pastor rightly observed, "The Bible has always been restricted in communist countries because it is an agent for change."[56] In a clever move, the government sometimes forces churches to claim that their outreach to the poor and the ill is not, in fact, church-based but relief activity by the government. Churches have to comply with this untruth to get some degree of space to operate. Given the confluence of different factors, it is no wonder that protest burst out at this point all over the country. Despite the roundup of anyone who resisted, a group of protesters even appeared outside the prison to protest Fr. Álvarez's detention and to demand his release.

Two years after the crisis and the arrest of Fr. Álvarez, things were, if anything, even worse for Cuba's Christians and citizens more generally. Catholics who spoke out against injustices were still receiving threats, though the government was careful not to make any high-profile martyrs. Masses were permitted in churches, but otherwise surveillance and control were everywhere. Fr. Alberto Reyes, of the Archdiocese of Camagüey, told ACI Prensa specifically about the situation of priests:

---

[55] Ramos, "Priest Beaten."
[56] "Christianity Once Considered a 'Disease.'"

If we also consider the prophetic mission of the Church as part of religious freedom ... there are continuous obstacles, because priests [and] men and women religious who have raised our voices have been harassed, publicly confronted by government partisans, and we have been summoned to State Security.... We have been threatened with being prosecuted and being imprisoned if we continue to publish our opinion on the situation in the country in the media when it doesn't agree with the official version of the government.[57]

Though there has been a delicate series of negotiations between Cuba's bishops and the regime and occasional efforts by the Vatican to broker some deals without provoking the Cuban leadership, the nation's priests have become even more direct and outspoken as the situation has worsened. Fr. Léster Zayas, O.P., the priest who, by 2024, had become the most visible figure in resisting the whole range of social, political, anti-religious injustices in Cuba, has explained why the priests continue in spite of seemingly impossible odds. And, in the process, he has expressed what may be the basis for hope for Cuba—and everywhere that Catholics are being martyred and persecuted in the twenty-first century:

Although I fear reprisals, I am even more afraid of not being faithful to my people.... People call me "brave," but I'm

---

[57] Eduardo Berdejo, "Priest: Cuban Government Threatening Religious Who Express Opinion on Country's Situation," Catholic News Agency, July 24, 2023, https://www.catholicnewsagency .com/news/254861/priest-cuban-government-threatening-religious -who-express-opinion-on-country-s-situation; brackets in the original.

not brave at all. I'm more afraid of hell for not being faithful to the truth and people's suffering than anything else.[58]

Venezuela

Of the socialist-Marxist regimes in Latin America, Venezuela is the third that is pressuring the Church in the twenty-first century and is distinctive in that its bishops have directly challenged the regime. Until the start of the twenty-first century, Venezuela was an oil-rich, basically prosperous Latin American country. But that status began to change with the approval of a new "Bolivarian" Constitution in 1999, which has had a huge impact on subsequent years. Hugo Chávez, a highly charismatic radical, took charge of the government and ruled until 2013, when he died of cancer. He was followed by Nicolás Maduro, who has ruled since then, including being "reelected" in July 2024 in elections widely viewed as clearly fraudulent. Election officials claimed he had received 51 percent of the vote, a modest claim in such circumstances, but given widespread protests against his impoverishment of the country and repression of all opposition—including the Church—which has forced close to eight million Venezuelans (perhaps a quarter of the population) to flee, even that gesture seemed highly implausible.

The Venezuelan bishops, in line with Church leaders in many Latin American countries, framed the political crisis in religious, even biblical, terms:

The words of Our Lord Jesus Christ, "The truth will set you free" (John 8:31), have insistently resonated in our minds

---

[58] Edgar Beltrán, "Why Cuba Is Getting Worse for the Catholic Church," *Pillar*, May 21, 2024, https://www.pillarcatholic.com/p /why-cuba-is-getting-worse-for-the.

and hearts, so we would like to reiterate the appeal to the National Electoral Council to … publish in detail the results of the electoral process carried out on July 28, in which the Venezuelan people's desire for change has been evident.[59]

Their plea has not been answered.

A Note on Haiti

Although Haiti, as a former French colony, is not part of Spanish- and Portuguese-speaking "Latin" America, it warrants brief attention here because not only does it suffer from extreme poverty, criminality, and government abuse, but it is perhaps the most lawless and chaotic nation in the Americas. Those who choose to live and work in Haiti—including priests, missionaries, and aid workers—know in advance that life is not much respected there and that violent attacks and death may come their way at any time. Such circumstances are particularly prone to producing John Paul II's "new martyrs" and Pope Francis's category of those who have offered an *oblatio vitae* in situations of sudden death. Among them all is almost a presumptive heroic witness and willingness to die for the faith, if not over theological differences, then in the carrying out of the Christian obligation to love one's neighbor in conditions where love is not evident.

Haitian society has a long history of disorder and violence from its very beginning as a nation. The Haitian Revolution started in 1791, and, in 1804, Haiti formally declared its independence from France—among the very first former European colonies to become

[59] Eduardo Campos Lima, "Venezuela Bishops Demand Government Come Clean about Election Results," *Crux*, October 19, 2024, https://cruxnow.com/church-in-the-americas/2024/10/venezuela-bishops-demand-government-come-clean-about-election-results.

independent (only the United States was earlier). In addition, it was one of the rare former colonies that would go on to be run for its entire history by black natives of the island nation. But that history has been marked by instability and political turmoil. Catholicism was the official religion until 1987. But Haiti had signed a concordat with the Vatican—an agreement that formally gives the Church special status and protection—in 1860, which remains in force. The island's Catholicism is also mixed with practices of voodoo, a West African import.

Among the many poor nations in the Americas, Haiti ranks as the very poorest. And as with those other nations, poverty and, above all, disorder have given rise to criminality on a truly staggering scale. In addition, in the twenty-first century, the island was hit by a series of natural disasters that have made traditionally bad circumstances markedly worse: in 2004, it was Hurricane Jeanne; then, in 2010, one of the most destructive earthquakes ever recorded; followed by another hurricane in 2016; and another powerful earthquake in 2021. And as if that were not enough, also in 2021, the Haitian president Jovenel Moïse was assassinated. Although there are many native clergy and Catholic institutions in Haiti, they are simply unable to manage so many social and humanitarian challenges, which has required the arrival of aid workers from abroad in large numbers. And despite the good they do, in Haiti, priests, nuns, brothers, and religious workers are often abducted—fourteen in the first half of 2024 alone—mostly for huge ransoms that religious institutions are utterly unable to pay.[60]

[60] Eduardo Campos Lima, "In Crime-Stricken Haiti, Catholic Priests and Nuns Are Targeted as Kidnap Victims," Religion News Service, April 1, 2024, https://religionnews.com/2024/04/01/in-crime -stricken-haiti-catholic-priests-and-nuns-are-targeted-as-kidnap -victims/.

According to reports, there is also some residual resentment against Catholic clergy as a holdover from the years in which the Church was partly subordinate to the brutal Duvalier family's leadership. Where it existed, that connection was outrageous. "Papa Doc" (François) Duvalier, who ruled the island nation from 1957 to 1971, was succeeded by his son "Baby Doc" (Jean-Claude), who continued the family dynasty until he was overthrown in 1986. Papa Doc had the churches he controlled change the Our Father they recited to say:

> Our Doc who art in the National Palace for life, hallowed be thy name by present and future generations. Thy will be done in Port-au-Prince and in the provinces. Give us this day our new Haiti and never forgive the trespasses of the anti-patriots who spit every day on our country; let them succumb to temptations, and under the weight of their venom, deliver them not from any evil.[61]

Through a clever manipulation of elements of voodoo (a further threat comparable to Santa Muerte in Mexico), Christianity, racism, and anti-communism — to say nothing of thousands of murders and intimidation by the Tonton Macoute, his personal paramilitary force — Papa Doc managed to stay in power and pass down the country to his son, even claiming divine spiritual status for himself: "I am neither the red nor the white but the indivisible bicolour of the Haitian people. I am already an Immaterial Being." He was nicknamed the "Lucifer of the Antilles."[62] And it's

[61] "Haiti," Concordat Watch, accessed February 14, 2025, https://www.concordatwatch.eu/haiti-s847.

[62] Fiona Cane, "Francois 'Papa Doc' Duvalier," LinkedIn, January 23, 2016, https://www.linkedin.com/pulse/francois-papa-doc-cuvalier-fiona-cane.

no wonder that the decades of Duvalier family rule, along with many other endemic problems, have left a chaotic mark on Haiti.

With the departure of the Duvaliers, the heads of the Haitian state have mostly had short, disorderly terms in office. When John Paul II visited in 1983, he said simply, "Things must change here"—an understatement if there ever was one. The Haitians twice elected an anti-Duvalier priest, Jean-Bertrand Aristide, near the beginning of the twenty-first century, but even he was unable to change Haiti's chaotic culture much. Among the many blows the nation has suffered, in October 2024, there occurred yet another that might serve as a symbol of the whole nation: a hospital run by Mother Teresa's Missionaries of Charity (which provided free medical care for fifteen hundred inpatients and more than thirty thousand outpatients) was looted and burned to the ground—while drugs and other items began to be sold by the gang in the surrounding neighborhood.[63]

Amid that chaos, attacks and murders occur that can't always be explained. A representative sampling:

- ❖ In 2010, Fr. Richard E. Joyal, a Canadian priest who had come to Haiti to help relocate students after the earthquake, was robbed and killed.
- ❖ In 2018, Fr. Joseph Simoly was killed in Port-au-Prince, possibly in a robbery, partly, according to rumors, with some government involvement for unknown reasons.
- ❖ In 2021, Fr. André Sylvestre was shot outside a bank where he had just withdrawn some money, but robbery

---

[63] "Convent of Mother Teresa's Missionaries Looted and Burned in Haiti," Zenit, October 31, 2024, https://zenit.org/2024/10/31/convent-of-mother-teresas-missionaries-looted-and-burned-in-haiti/.

apparently was not the motive, since the money was not stolen.

❖ In 2022, a similar incident involved Sr. Luisa Dell'Orto, an Italian nun who had worked for twenty years in Haiti. A priest commented, "It seems it was not a robbery or even a kidnapping attempt, but one of the many cases of absurd violence that the proliferation of weapons allows. Luisa had no enemies." The nun's sister added: "She was aware that something might happen; even in her last letter she said that the situation was very difficult."[64]

❖ In 2024, Bishop Pierre André Dumas was injured in an explosion. Some say it was merely an accident, others that it was the result of his offering himself in exchange for six nuns being held hostage.

Conditions in Haiti offer an almost textbook case of what Pope Francis was getting at in designating *oblatio vitae* – offering oneself on the spot as a form of heroic Christian witness. In a place like Haiti, that is something that everyone involved in the Church's mission knows may be demanded of them on any day, at any hour.

---

[64] Inés San Martín, "Four Priests, One Religious Sister Murdered in One Week," *Crux*, June 28, 2022, https://cruxnow.com/church-in-africa/2022/06/four-priests-one-religious-sister-murdered-in-one-week.

2

The Middle East

"A voice is heard in Ramah,
  lamentation and bitter weeping.
Rachel is weeping for her children;
  she refuses to be comforted for her children,
  because they are not."

Thus says the LORD:
"Keep your voice from weeping,
  and your eyes from tears;
for your work shall be rewarded,
  says the LORD,
  and they shall come back from the land of the enemy.
There is hope for your future,
  says the LORD,
  and your children shall come back to their own country.

—Jeremiah 31:15–17

The Rise of Islamic Radicalism

The attack on the Twin Towers in New York City and the Pentagon in Washington, D.C., on September 11, 2001, announced to the whole world a new reality that has squarely confronted Christians and others in the first quarter of the twenty-first century. An Islamic fundamentalism has emerged with the means to cause mayhem and havoc anywhere on earth. It had been developing for several decades in the Middle East and on the Mediterranean Coast of Africa (and had even attacked the World Trade Center less successfully in 1993) and was determined to destroy the West—by which it meant America and Europe—and what it regarded as the presence of "Christian crusaders" in historical Muslim lands.

Even prior to 9/11, however, several Muslim countries from Morocco to Algeria to Libya to Egypt, as well as Lebanon, Syria, and Iraq—home to historically second-class but tolerated Christian minorities—had found themselves beset by radical Islamist movements that not only targeted Christians but even struck at Muslim communities that the Islamists deemed insufficiently radical. The circumstances varied from country to country, to be sure, but the results were basically the same—and deadly for many Christians who had long lived in otherwise quiet and relatively safe enclaves. And the rise of Islamic radicalism in the Middle East would influence similar developments in Africa and the Far East, as will be examined in subsequent chapters of the present work.

These threats to Christians in many parts of the world raise uncomfortable questions about the relations between religions—for those of us in the West. In the West, where religious belief plays an increasingly minor role in public affairs, there is an assumption that coexistence among various faiths is easy. All that is required is a live-and-let-live attitude in public spaces that are—in theory—neutral among various kinds of belief and even unbelief. That has been a difficult stance to maintain, but it has worked tolerably well in some countries, within some very clear limits. (And even in those countries, the achievement of religious toleration is now under strain from movements such as "Satan worship," the radicalism of recent Islamic migrants, and other post-Christian currents in public life.) But the ease of mutual toleration is a false—Western—assumption with regard to religion globally.

Religious toleration is necessary and urgent in Western nations where pluralism is a social *fact*, and a peaceful social order depends on some degree of mutual goodwill and shared understandings for the sake of the common life. But that otherwise admirable attitude can be a hindrance to a proper appraisal of realities elsewhere, not least in the case of militant Islam in the Middle East.

As will become clear in the chapters that follow, these Western assumptions and aspirations are not shared everywhere in the rest of the world, and least of all by Islamic militants. In some places, to be sure, religions are used as mere political tools. That seems to be the case in twenty-first-century India. Fundamentalist forms of Hinduism, a religion that historically has not had a theological imperative to impose itself on others, is being utilized by various political actors to promote national identity against the powerful cultural forces coming from the West. Many Western observers tend to believe that *all* religious clashes are really, at bottom, political or economic or cultural—categories that Westerners are more comfortable in dealing with. And in India, that approach explains, to a large degree, the recent rise of a nationalist Hinduism that has taken an aggressive stance against Christians—and, owing to longstanding tensions, against Muslims as well.

There are, however, other religious forms that do not fit into this first-world perspective. Radical Islam is, in the twenty-first century, the most conspicuous instance of a faith with a *militant theology*. The vast majority of Muslims are not terrorists and have, in the past, been able to live relatively peacefully with other monotheistic believers. But individual countries vary in their stances. Jordan, for example is (relatively) tolerant and has accepted hundreds of thousands of Christian refugees fleeing from the wars in Syria and Iraq. The king of Bahrain has allowed a Christian basilica, Our Lady of Arabia, and a Christian study center to be built on the island to accommodate Catholics living in his country. But Iran and Saudi Arabia, of course, and several other majority-Muslim countries impose very severe restrictions on Christians in public spaces. One of the particular features of radical Islam or Islamism is precisely that it is *international* and doesn't much care about national differences in its pursuit of a new "caliphate."

Such distinctions do not, in any case, go to the heart of the question of whether there is a new type of Islam—or rather an old type that has experienced a recent resurgence—that bears many of the marks that we usually associate with large political tyrannies such as the communism, fascism, and Nazism of the twentieth century. Indeed, many Westerners tend to dismiss this kind of analysis because it challenges the generous hope that, in open, liberal societies, everyone may be accommodated under a kind of Enlightenment rationality. Violent Islamic groups, therefore, are often defined as not representative of their own tradition or as merely political or economic or cultural actors. Yet radical Islamists claim to find in the Quran and the Hadith justifications for expelling "infidels" from their nations, and they see the history of Islamic caliphates as the proper form of social organization—and an authorization for violent action wherever the faith or the Prophet are not respected.

Salman Rushdie, a novelist of Indian-Muslim birth, who has lived and worked in the United Kingdom and America for much of his career, became a cause célèbre internationally when he published in 1988 *The Satanic Verses*, a magical-realist novel that portrayed Muhammad as having accepted some disputed verses about pagan divinities in the Quran. A fatwa authorizing Rushdie's murder was issued by the Iranian supreme leader, the ayatollah Ruhollah Khomeini, and Rushdie had to go into hiding, protected for years by British authorities. The novel was banned in dozens of Muslim nations, threats were made against him personally and against the publishers of his work, and terrorist attacks were carried out in various places with the explanation that they were in retaliation for his insults to Islam. The animus against him was so great that, thirty-four years later, in 2022, he was stabbed in New York by a Muslim carrying out the fatwa and lost an eye. As mentioned in this book's introduction, he commented on Islamic militancy, "After having overcome fascism, Nazism, and Stalinism, the world now faces a new totalitarian global threat: Islamism."

Such a statement coming from someone with his origins should give pause. There are certainly political, economic, and cultural factors behind the rise of militant Islamism. But there are, beyond all doubt, religious elements within Islam itself that should not be ignored by assuming that an American or Eurocentric view of religion as a minor motivation in public affairs is true everywhere and for every religion. The vast majority of Muslims in the world, to repeat, lead peaceful lives. But at the same time, when America was attacked on September 11, 2001, many Muslims around the world celebrated the fact, which brought home a new reality in the twenty-first century: a generalized resentment of America and the West that spread to many other nations—and an Islamist theology that justified the deliberate persecution and killing of Christians. As one analyst observed:

> The suicide bomber, be it noted, is not considered to be violating any [Islamic] "law." Rather, he is following a law.... In fact, he sees himself obeying the "law" or "will" of Allah. We do have instances of Western religious leaders sympathizing

with suicide bombers on the grounds that their pain is so great they must lash out. But the "oppression" is usually itself defined in terms of Western political philosophy that no suicide bomber himself would ever follow.[65]

Westerners often talk about respect toward the religion of others. One way that respect needs to be shown toward militant Islam is to accept its adherents' claim that they are motivated by faithfulness to their tradition, as they see it. This is an uncomfortable, very much non-Western stance. But not to recognize it for what it is would be to impose Western categories on people who challenge those very categories. For instance, Western nations have rightly charged ISIS militants with "war crimes" and "crimes against humanity." These are Western categories of evil behavior and make sense to all who accept the liberal internationalist foundations that they presume. But ISIS and other radical Islamist groups presume no such thing and cannot be considered as merely rogue bands, the way the West might think of pirates in the Persian Gulf or drug (and human) traffickers in Africa or Latin America.

There is a clear ideology in ISIS and related Islamic groups aimed at bringing the whole world into submission in the *Dar al-Salam*, the "house of peace." It's ironic from a Western perspective, of course, that this goal—which requires bloody military action to achieve—is contrasted in the extremist ideology with the *Dar al-Harb*, the "house of war," meaning the world outside of Islamic control. This very division is alien to non-Islamist thinking, but it is real for its believers. For them, Christianity itself—with its belief in Jesus as God incarnate—is blasphemy and an idolatry offensive

---

[65] James V. Schall, S.J., "9/11 Revisited," *Catholic World Report*, September 10, 2024, https://www.catholicworldreport.com/2024/09/10/9-11-revisited/.

to Allah. Islamists may take different approaches to the elimination of those offenses, but the goal is the same and deeply held.

U.S. president Barack Obama, generously trying to distinguish between those he believed to be true Muslims and those, he considered, who falsely claim the name, argued in a 2014 speech that ISIS is not Islamic because no religion sanctions the killing of innocent people. He was making the case that Islam, as has often be said, is "a religion of peace." That assertion may be largely true in modern times, though religious beliefs worldwide have shaded off into some truly bizarre channels; one need only think of Aztec human sacrifice of captured innocents. And it's precisely the contention of Islamists that Christians are blasphemers and "crusaders," and therefore not entirely innocent. In this same perspective, moderate and modernizing Muslims may be judged by Islamists as "apostates" in one way or another, and so are equally not "innocent." It is only because of these *theological* judgments that the killing of Christian clergy or laypeople (and disfavored Muslims) can be seen as "holy" and, in the case of suicide bombers, heroic martyrdom.

The Western coalition that brought pressure to bear on ISIS in Syria, Iraq, and the rest of the Middle East shrank the territory it controlled to virtually nothing by 2019. But as the persecution and death of Christians across much of Africa attests, the ISIS affiliates, operating on some of the same premises and with the same goals as the central Middle Eastern groups, in the 2020s became some of the worst nations for anti-Christian persecution in the world. As an Al Jazeera guest warned around the time of the shift in activity, "ISIL is not dead; it just moved to Africa."[66] That is a

---

[66] Quoted in Jason Warner, with Ryan O'Farrell, Héni Nsaibia, and Ryan Cummings, *The Islamic State in Africa: The Emergence, Evolution, and Future of the Next Jihadist Battlefront* (New York: Oxford University Press, 2021), 19.

story for the following chapter. But here it's necessary to examine the record of some of the nations where Islamist fundamentalism did the greatest damage, in the Middle East.

Iraq

Most people in the West were barely aware of the nation of Iraq until it invaded Kuwait in 1990—and was, in turn, attacked and driven out of that country by a coalition of forces led by the United States. That war—the First Gulf War—was followed by another in 2003 after the attacks against New York and Washington on September 11, 2001, because of the widespread belief—contested at the time and subsequently shown to be greatly exaggerated—that the regime of Saddam Hussein possessed large numbers of weapons of mass destruction. But the territory that modern Iraq occupies has had a long and storied history as both the "cradle of civilization" in Mesopotamia and a threat to several civilizations—indeed, the whole world—by developments in the twenty-first century.

The persecution and death of Christians in Iraq at the beginning of the twenty-first century was part of the general rise of Islamist fundamentalism in the whole Middle East, but it also had complicated ties to Iraq's particular political and military history. Under Saddam Hussein, Christians had been generally tolerated. There were even Catholics in influential political and military positions in his regime. As he neared the end of his rule, however, Saddam Hussein began to foster greater Muslim dominance over all other groups in the nation, but nothing like the repression and slaughter of Christians that arose in the chaotic situation after he was driven out. Still, the fatal identification of Christians with the West was taking on radical forms even under Saddam Hussein.

In what was a harbinger of things soon to come, Sr. Cecilia Moshi Hanna, an Assyrian Catholic nun, was assaulted in Baghdad at the Monastery of the Sacred Heart of Jesus on August 15, 2002, the feast of the Assumption of the Blessed Virgin Mary. She was seventy-one years old, a native Iraqi, and the kind of quiet woman religious who had worked throughout her life with the poor and the sick. Clearly, there could have been no personal reason to attack her, and, as the particulars of her case showed, robbery was not the motive either. Three men entered her monastery with knives, stabbed her multiple times, and cut off her head. Two other nuns who lived at the monastery were out at the time of the attack and survived, but they seem to have been targeted as well. It was also the day before what has been described as a "nationwide spiritual retreat." Such an obvious Islamist attack on a harmless Christian—and on a Catholic feast day—was meant to induce terror. The Hussein regime did little to investigate, and within Iraq there was speculation that the government even encouraged such lawlessness in anticipation of the Western invasion, which did not occur until the following year.[67]

Unlike other places in the Middle East, where such outrages did not really get into full swing until 2011, at the beginning of the "Arab Spring," Iraqi Christians experienced not only personal assaults but large, brutal attacks immediately following the fall of Saddam Hussein's Ba'athist regime in 2003. For example, on August 1, 2004, Islamic forces—claiming to be replying to a Western "crusade"—attacked ten churches with car bombs, within a few minutes of each other, in Baghdad and Mosul, wounding hundreds

---

[67] "Assyrian Nun Savagely Murdered in Baghdad," Assyrian International News Agency, August 31, 2002, http://www.aina.org/releases/cecilia.htm.

and killing at least a dozen Christians. There was a kind of Christian ecumenism in this well-coordinated assault, what Pope Francis has rightly called "an ecumenism of blood." Bombs struck at Syrian Catholics, Armenian Catholics, Latin-Rite Catholics, and others. Displaying the unwillingness or inability to distinguish between the Western political and military forces on the one hand and the age-old Christian communities of the region on the other, the attackers claimed, "You wanted a crusade; so here are the consequences. We have warned you. The mujahideen brothers have struck painful blows against the lairs of the crusaders, the laws of evil, of corruption, immorality and Christianization, by detonating car bombs."[68]

How Iraqi Christians—not coalition military forces—"wanted a crusade" or how their churches, which had existed for centuries in Iraq, were "lairs of the crusaders" was, to say the least, not clear. But in the blind fury of the moment, Christians praying at Mass were an easy target. Similar attacks on multiple churches, also coordinated to be simultaneous, occurred twice more in 2004; six churches were hit on a single day in January 2006; and a whole series of terror waves against Christians was to continue sporadically for more than a decade afterward. In several respects, this reflected the generalized violence in Iraqi society in those years. But it cannot be ignored that these were Christian *churches* being specifically targeted. Merely attending a Mass or another Christian gathering was thus to risk becoming a victim of *odium fidei*, hatred of the faith. The Church has not formally declared most of the

---

[68] "The Names of Those Killed While on Mission in the Year 2005," Agenzia Fides, December 30, 2005, https://www.fides.org/en/missionaries/6461-THE_NAMES_OF_THOSE_KILLED_WHILE_ON_MISSION_IN_THE_YEAR_2005.

casualties to be martyrs just yet. But it's difficult not to think that the fidelity and courage it took for those many hundreds of Christians to stay in their communities and practice their faith was a kind of everyday, but heroic, form of witness.

Many other Iraqi Christians chose not to stay, beginning from the first days after the coalition forces invaded. The multiple church bombings drove tens of thousands more out of major cities, once thought of as basically safe for Christians and other minorities. These waves of refugees amounted to a major flight of Christians, both individuals and whole communities, from the Middle East. Iraq is a rather large nation, with a population of more than forty-five million people (about the size of Spain), the vast majority Muslim. But prior to the recent wars, there were probably close to a million and a half Christians living in Iraq. They belonged to various churches, reflective of the region's complicated history and ethnic makeup, some claiming lineages back to the first century A.D. and St. Thomas the Apostle, the patron saint of the Church in Mesopotamia. Despite more than two thousand years of continuous presence—a presence that had survived Muslim conquest, the Ottoman Empire, the rise of authoritarian modern rule, and especially the emergence of ISIS—at least two hundred thousand Iraqi Christians fled to the northern region of Kurdistan, and a large number of other refugees were driven out of the country entirely.

Though the storied region of Mesopotamia lies within its modern borders, the Republic of Iraq dates only to the years after World War I, when the Ottoman Empire was dissolved and several former regions—Turkey, Syria, Iraq, Lebanon, and others—became independent states after brief rule by France and Great Britain. Christians in the Ottoman Empire were generally protected as *dhimmi*, which means they paid a tax for an uneasy toleration—an important source of revenue for the Muslim rulers. But they were periodically victims of massacres in various places within the empire as well, notably the Armenian genocide between 1915 and 1917 and later outrages as the Ottoman rule was coming to an end.

Christians in Iraq survived these and many other challenges, as they had for millennia. But as a result of recent wars, estimates are that this historical Middle Eastern Christian community numbers only about half of its earlier size, perhaps five hundred thousand now. Observers believe, for example, that at the height of the attacks, for the first time since the coming of Christianity, there were no longer any Christians in the region of Nineveh (where Jonah once prophesied), which is part of the modern city of Mosul. And those who remained elsewhere often found themselves in precarious conditions, pressured by militant Islamists, and, in several cases, died as martyrs. By the 2020s, some Catholics had returned and the cathedral was restored, but the situation of Christians in their historical homeland remained dangerous.

Among the cases that have reasonably full documentation, two are exemplary of many more: those of Fr. Ragheed Ganni and Bishop Paulos Faraj Rahho, both of the Chaldean Diocese of Mosul. According to reports by the Chaldean Catholic Church of Mesopotamia, a church in communion with Rome, Fr. Ganni was killed along with three subdeacons (Basman Yousef Daoud, Ghasan Issam Bidawid, and Waheed Hanna Isho'a) on June 3, 2007; his bishop was kidnapped just a few months after, on February 29, 2008, and found dead two weeks later. Three people were also killed during the bishop's kidnapping.[69] The perpetrators were members of the Islamic State of Iraq and the Levant (ISIL),

---

[69] Rebwar Audish Basa, *Un sacerdote cattolico nello stato islamico: La storia di Padre Ragheed Ganni* (Rome: ACN, n.d.), 15.

an ISIS affiliate. It was a period when Islamic militancy was at its height and historic churches, including even a stone plaque commemorating the long history of the Christian church in Iraq, were being obliterated. Amid other ethnic and religious clashes, the Iraqi government, such as it was, was unable to do very much about the daily violence.

It's an additional tragedy that all this transpired in a land so rich in history—not only figures such as Daniel and Nahum in the Jewish Scriptures and more recent Christian connections but the history of Babylon and much more. The recent violence has respected no religious boundaries. Christians have been killed by bombs at Mass, priests attacked during the celebration of the Eucharist, and one—Fr. Thair Sad-alla Abd-al—was assailed even while he was reconciling penitents to God in the confessional. And the desecration hardly stops there. Large numbers of Iraqi lay Christians have suffered decapitation, had limbs cut off, and been tortured. It takes the wider understanding of what it means to be a martyr to appreciate what life is like for Christians amid such constant threats. As some have said, it makes you see what it's like not only to die a martyr, but to *live* daily with the constant possibility of becoming one.

The Chaldean Catholic archbishop of Mosul, Paulos Faraj Rahho, was quite aware of those daily dangers and still bravely continued to celebrate Mass and participate in other public events. He also spoke out about the way that the post-invasion government was being organized, particularly the process of inserting sharia law into the new constitution—a step that couldn't help but bring trouble to the various Christian communities in Iraq. His activities certainly brought trouble to him. He was repeatedly threatened, and he alerted officials in the Vatican, during a visit to Rome, about the possibility of his being killed. When he was kidnapped and thrown into the trunk of a car, he was somehow able to get to his cell phone and call his colleagues in the Church. He made it clear that he didn't want them to pay a ransom, which would be money better spent taking care of the poor and the displaced. He was posthumously given the Path to Peace Award the following year.

A prominent priest of the bishop's diocese, Fr. Ragheed Ganni, was repeatedly sent bullets by mail and warned by telephone that he should close his Church of the Holy Spirit in Mosul. In the very real face of violent consequences for refusing—conditions he described as "worse than hell"—he kept the parish open and functioning. His family reported that just before he was murdered in 2007, the year before the death of his bishop, an assassin asked him why he didn't obey and close the church. It seems that his last words were "I can't close the house of God."[70]

Fr. Ganni was born in Karemles on the Nineveh Plain, a small town in which the inhabitants were Chaldean Catholics and spoke Aramaic, the same language Jesus spoke when He walked the earth. He was both an intelligent and pious boy, and his first intention when he was admitted to university—during the First Gulf War—was to become an engineer. He graduated easily, despite all the turmoil of that period. Though he was increasingly thinking about the priesthood, the bishop of Mosul, a longtime friend, counseled him to perform his military service first and see if a vocation was really the right thing for him. In 1993, when he entered his obligatory service for a year and a half, the country was not at war—only under an embargo—but the regime of Saddam Hussein was not an easy one for any Iraqi to serve, let alone Catholics, who were often discriminated against and placed in the front battle lines as cannon fodder. Fortunately, as hard as life as

---

[70] Audish Basa, *Un sacerdote cattolico*, 33.

an Iraqi soldier was, Ganni survived and returned to civilian life convinced that he was called to be a priest.

His bishop, seeing what an intelligent and energetic man he was, decided to send him to Rome right away. In 1996, he began five years of study at the Angelicum, the university run by the Dominicans there. After that, he was ordained, taking as his motto the ominous words of Jesus as He was facing arrest and Crucifixion: "Father ... not my will be done, but your will."[71] He had made many friends in Rome and learned several languages, including English, Italian, and French along the way. And he said his first Mass at the Pontifical Irish College. He wrote his bishop, offering to return immediately to Iraq. But he asked if he could stay on an additional two years—his scholarship, provided by Aid to the Church in Need, covered the extra time—to get a licentiate in ecumenical theology at the Angelicum. Given his obvious gifts, the bishop agreed. He wanted the very best Ragheed that Rome could give him. The bishop might well be thinking that a man like Ragheed could one day be a bishop himself. When he did return to Iraq, he began working with the bishop as his secretary on the very first day. He was also named pastor of a new parish and began teaching philosophy and theology in Baghdad at the Pontifical Babel College.

The situation in Iraq after the American invasion was horrible, "worse than hell," as the priest said. But it became still worse after September 12, 2006, when Pope Benedict XVI's lecture at Regensburg (described in the introduction to the present volume) was misinterpreted as an intentional insult to the Prophet and Islam. A Syrian Orthodox priest, Paulos Eskander, was kidnapped, terribly tortured, and killed—decapitated—in the area around Mosul. Fr. Ganni and his parishioners did not escape the violent reactions.

[71] Audish Basa, *Un sacerdote cattolico*, 45.

The parish was attacked five times in the days after the lecture. The priest was himself threatened multiple times even before the kidnapping of Fr. Eskander. He survived primarily, it seems, because he took great precautions as he moved around from one place to another. He was scheduled to fly to Europe on September 18 but postponed his departure twice, he said, "because I cannot leave the city given these conditions." If the process for his canonization needs confirmation of heroic virtue and a willingness to die because of his faith, the evidence is abundant in this instance. In his view, Christians in Iraq were enduring double suffering owing to the generalized chaos affecting all Iraqis after the American invasion—and, on top of it, because of their faith.

He was to die on a Sunday, shortly after saying his last Mass. The wife of one of the subdeacons who died with him said that they were driving that same day to a government office to get his identity card renewed. He stopped first at his parents' house and gave them a copy of the photo he was going to use for the renewal and told them that he had had it enlarged, adding, "This is for my funeral, so don't worry about it." The group left. Five or six masked men with machine guns stopped them along the way and made them get out of their car. Hands up. Shouts that the Christians were blasphemers. Bursts of gunfire. The killers fled in their car—and stole the subdeacon's as well.

The assassination influenced us, said the wife of the murdered subdeacon later. How can you go on the same as before after that? But it didn't change our faith. The priest's mother reported that he had said, "If I die today or die in ten years, it will be the same death." He had received many invitations to leave and work in Switzerland or Italy. But his view was that "if everyone who becomes a priest leaves to go abroad, there won't be anyone [presumably any Christians] left here. Whatever happens, let it happen!"

His mother, when asked how, given all the threats, she could let her son come and go to and from his parish, answered, "It's true that he was my son and I brought him up, but he became a son of the Church. I then had no authority over him." At the funeral for him and his companions, which was attended by thousands of people, the Chaldean patriarch and all the bishops of the Church in Iraq, along with representatives of all the Christian churches, deplored the scandalous act and made a point of describing it as an act committed

> against God and against Humanity, and against their broth-
> ers who are faithful and peaceful citizens, in addition to
> being men of religion who have offered their prayers and
> their supplications to Almighty God that He will bring
> peace, safety, and stability to all of Iraq.... The Bishops
> ask everyone for their unity and solidarity in this difficult
> moment, this sad occasion, and repeat what they have
> previously declared with regard to the persecution against
> Iraqi Christians, their forced emigration, and their being
> pushed to renounce their faith, calling on the responsible
> Iraqi officials and the international organizations to inter-
> vene, taking the necessary previsions to put an end to these
> criminal acts.

Noble and moving sentiments, which, tragically, had almost no effect on the situation.[72]

In fact, many of those present at the funeral were themselves persecuted, martyred, or displaced to other nations, particularly

[72] Audish Basa, *Un sacerdote cattolico*, 71, as reported in the *Servizio Informazione Chiese Orientali* (Rome: Congregazione per le Chiese Orientali, 2007), 172–173.

after the emergence of the Islamic State in 2014. They, too, heroically remained, despite the threats. As the patriarch of Baghdad, Cardinal Emmanuel Delly affirmed, "We are staying here until the end, because our roots go back thousands of years in this dear homeland.... God is with us. We stay here as good seed. The blood of our martyrs is this holy seed."

Pope Benedict sent a telegram to the Iraqi bishops proclaiming that "their sacrifice is hastening the dawn of reconciliation, justice and peace in Iraq." Cardinal Bertone, then Vatican secretary of state, wrote at greater length that the Holy Father "prays that their costly sacrifice will inspire in the hearts of all men and women of good will a renewed resolve to reject the ways of hatred and violence, to conquer evil with good and to cooperate in hastening the dawn of reconciliation, justice and peace in Iraq."[73]

For their part, the Islamic militants did not leave Fr. Ganni at peace even in death. After one of the periodic attacks on a church near where he was buried, they broke up the tombstone that had been raised over his grave.

By 2024, however, ISIS was almost entirely suppressed, and Christians began to return to some of their historical lands. There was no more "persecution," according to Chaldean Catholic archbishop of Erbil, Bashar Matti Warda, in the sense that there was no more than what ordinarily confronts Christians in every Muslim society. As he told an interviewer:

> One of the facts that we have to be fully aware of is that once you live in the land of Islam, there is no freedom of

---

[73] "Benedict XVI Mourns Clerics Slain in Iraq," Byzantine Catholic Church in America, last updated February 19, 2013, https://www.byzcath.org/index.php/news-mainmenu-49/1026-benedict-xvi-mourns-clerics-slain-in-iraq.

religion, though there is a freedom of worship. The Iraqi constitution is based on Islamic *Shariah*, which means that evangelization outside the Christian community is forbidden. We have 1,400 years of dialogue of life with Islam, and we know that we cannot do that. We sometimes hear reports that there is no freedom of religion in this part of the world. but where is the surprise? This is something that we know as Christians. We cannot [convert Muslims], because that would be endangering the lives of the Muslims seeking baptism, or endangering the Christian community.[74]

Syria

Syria, historically another region of the former Ottoman Empire, and more recently an independent nation, contains some of the very oldest Christian communities. St. Paul famously had his conversion experience on the road to Damascus, where there were already other Christians who took him in and which, almost two thousand years later, is still a large, flourishing city. It is now, of course, the capital of the Syrian Arab Republic, one of several nations that had been formed after the fall of the Ottoman Empire in 1922. Like those other nations, it was first placed under a European "protectorate"—in Syria's case, under France, as a means of maintaining order as it transferred to a more permanent system run by native Syrians. When independence came, that order quickly evaporated into decades of dictatorships, military coups, even a brief union with Egypt. But the nation finally achieved

---

[74] Filipe d'Avillez, "Warda: 'The Whole Middle East Is Burning,'" *Pillar,* November 1, 2024, https://www.pillarcatholic.com/p/warda-the-whole-middle-east-is-burning; brackets in the original.

some stability in 1970 under the heavy hand of Hafiz al-Assad—an Alawite, a somewhat eclectic Muslim sect that also operated via ethnic ties in the region.

That stability came at a high cost. The Syrian Army ruthlessly put down resistance. By 1980, the radical Muslim Brotherhood was challenging the regime in various terrorist attacks against politicians, the military, and even civilians. Government forces responded with savage brutality. In one incident alone—the Hama massacre in 1982—tens of thousands of Syrians regarded as opponents of the regime perished, a stunning body count even for an unsettled Middle East. But Hafiz al-Assad at least managed to maintain some semblance of political order. The Syrian government also carefully calculated its position in regional affairs, even joining with Western forces in the First Gulf War against Iraq after Saddam Hussein's invasion of Kuwait. The Syrian strongman's grip at home, however, remained mercilessly tight.

Hafiz al-Assad died in 2000. His son, Bashar al-Assad, succeeded him. A medical doctor, a trained ophthalmologist, who studied partly in the United Kingdom and seemed comfortable with Western ways, Bashar al-Assad had not been groomed for a political role. But when his elder brother died in an automobile accident, the post was thrust upon him. Initially, he was welcomed in the West as a potentially liberalizing reformer. Flattering articles about him and his attractive and stylish wife appeared in the world press, and it seems that he might have at least softened the grip of the regime somewhat if the Syrian Civil War (2011–2019) had not occurred. But as disorder spread in the country and he had to use the Syrian Army to repress "democratic" dissent, opinions among Western nations flipped. The West turned its back on him because of his regime's brutality. France broke off formal diplomatic relations in 2011, the United States did the same the following year, and NATO began sending arms to the insurgents. Russia and Iran, however, supported his regime and stepped into the gap. As things escalated into full-blown civil war, other forces emerged as well.

Most prominent initially was the Free Syrian Army (FSA), an umbrella organization at its founding in 2011, which included several former officers of the regular Syrian Army who professed to want to shelter Syrian citizens from the regime. The FSA went through various permutations and orientations as time passed. But within a few years, another major threat emerged—ISIS—an even more serious force that took control of a large area that straddled western Iraq and eastern Syria, declaring the territory an Islamic caliphate. And still other groups, among the most significant the al-Nusra Front, arose with similar Islamist tendencies. Christians and other minorities in Syria naturally fell afoul of the various Islamists in a civil war that was both political and religious.

As had once been the case in much of the Middle East, the Syrian government—though later allied with Russia and Iran—was, to a degree, a protector of Christians and other minorities, especially if they remained loyal to the government. The regime appreciated any support amid a welter of political dissidents demanding "democracy," radical Islamist factions (often enough at war with one another), Kurdish rebel armies, and even the occasional raid from nearby Turkey. The Catholic Melkite archbishop of Aleppo, Jean-Clément Jeanbart, observed that, amid all the factional violence and the tragic international rivalries and divisions, where the government ruled, the Church was relatively safer. Relatively. Otherwise, she was at the mercy of the Islamists and others.

The Syrian Civil War displays many of the complexities that also trouble several Muslim nations in North Africa, the Middle East, and East Asia. In a way, it began in Tunisia—and on social media. There, in 2010, a democratic uprising broke out when a street vendor, Mohamed Bouazizi, set himself on fire in protest against the mistreatment he and others were getting under the Tunisian regime. Similar unrest had been growing just beneath the surface in several other Arab nations against corrupt and repressive rulers. Protest spread rapidly via the Internet, something that could not have happened earlier when means of communication were slower and spotty. And the various clashes that followed—raising democratic hopes all over the Arab world—subsequently became known as the Arab Spring. In 2011, when the Syrian Civil War started, there were many armed groups—often at odds with one another as well—who began attacks on the government. The government was quite willing to respond with equal savagery.

The killing of Christians started at once. Syria has been home to several Christian communities over thousands of years. Prior to the civil war, there were substantial Greek and Syriac Orthodox churches. Catholics were spread among several bodies. Most Syrian Catholics were Melkites, but there were numbers of Maronite, Armenian, Chaldean, and Syriac Catholics as well as a few Latin-Rite Catholics—and some ancient communities that don't neatly fit the usual Western categories. When the war began in 2011, they were all immediately in peril. Reports reaching Aid to the Church in Need specified that, around Christmas of that year, Christians were already being murdered and kidnapped throughout the country.[75] According to the Voice of the Martyrs and other reliable sources, Islamists not only targeted churches but frequently marked out Christian homes of all members of the faith groups

---

[75] George J. Marlin, *Christian Persecution in the Middle East: A 21st Century Tragedy* (South Bend, IN: St. Augustine's Press, 2015), 108.

with a cross, which they used to identify men who were then kidnapped, women raped, both sexes tortured and murdered. All this continued unabated until the civil war petered out in 2019 and sporadically after that.

One of the most ironic stories of the ISIS period in the Middle East was the murder of the American photojournalist James Foley early in the Syrian Civil War. A graduate of Marquette University in Wisconsin and a lifelong Catholic, according to his mother, he chose to become a freelancer in war zones because he "wanted to inspire us to reflect on what really happens in a war."[76] What happened to him was that he was kidnapped—twice—by Islamists, first in Libya, where he was held for forty-four days in 2011 while he was documenting the Arab Spring and the fall of the Libyan strongman Muammar al-Gaddhafi. Asked about that experience, he said that praying had gotten him through: "I began to pray the Rosary.... It was what my mother and grandmother would have prayed. I said 10 Hail Marys between each Our Father. It took a long time, almost an hour to count 100 Hail Marys off on my knuckles. And it helped to keep my mind focused." He even attributed a certain spiritual liberation to his prayer in captivity: "If nothing else, prayer was the glue that enabled my freedom ... an inner freedom first and later the miracle of being released during a war in which the regime had no real incentive to free us."[77]

---

[76] Quoted in Stacey Stowe, "Life after Horrific Death for the Journalist James Foley," *New York Times*, December 21, 2018, https://www.nytimes.com/2018/12/21/arts/design/james-foley-bradley-mccallum.html.

[77] Adelaide Mena, "Prayer a Stronghold in Life, Death of Catholic Journalist James Foley," Catholic News Agency, August 20, 2014, https://www.catholicnewsagency.com/news/30331/prayer-a-stronghold-in-life-death-of-catholic-journalist-james-foley.

Undaunted, he went to Syria the very next year and was taken hostage in Northern Syria while covering the civil war. He was held captive there for much longer, twenty-one months—during which he also maintained a regular prayer life—and then was brutally beheaded by members of ISIS. The grizzly event was videotaped and then posted on the Internet by his killers, showing in its own way what was "really happening" in the Syrian war. ISIS said that his execution was in retaliation for U.S. air strikes against the group and threatened further assassinations if America persisted. Bishop Peter Libasci of Manchester, New Hampshire, Foley's home diocese, remarked of him, however, "All I can think of is here was this young man who was pointing the way toward truth, here was a man who pointing out what was happening in the country of Syria, here was a man who was pointing to what we should be aware of."[78]

James Foley's case may be just a bit too distant from a specifically Catholic death to make him formally a martyr—even under the expanded categories promulgated by John Paul II and Pope Francis. But it shows how doing ordinary things inspired by the faith in a variety of current circumstances can in themselves be a kind of Christian witness.

In the widespread violence of Syria's civil war, however, multiple beheadings and mass rapes became a commonplace. Among many inhumane tactics, the militants would sometimes shoot one person in a group and then hide and wait until rescuers returned—which permitted them to rack up an even larger body count. There were reports of some groups, such as the Alawites—the Muslim sect to which the Syrian president Bashar al-Assad belongs—gathering together when they faced capture and

---

[78] Mena, "Prayer a Stronghold."

committing mass suicide to forestall the serial torture and death they knew awaited them.

Savagery was directed toward Christian groups and even toward Christian buildings. A French relief worker for SOS Chrétiens d'Orient described what happened in the Church of St. George in Maaloula, a Christian city, early in the conflict:

> We had already seen the distortion of the church's façade, where the mosaic of Christ had been damaged by bullet holes. And now we discovered the carnage inside: icons slashed with knives, their eyes gouged out, claw marks that made it feel like the devil himself had been there in a bout of fury, and paintings that were charred or blackened from fire. Even the church doors had been damaged; where once there had been images of the chalice, the cross, and other Christian symbols, now there were great holes, dug out with knives. Not a single icon or painting in the entire church had been spared.[79]

This was in a small out-of-the-way church, but as the fighting spread everywhere, large, historical basilicas in cultural centers such as Aleppo and numerous other places of worship were not spared similar outrages. Indeed, some native Iraqis have said that the destruction visited on their cities by the civil war reminded them of Hiroshima and Nagasaki after they were hit by nuclear bombs.

In 2013, one of the first priests whose name we know (among the many whose identity we do not know), Fr. François Murad, was martyred at the Convent of the Custody of the Holy Land in Ghassaniya. Fr. Murad was a native Syrian and a Franciscan. There

---

[79] Alexandre Goodarzy, *Kidnapped in Iraq: A Christian Humanitarian Tells His Story* (Manchester, NH: Sophia Institute Press, 2022), 53.

has been a considerable presence of Franciscans in the Middle East ever since the visit there of St. Francis of Assisi himself in the thirteenth century. He was one of the sources behind what came to be known as the Custody of the Holy Land, a Franciscan organization headquartered in Jerusalem with the responsibility of looking after the sacred Christian sites, not only in Israel but in Jordan, Lebanon, Syria, and even in Egypt and Cyprus, along with a few other places. The Syrian Civil War affected many Catholic sites that had existed continuously in these nations for eight hundred years.

Fr. Murrad had been living at the Monastery of St. Simon, which he had been forced to leave when it was bombed by Islamist rebels. He moved on to the nearby convent of the Custody of the Holy Land, as did those same rebels. The priest tried to protect the nuns there but was killed during the assault. In the fog of war, it's often difficult to know the exact way in which such outrages take place. At first, it was believed he was beheaded. But the perpetrators themselves clarified that he was shot inside the church. The Custody of the Holy Land announced, "Islamists attacked the monastery, ransacking it and destroying everything.... When Father François tried to resist, defending the nuns, rebels shot him."[80] That is to say, they shot a fellow Syrian who, during his whole life, had simply carried out his priestly duties and protected Syria's historical Christians and Christian sites from harm.

That was 2013. In 2014, a foreigner and a Jesuit suffered a similar fate. A Dutch priest, Fr. Frans van der Lugt, S.J., who had been working in Syria for fifty years, was pulled from a monastery in the city of Homs, where about two dozen other Christians

---

[80] "Vatican Confirms Catholic Priest Was Killed in Syria," BBC News, July 2, 2013, https://www.bbc.com/news/world-middle -east-23138679.

had come for refuge. Tragically, the Old City of Homs was being attacked on two fronts: bombarded by the Syrian army and being held by rebel forces. Fr. van der Lugt had mostly worked with children with disabilities over decades and had just succeeded in getting UN aid for three thousand people dying of hunger in the city. A masked gunman shot him twice in the head. Both sides in the conflict claimed to be appalled at this cold-blooded murder, but the preponderance of the evidence was that a radical Islamist group had decided to eliminate him.

Fr. van der Lugt was seventy-five years old at the time and decided to remain with the people sheltering at the monastery even though he had been provided with a way of escape. Just before he was killed, he declared, "I am here for all Syrians. When all Christians would leave, I would stay because I am here to serve all Syrians." His is a virtual textbook case of a Christian shepherd staying with the flock—which included some Muslims—instead of fleeing when the wolf was at the door.[81]

There were, of course, many comparable cases during the course of the civil war, and they touch every Catholic religious order and ethnic group and even those who had dedicated themselves to dialogue. An Italian, Fr. Paolo dall'Oglio, a man who bravely ran a multifaith center (and was even briefly expelled from Syria for criticizing the Syrian government), sponsored meetings between Christians and Muslims. Despite all that, he was kidnapped in 2013 by Islamists. Unlike most of the brave religious men and women who were taken for one reason or another, he was never

---

[81] Peter Jesserer Smith, "Jesuit Priest Martyred in Syria: Remembering the Holy Witness of Father Frans van der Lugt," *National Catholic Register*, April 29, 2014, https://www.ncregister.com/news/jesuit-priest-martyred-in-syria.

returned, and his fate has never been revealed. Some sources say he was killed shortly after his capture. As late as 2019, some reports surfaced that—improbably after being held for six years—he was still alive. Now, more than a decade after his disappearance, his status—along with that of thousands of others—remains unknown.

It's good to have all the names of individuals who died like this Franciscan and Jesuit and Italian, but whole groups of nameless people have perished as well. The Martyrs of Damascus, almost a dozen who were slaughtered in 1860 by a Druze militia, were a landmark group of martyrs that Pope Francis decided to canonize in 2024—perhaps to make a point about religious-motivated violence. But horrible as their deaths were, even much larger groups of Christians were eliminated during the twenty-first century Syrian Civil War. Thousands of Christians are thought to have been killed and millions of all faiths and backgrounds, displaced. But large groups of Catholics and others—a whole series of them—were deliberately targeted.

Even a cursory look, almost year by year, gives the general outlines of the picture. A dozen nuns were abducted in December 2012. In 2013, during the notorious Adra massacre, dozens of minorities—including Christians—were specifically targeted for their faith by the al-Nusra Front and killed. Also in 2013, five Melkite Catholics were "disappeared" by jihadists from the Christian town of Maaloula; their remains were discovered and identified only five years later. By the end of 2013, three thousand Christians had died in the city of Homs alone. When ISIS got control of the northern city of Raqqa in 2014, it threatened the entire Christian population with a stark choice: conversion, return to dhimmitude, or death. Churches—including the Church of the Martyrs of the Armenian Catholic Church—and even mosques that did not follow the extremist line were destroyed. Hundreds of Christians disappeared.

In Homs, the Catholic archbishop recorded ninety-six martyrs. In 2016, the Islamic State killed at least twenty-one Christians in al-Qaryatain, with five more missing.

And the list could easily be extended at great length, though a full accounting of such widespread mayhem is probably impossible.

By 2019, the Syrian Civil War was on its way toward an end. Yet an Armenian Catholic priest died in one of the many random attacks on clergy that were still taking place. Three others—including his own father—were riding with him in a car on the way to help rebuild the Church of the Martyrs in Deir ez-Zor when two assailants on motorcycles sprayed the vehicle with bullets. The priest's father died on the spot; the priest succumbed later in a hospital. The others were wounded but escaped. Fr. Hovsep Hanna Bedoyan was the pastor of the Armenian Catholic parish of St. Joseph in Qamishli, part of the Armenian Christian community that had fled the Turkish genocide in the early years of the twentieth century and built up a considerable network of Armenian Catholic churches and other institutions. Such attacks are much reduced since the end of the civil war, but they have continued.

It's no surprise that the number of Catholics in Syria declined as they were either killed in droves or fled elsewhere. Before the civil war, it was generally believed that the ancient Christian communities in Syria counted for about 10 percent of the population, about 2.1 million people. By 2022, according to Aid to the Church in Need, there were only about 300,000 left, maybe less than 2 percent. Many fled to Jordan or Lebanon, some to places as far away as Sweden and Canada, but a significant number went to Europe, especially after an invitation from the president of France, Syria's former "protector."

And on December 8, 2024, the feast of the Immaculate Conception, Syria was struck by another upheaval. The Assad government fell under a sudden attack by Hay'at Tahrir al-Sham (HTS), an offshoot of al-Qaeda, but maintained an Islamist orientation. It was aided in the overthrow of the government by the rebel Syrian National Army, operating with Turkish assistance. Assad fled to Russia, which had supported his government for years during the most tumultuous periods. The HTS regime, at least in its first weeks in power, has been careful to present itself to the world as pursuing "moderate" Islamic rule and respect for religious and ethnic minorities. But anecdotal reports from a very fluid situation indicate that the Alawites—the religious sect to which the Assad family belonged—were being hunted down. Reports from Christian communties were mixed, some saying that Masses and other religious practices were going on unmolested, others saying that Christian schools and other institutions were coming under random attacks. As the 2025 Jubilee Year was beginning, the future of the remaining Christian communities in Syria seemed to be teetering and in danger of falling back into the persecution and martyrdom of recent decades.

It's difficult for a Christian to understand why God allows such things to overtake His people. But their heroic witness in many places continues. The old saying that the blood of the martyrs is the seed of the Church is something of a cliché, but it is the truth. Indeed, rebuilding the Church and the nation after the civil war in order to encourage an ancient Christian people "to stay" had become a kind of spiritual as well as political and economic crusade in Syria. One French aid worker may also have expressed something about the Christian life in such circumstances, not nearly so evident in more settled, prosperous nations: "Here [in Syria], being Christian means something."[82]

---

[82] Goodarzy, *Kidnapped in Iraq*, 116.

Israel

Religious extremism of all kinds leads to bad behavior, even in a Western-friendly nation such as Israel. As a modern democracy, the Jewish nation accepts and tolerates other faiths, including Christians. But a segment of Ultra-Orthodox Jews in Israel has demonstrated persistent bias against Christians, spitting on clergy, and intimidating people—typically Christians—who work or travel on Saturdays, the Jewish Sabbath. And things have gotten even worse with Christian graves and holy sites being defaced. In 2012, a Trappist monastery in Latrun, a town about halfway between Jerusalem and the Ben Gurion Airport, had its doors set on fire and the walls were spray-painted with the insult "Jesus was a monkey." Though clearly the work of extremist Jews, it was shocking that this could occur in the very heart of Israel proper.

The Vatican took the unusual step of issuing a formal statement, signed by several officials in the Curia, criticizing the Israeli government for not controlling such expressions of hate. The custodian of the Holy Land at the time, Archbishop (later Latin patriarch) Pierbattista Pizzaballa, commented, "The time has come for the authorities to act to put an end to this senseless violence and to ensure a 'teaching of respect' in schools for all those who call this land home." He added, "When I came to the country, I was told that I should know that if I walk around with a frock in the city [of Jerusalem], people would spit on me, and I shouldn't be offended, it's normal."[83] But of course, even if common, it

---

[83] Jacey Fortin, "Vatican Official Condemns Israeli Discrimination against Christians," *International Business Times*, September 7, 2012, https://www.ibtimes.com/vatican-official-condemns-israeli -discrimination-against-christians-780879; brackets in the original. The Vatican statement was published in the Italian newspaper *La Stampa*.

shouldn't be normal, and Christians experiencing such attitudes are "offended."

The 2012 attack on the Trappists was not the only such serious event. In 2015, the Church of the Multiplication of the Loaves and the Fishes was also hit with arson by Jewish anti-Christian extremists and painted with slogans. More than 150 similar anti-Christian assaults have been reported within a decade. In 2023, tensions came to a head in Haifa with multiple clashes between Jews and Christians at the monastery on Mount Carmel. Christian officials speculate that many more attacks have taken place that were never reported to Israeli authorities, and they deplore what they believe is the government's general passivity about such acts, which has allowed a virulent anti-Christian attitude to spread.

There are also places in Israel, of course, where Christians not only survive but flourish. Nazareth, for example, has Christians in prominent political, business, and education positions. But places associated with Jesus—Nazareth in Israel and Bethlehem in Palestinian territories—have come under increasing pressures from Islamist currents pervading the whole Middle East. The flight of Christians from Bethlehem has been particularly noteworthy. In 1950, Bethlehem was more than 80 percent Christian. Well into the 1990s, Christians still made up a majority of Bethlehem's population. Various political and military factors—notably the border wall that Israel built in 2003 because of Islamist threats from Gaza—put pressure on the lives of Christians in the town. But those Islamist currents themselves also threatened Bethlehem's Christians. So it's no surprise that in the place of Jesus' birth, as the twenty-first century has progressed, the Christian population in Bethlehem has shrunk to around 12 percent.

Besides the general day-to-day grind, various events have contributed to the sharp decline. In 2022, for instance, Israeli Defense

Forces surrounded the Church of the Nativity in Bethlehem. Several dozen Palestinian militants had sought sanctuary there. The accounts of this event differ. Palestinians claim they were only seeking safety by entering the church. Israel claims that they had taken hostage the Franciscans living there. Whatever interpretation might be given to the siege that resulted, it's emblematic of the kind of clashes that make Christians in the very birthplace of the Prince of Peace ready to flee elsewhere. And they have been doing so by the thousands. Even before the murderous cross-border raid by Hamas on October 7, 2023—a raid that resulted in the deaths of at least twelve hundred Israelis and the taking of hundreds more as hostages—Christians in the area around Bethlehem reported that militants invaded Christian homes and used them as bases for snipers to fire into Israel. Under such circumstances, few Christians are willing to remain in their historical homeland.

Christians in Muslim-dominated territories of Israel face the usual challenges as in the rest of the Middle East. Though there is perhaps a slightly more tolerant attitude, since 2002, sharia law has been authoritative in the Gaza Strip and the West Bank. The legal system is complicated, but according to article 4 of the 2002 Basic Law, which is supposed to operate in an independent Palestinian state, should one ever come into existence:

1. Islam is the official religion in Palestine. Respect for the sanctity of all other heavenly religions shall be maintained.
2. The principles of Islamic Shari'a shall be the main source of legislation.
3. Arabic shall be the official language.[84]

---

[84] "Palestine 2003 (rev. 2005)," Constitute, https://www.constitute project.org/constitution/Palestine_2005.

It's not surprising that, as elsewhere, this portends the usual constant pressures for Christians to convert, the assigning of second-class social status to Christian inhabitants, and periodic eruptions of interreligious clashes.

Especially since Hamas has come to dominate in Gaza, the situation of Christians has worsened. In the simplistic way that media often cover such complicated situations, much of the reality of anti-Christian persecution has been left out, as if Israel were solely to blame for the plight of Palestinian Christians. But people close to the situation see it quite differently. A Muslim journalist, Khaled Abu Toameh, has observed, "The attacks by Muslims on Christians are often ignored by the international community and media, who seem to speak out only when they can find a way to blame Israel." And he notes that intimidation of Christians in Gaza has even led to a kind of forced self-censorship: the "disturbing situation is that the leaders of the Christian community in the West Bank are reluctant to hold the Palestinian Authority and their Muslim neighbors responsible for the attacks. They are afraid of retribution and prefer to toe the official line of holding Israel solely responsible for the misery of the Christian minority."[85]

What all this—the attacks on Christians from Ultra-Orthodox Jews in Israel as well as Muslim pressures on Christians in the Palestinian territories—means is that many of the same anti-Christian elements common to the whole Middle East exist, if in a somewhat different form and to a lesser degree, in Israel as well.

---

[85] Raymond Ibrahim, "The Persecution of Christians in the Palestinian Authority," Middle East Forum, December 25, 2022, https://www.meforum.org/persecution-of-christians-in-the-palestinian-authority.

A Note on Lebanon

Of all the misfortunes that have overtaken Christians in the Middle East in the twenty-first century, perhaps none is more tragic than the radicalization of different sectors of the population in Lebanon. Like the other new nations that were created after the dissolution of the Ottoman Empire in the wake of World War I, the region along the Mediterranean Coast that came to be known as Lebanon was placed under a European "mandate," which, for Lebanon, meant France. Initially, this promised to be a rare, happy development for the various religious communities within the territory. Though all the new states had their boundaries drawn in ways that often did not reflect the underlying populations very well, Lebanon at least sought a way to respect religious differences. Notably, unlike any other of the new Middle Eastern nations, when an independent government was inaugurated in the 1940s, it formally required that a Christian head the state. Henceforth, a Maronite Christian would be the president, a Sunni Muslim would be the prime minister, a Shia would be the speaker of the parliament, and a Greek Orthodox would be the deputy speaker. This effort at incorporating all groups into the political system was hopeful but unrealistic in a situation that was bound to create rivalries—and soon succumbed to conflicting interests from inside Lebanon and interference from outside.

It had been possible to reserve the Lebanese presidency to a Christian because, when the country was first being governed by the French, perhaps more than 80 percent of the population was Christian. As turmoil would grow over the decades and into the twenty-first century, that percentage would shrink to around 30 percent. Reliable estimates of the casualties of the civil war in Lebanon are difficult to establish, but by 1990 it appears that something on the order of 125,000 civilians were killed, more than three-quarters of them Catholic. Maybe another quarter million fled, owing largely to the emergence of various radical Muslim currents but especially to the rise of the radical Iranian-backed group Hezbollah. Indeed, Hezbollah became so powerful that, by the first decades of the twenty-first century, it had established de facto control of the government. The terror group insinuated itself into the Lebanese military, the educational system, and political institutions and began a subtle—and sometimes not so subtle—process of Islamizing the nation.

Though Lebanon's constitution protects all religions, Hezbollah has been curtailing Catholic activities, closing a Catholic television station, imprisoning Catholic journalists, and hacking Catholic websites and replacing their Christian material with Muslim messages. Even worse, it has damaged or destroyed hundreds of historical Christian sites. Despite constant persecution and intimidation—kidnappings, extortion, murders, and even demands that Christian women wear hijabs—other Middle Eastern Christians have regarded Lebanon as a place of refuge. Many Iraqi Christians sought shelter there in 2007 after the American invasion. Indeed, when the Syrian Civil War broke out in 2011, more than a million Chaldean Catholics fled into Lebanon. Rivalries among Muslim groups also played into this dynamic. Hezbollah opposed ISIS—which was then trying to form a "caliphate" over parts of Syria and Iraq. Hezbollah fought against this Islamic throwback not only by mobilizing Muslim troops but also by training Christians as soldiers. In the complicated ways of the Middle East, that was something of an unusual, if temporary, collaboration.

Earlier, the various religious groups had opposed and committed massacres against one another, in a sickening cycle of atrocity and counteratrocity. Thousands died in the civil war that raged from 1975 to 1990, at various hands, including those of the

Christian phalangists. The phalangists were a Christian Democrat group and also followers of the "personalism" of various Catholic thinkers. Yet they were caught up perpetrating and suffering the social violence that spared no one. In 1989, Pope John Paul II wrote an apostolic letter to all the Catholic bishops of the world, observing that "the disappearance of Lebanon would be one of the world's greatest sorrows." He also urged the international institutions to make saving Lebanon "one of the most urgent and noble tasks"[86] and called the nation "more than a country; it's a message."[87]

The civil war came to an end with Syria taking control of Lebanon for the fifteen years between 1990 and 2005. Lebanon then became independent again with the Cedar Revolution, in which the Kataeb Party—the party of the Christian Democrats—played a prominent role. But even independence did not entirely help. Some party leaders and elected officials were assassinated in short order.

All this troubled history did not bode well for Christians or any other group in Lebanon at the opening of the twenty-first century. These large-scale conflicts are somewhat distant from what might be more properly called persecution or martyrdom. And it would be difficult to point to any political or religious figure as a unifying leader, given the back-and-forth of party politics and sectarian strife. At the same time, beneath these tangled and usual forms of violence, many Lebanese Christians have become victims. And as Maronite Catholic Michael Aoun, later president of Lebanon,

---

[86] Messaggio di Giovanni Paolo II a Tutti i Vescovi della Chiesa Cattolica sulla Situazione nel Libano, September 7, 1989.

[87] See Romy Haber, "10 Things to Know about the Catholic Church in Lebanon," Catholic News Agency, October 26, 2024, https://www.catholicnewsagency.com/news/260065/10-things-to-know-about-the-catholic-church-in-lebanon.

a leader of the Free Patriotic Movement, said in 2006, the large numbers of Lebanese Christians—his party was then the largest Christian party in the parliament—act as a "moderating force." He was also hopeful that they could become "like a transitional culture between the West and the East ... like a human bridge between both sides."[88]

That was an optimistic forecast, especially because the human bridge was to Hezbollah on the Muslim side, which was already worrying because of its militancy and would only become more so.

In the early 2000s, multiple car bombs, placed by various perpetrators in a seeming attempt to intimidate native Lebanese Christians, exploded in predominantly Christian areas. Suicide bombers struck at several Christian enclaves. Cardinal Nasrallah Boutros Sfeir, the Maronite patriarch, was the target of an assassination attempt in 2010 when he was scheduled to consecrate a new church in Zahle, which is the largest predominantly Christian city in the Middle East and was the target of several Muslim plots.[89] The car bomb detonated too soon, however, and killed only one local resident and wounded others.

In 2012, Pope Benedict XVI visited Lebanon and released an apostolic letter that reflected the discussions at an earlier Middle Eastern Bishops' Synod. The hope was that the visit and the letter would energize a new round of collaboration and understanding. That hope was dashed a few months later when eight Christians

---

[88] Doreen Abi Raad, "Christians Are 'Moderating Force' in Lebanon," *National Catholic Register*, April 10, 2006, https://www.ncregister.com/news/christians-are-moderating-force-in-lebanon; ellipsis in the original.

[89] Marlin, *Christian Persecution*, 101.

were killed and a hundred others wounded in Muslim attacks in Beirut and elsewhere.

The United Nations has estimated that, by the end of the Syrian Civil War in 2019, close to two million Syrian refugees, mostly Christians, have sought asylum in Lebanon, effectively constituting a large percentage of the inhabitants. While this has created a vast humanitarian crisis, it also points to the potential for an even greater problem if the situation becomes more destabilized. As the group In Defense of Christians observed in 2019, Lebanon is "the last safe haven for Christians in the Middle East, and it is at a crossroads."[90] That was before the outbreak of yet another clash between Hezbollah and Israel in 2023 set all groups within the country on edge and made the future of Christians in this "last safe haven" even more uncertain.

[90] "Lebanon on the Brink: Syrian Crisis Threatens 'Last Safe Haven' for Christians," Catholic News Agency, November 20, 2019, https://www.catholicnewsagency.com/news/42873/lebanon-on-the-brink-syrian-crisis-threatens-last-safe-haven-for-christians.

3

Africa

And behold, an Ethiopian, a eunuch, a minister of the
Candace the queen of the Ethiopians, in charge of all her
treasure, had come to Jerusalem to worship and was returning;
seated in his chariot, he was reading the prophet Isaiah.... Now
the passage of the scripture which he was reading was this:

"As a sheep led to the slaughter
or a lamb before its shearer is dumb,
so he opens not his mouth.
In his humiliation justice was denied him.
Who can describe his generation?
For his life is taken up from the earth."

—Acts 8:27–33

Many Western Christians would be hard put even to identify on a map the location of an African nation like Burkina Faso. But Islamist forces have had no difficulty in doing so and in carrying out massacres against Christians. Indeed, as in several other African nations, they exert relentless and murderous pressures on Catholics and others who don't conform their lives and beliefs to Islamist ideology. And in large numbers: In mid-2024, for example, over a period of three months, Islamists in Burkina Faso murdered at least 100 Christians and kidnapped, according to local sources, many more. On August 25, 2024, in the village of Sanaba, 26 people were taken to a church and had their throats cut. On the day before, somewhere between 150 and 250 were slaughtered in the town of Barsalogho. Shocking as such numbers are, they are fairly representative of what had been going on for years in the whole region.

Besides the mass slaughters, individuals are targeted. In 2019, Fr. Fernando Hernández; four years later, Fr. Jacques Yaro Zerbo; the year after that, the catechist Edouard Yougbare, along with other catechists and religious. The security situation was so bad that the Catholic Bishops' Conference of Burkina Faso–Niger (CEBN) decided to call for a formal triduum of prayer for peace in September 2024: "At this grave hour, when our families, villages, and communities are tormented in body, mind, and soul by death, fear, and ongoing insecurity, we call all Christian faithful to fervent prayer." The bishops added an urgent wish: "All Christians who are able are called to fast for the forgiveness of our sins and for the blood spilled like water on the sacred ground of our villages and cities."[91]

There has been an unfortunate tendency among Christians and others in the West and in the international community to regard religious persecution and martyrdom in Africa with a certain indifference, as if there is simply nothing to be done in countries

---

[91] Jude Atemanke, "Catholic Bishops Declare Triduum Prayer for Peace in Burkina Faso, Niger amid Surge in Insecurity," ACI Africa, September 12, 2024, https://www.aciafrica.org/news/12059/catholic-bishops-declare-triduum-prayer-for-peace-in-burkina-faso-niger-amid-surge-in-insecurity.

still finding their way after long years of colonialism and economic exploitation. There's no question that conditions in much of Africa make it difficult to achieve a tolerable level of social order and the rule of law. And the injection of radical Islam, mostly an import from the Middle East in the twenty-first century, has made a bad situation worse. But at the same time, at least for Christians, hopelessness is simply not an option. In recent decades, much of the growth of Christianity in the world has taken place in Africa. Indeed, Christian growth in Africa dwarfs whatever gains are being made in other parts of the world and is a significant counterweight to the shrinking of Christianity in its historical European and Middle Eastern homelands. And protection of Christian populations is of importance not only in Africa itself; it has an impact on immigration, international institutions, and the status of human rights in much of the rest of the world as well.

Christians number 2.4 billion, almost 32 percent of the global population. Of those, African Christians are about one-third, around 750 million—and growing rapidly, not only in absolute numbers but as a percentage of the whole. And that growth favors Christianity in its current clashes with Islam. According to Philip Jenkins, author of *The Next Christendom: The Coming of Global Christianity*, despite appearances, young African Christians outnumber young Muslims four to one.[92] Indeed, that may be one reason why ISIS affiliates, which have been curtailed in the Middle East, remain quite active in Africa—an effort to stem a tide that could change the religious makeup of the continent. Anyone concerned for the future of the faith—indeed, of the whole world—must also be concerned about Africa and its future.

[92] Philip Jenkins, *The Next Christendom: The Coming of Global Christianity* (New York: Oxford University Press, 2002).

In the first two decades of the twenty-first century, several world developments have made conditions in Africa more perilous for the continent's Christians. But, as noted earlier, the main factor was how ISIS moved to Africa. It's difficult to explain entirely why this has happened. The attractions of a growing and charismatic Middle Eastern Islamist movement in the prior two decades help account for the initial spread. The fact that African governments were weak and did not attract the kind of Western military forces that suppressed ISIS in the Middle East is certainly another factor. But it probably should also be said that there is a conspicuous lack of concern for what happens in Africa, even among Western Christians. Some might claim that this is the result of racism, but a simpler explanation might be that the developed world has lower expectations and practices its own form of postcolonial restraint from interventions since the wave of independence movements in the second half of the twentieth century. But whatever the explanation, Western Christians and African Christians themselves have paid the greatest price. Open Doors, which tracks persecution and martyrdom of Christians all over the world, puts five African nations—Somalia, Libya, Eritrea, Nigeria, and Sudan—among its top ten countries of concern for religious liberty; and it identifies twenty African countries among the fifty worst globally.[93] The worst of the worst in terms of sheer numbers is Nigeria, where

---

[93] Besides the five already named, Open Doors names, in descending order of seriousness, Mali, Algeria, Burkina Faso, Mauritania, Morocco, Niger, the Central African Republic, Ethiopia, Tunisia, Egypt, Mozambique, the Democratic Republic of the Congo, Cameroon, and Comoros. One can only hope that persecution will soon evaporate and full accounts of the destruction and mayhem in all these nations can be written.

in 2023–2024 more Christians were martyred than in the rest of the world combined.

Nigeria

In 2020, one of the most heroic twenty-first-century martyrdoms in all of Africa took place. A seminarian, Michael Nnadi, who was only eighteen years old, was abducted by Muslim raiders, as were three fellow students from the Good Shepherd Seminary. The others were eventually released. Nnadi was not because, according to his captors, he was adamant in telling them repeatedly that they must repent and turn from their evil ways. This embarrassed them because he implied that they were bringing disgrace on their own religion. He also urged them to convert to Catholicism. Mustapha Mohammed, the leader of the gang and the person who killed Nnadi, was captured later and admitted that he admired the young seminarian's "outstanding bravery." The raiders also abducted a Catholic laywoman, Bolanle Ataga, and her two daughters and killed the mother when she repelled their attempt to rape her.[94]

The year 2020 was an especially bad one for Catholics in Nigeria. At the end of the year, the Pontifical Institute for Foreign Missions (PIME) totted up the mayhem and determined that "eight priests, three religious women, one male religious, two seminarians, and six lay people" had been martyred in that nation during the previous twelve months.[95] In its own commentary on these and

---

[94] "Nigeria: Michael Nnadi and Bolanle Ataga—Martyrs Walking toward the Barking Dogs," Aid to the Church in Need, May 11, 2020, https://www.churchinneed.org/nigeria-michael-nnadi-bolanle-ataga-martyrs-walking-toward-the-barking-dogs/.

[95] "Michael Nnadi," *Inside the Vatican*, January 1, 2021, https://insidethevatican.com/magazine/people/top-ten-people/michael-nnadi/.

many other separate incidents, a Muslim offshoot of ISIS and Boko Haram released a video saying that the terror was a warning to "all those being used by infidels to convert Muslims to Christianity."[96]

Though this statement of intent was as clear as anything could possibly be, it's not always easy to determine the motive behind such outrages. For example, Nigerian lawlessness also often involves sexual assaults on women, which at times may simply be crimes or, more typically, are a way in which anti-Christian elements in Islamic societies disrespect and demoralize Christian minorities. Ironically, one such attack may have given Nigeria a Christian saint—the country's own version of the well-known witness of St. Maria Goretti.

Vivian Uchechi Ogu was a teenage Catholic in 2009 when she was kidnapped and dragged into a nearby wood. The perpetrators may have simply been criminals, but according to local sources, they were more likely to have been Islamic extremists who were also outlaws looking for opportunities to spread terror. Like Goretti, Vivian refused to let the kidnappers rape her. Significantly, she had earlier that day delivered a talk to her fellow teens in St. Joseph Church in Benin City about sexual purity and martyrdom. She had her words put to the test later that evening and chose death over dishonor.

People who knew her said that, young as she was, she displayed extraordinary maturity, charity, and commitment. In May 2024, the Vatican announced that she may be referred to as "Servant of God," a first step toward potential declaration of sainthood. Maria Lozano, director of Aid to the Church in Need, remarked, "The beatification of Vivian would serve as a powerful source of inspiration for Nigerian Christians, particularly the youth. . . . The example and the testimony of a young girl of unwavering faith in the face of extreme adversity could encourage others to remain steadfast in their beliefs

---

[96] "Michael Nnadi," *Inside the Vatican.*

despite the threat of persecution, corruption and criminality."[97] It says something about the several evils that work together within Nigeria that she included these three elements in this comment.

At least Michael Nnadi, Bolanle Ataga, Vivian Uchechi Ogu, and the several other Catholics martyred can be identified by name. But there are many, many more—hundreds and thousands of other nameless, unidentified Christians—killed singly or in whole groups in Nigeria, year after year.

The world doesn't pay much attention to Christian martyrdom and persecution despite the fact that Christians are attacked and repressed in more countries and to a greater degree than any other religious group. But even people who do not much care about or pay little attention to these matters must almost intentionally avert their gaze not to notice the steady stream of Christian casualties in the central African nation of Nigeria. The situation in Nigeria is clearly the most openly bloody instance of religious persecution and martyrdom of Christians in the twenty-first century.

According to Open Doors, 4,998 Christians perished in Nigeria in 2023; "there were more people that were killed because of their Christian faith than all other places in the globe combined." And that was only one year. In the four-year stretch from 2019 to 2023, 33,000 Christians of various denominations and several thousand moderate Muslims were killed by Islamic extremists belonging to Boko Haram, Fulani militants (formerly mostly Muslim "herdsmen" involved in land disputes with Christians), and the Islamic State West Africa Province (ISWP), among others. Over an even

[97] Ngala Killian Chimtom, "Nigeria's Own Teenage Sainthood Candidate a Potential 'Game-Changer,'" *Crux*, May 25, 2024, https://cruxnow.com/church-in-africa/2024/05/nigerias-own-teenage-sainthood-candidate-a-potential-game-changer.

longer period (2009–2021), the International Society for Civil Liberties and the Rule of Law (Intersociety)—a Nigerian watchdog group—has documented 43,000 Christians killed, 18,500 Christians "disappeared," 17,500 churches attacked, 2,000 Christian elementary schools destroyed, and much else.

Mixed in with these clearer religious motives, of course, are conflicts over land, abductions for ransom (especially of Catholic priests), and other crimes and disorders. But there's no denying the specifically anti-Christian animus behind most of these murders.

Though most of the mayhem comes from radical Islamists, the national government is not entirely innocent in these matters. While the constitution proclaims that Nigeria is not a "confessional state," the nation is a member the Organization for Islamic Cooperation, which is dedicated to preserving and advancing the Islamic inheritance and revitalizing it throughout the world. Christians and other minorities have pointed out that the 1999 constitution contains several provisions that favor Muslims and disfavor Christians. And the federal government of Nigeria does little, often nothing, to protect Christians from Islamic militants. In the state of Kaduna, for instance, an Islamic terror group has set up what amounts to a parallel governing authority that controls all economic and political activity—with all but no pushback from the proper authorities. The bishop of Makurdi in the state of Benue, Wilfred Anagbe, has called all this "creeping genocide."[98]

This is why it was puzzling when the administration of U.S. president Joseph Biden removed Nigeria in 2021 from the list of Countries of Particular Concern over religious liberty. It's true that the

---

[98] "Nigeria," Aid to the Church in Need, accessed February 14, 2025, https://acninternational.org/activity/church-in-africa/nigeria -in-2021/

Nigerian *government* is not directly involved in attacks on Christians, as are the government of nations such as North Korea, Sudan, and Iran. Nigeria's constitution affirms in principle the right to religious freedom as well as free speech, propagating religion through public instruction, and protections against religious discrimination. But the forces of the state have not been of much help in stopping the carnage.

This is a serious problem in the most populous nation in Africa, with around 250 million people almost equally divided between Muslims and Christians. In addition, because of quirks in the constitution, individual states have a right to adopt a religion. Early in the twenty-first century, a dozen out of the thirty-six states chose to become officially Muslim and apply sharia law within their borders. Christians and members of minority faiths objected, but the move was technically legal. Historically, Muslims were mostly concentrated in the northern half of the country—where the twelve states had embraced sharia—while Christians largely occupied the south. Naturally, public clashes followed between the two groups where sharia law was put into effect, mostly in the north. In 2020, the bishop of Sokoto, Matthew Hassan Kukah, claimed that many of the northern Muslims believed in restoring the former Nigerian caliphate that had once ruled the country (1804–1903). Ironically, they considered Christianity a tool of colonialism, whereas their own Islamic faith had practiced what could be characterized as Islamic colonialism, only a few centuries earlier.

On a day-to-day level in those northern states, Christian education is not allowed in public schools, Christian students can't get scholarships to study, graduates are discriminated against in the workplace, permits for building churches are denied, and religious buildings are taken away without compensation. Local police forces, in violation of federal law, harshly treat Christians for sharia violations, imposing punishments that include the death penalty, amputations, and beatings. They enforce on Christians sharia regulations about dress, public eating and drinking during Ramadan, and other such rules. Observers also rightly mention, however, that these clashes are not universal: in Nigeria's west, where more moderate Muslims dominate, relations are very different with Christians, and toleration prevails for the most part.

The modern nation of Nigeria gained independence in 1960, emerging from the British protectorate that had ruled the area since the late nineteenth century. The usual postcolonial political and military turmoil followed for several decades. Nigeria has had a major advantage over other postcolonial African nations in that it stood on large oil reserves and became one of the leading exporters of oil in the world. The wealth, however, was not much used to improve the general well-being of the population. It was not until 1999, with the establishment of the Fourth Nigerian Republic, for example, that relative stability was achieved. Nigeria remains an economic leader in Africa, despite everything, but the bloody religious conflicts that have marked twenty-first-century Nigeria have overshadowed many other developments.

In 2014, for example, Boko Haram—then a growing militant Islamist sect—perpetrated the massacre of multiple villages in what came to be known as the Gwoza massacre. (The name Boko Haram has been translated as meaning "Western Education Is Forbidden," but their formal name is "Group of the People of Sunnah for Dawah and Jihad.") The militants, dressed as government soldiers, destroyed cellular towers, which made it difficult for local officials to call for help from federal authorities. The attack targeted both the government and the Church; administrative offices and a Catholic church were burned to the ground. And the carnage was so widespread and drove so many to flee into neighboring Cameroon that it became all but impossible to arrive at reliable figures regarding what happened, though probably as many as five hundred were killed.

This was an inflection point for the movement, which had restarted attacks in 2009, after being suppressed by the government in 2002. The goal was to "purify" Sunni Islam from other influences within the faith and to eliminate Christians and others in the effort to create an Islamic caliphate. And it was a harbinger of worse things to come. Boko Haram became formally affiliated with ISIS around 2015, just as that insurgency was ramping up operations in the Middle East. In another raid that took place just a year before that affiliation, Boko Haram kidnapped 256 mostly Christian schoolgirls from the town of Chibok, an outrage that gained a great deal of international attention. Similar raids involving thousands had been occurring both before and after that resulted in young girls being forced into sexual slavery as well as dying during their detention yet were all but ignored in Western media and political circles.

So it's no surprise that, according to the Global Terrorism Index, Boko Haram—which killed 6,644 people in 2015—was even outstripping ISIS. This reflected a rapid increase in attacks—in that one year, "the largest increase in terrorist-caused deaths ever recorded by any country," according to observers, making Boko Haram the world's deadliest terror organization.[99] And the carnage wasn't restricted to Nigeria; though Boko Haram focused on Nigeria, it was also active in Chad and Cameroon.

But Boko Haram was far from being the only force attacking and killing Christians in Nigeria. As the twenty-first century has

---

[99] Rose Troup Buchanan, "Isis Overtaken by Boko Haram as World's Deadliest Terror Organization," *Independent*, November 17, 2015, https://www.independent.co.uk/news/world/africa/boko-haram-overtakes-isis-as-world-s-deadliest-terror-organisation-a6737761.html.

progressed, another major persecutor has been the Fulani Ethnic Militia (FEM). Before the religious and ethnic side of the group consolidated itself, the Fulani were sometimes described as merely Muslim cow "herdsman," which they were, and in conflict over grazing lands with Christian farmers, which they also were, but not exclusively. As the end of the first quarter of the century approached, they became ever more involved in targeting Christians—individuals and whole groups in small towns—to such a degree that when the Observatory for Religious Freedom in Africa (ORFA), totted up the numbers between 2020 and 2024, it was clear that the FEM body count had surpassed even Boko Haram's over that four-year period.

The report that ORFA issued in August 2024 made clear in its very title—*Countering the Myth of Religious Indifference in Nigerian Terror*[100]—that there were not "land disputes" but anti-Christian animus behind the majority of FEM-Christian clashes. Two incidents that offer evidence of this occurred in 2023: On Good Friday, in a FEM attack on Christians, thirty-five died, and many others were wounded. That same year, a Christmas attack on Nigerian Christians left around two hundred dead in twenty-six villages in Nigeria's central Plateau region. The timing (Easter and Christmas) and the targets chosen clearly show that these kinds of assaults are carefully planned and executed—and intended as part of a deliberate and wider strategy of terrorizing and driving out the Christian population.

ORFA's calling attention to the religious dimension of such events is well warranted. Many secular news outlets try to play

---

[100] Observatory for Religious Freedom in Africa, *Countering the Myth of Religious Indifference in Nigerian Terror*, August 29, 2024, https://orfa.africa/wp/wp-content/uploads/2024/08/26082024-ORFA-4-YEARS-REPORT.pdf.

down or entirely ignore the religious dimension. In this particular case, Britain's *Guardian* and Reuters news service, along with the German newspaper *Die Zeit*, claimed that "climate change" was responsible, to some degree, for the clash with the Fulani. Sadly, even some in the Church have taken up the same excuse. Fr. Benedict Kiely, however, who follows Christian persecution and martyrdom in several places around the globe, highlighted countertestimony by people close to the event:

> This is the narrative of the post-Christian globalist West. How could they dare admit there is a genocide going on in Nigeria perpetrated by Muslims against Christians — it would demand action. I remember hearing the words of the Bishop of Ondo in Nigeria last year, when more than 40 of his people were killed at Pentecost Mass — he said, "40 of my people were not killed because of global warming, but because they were Christians.[101]

Other sources have documented that, in 2022, thirty-nine Catholic priests were killed and another thirty abducted. Fairly typical of the random violence against priests was the death of Fr. Charles Igechi in Benin on June 7, 2023. He had been ordained only in the previous August and was shot while returning from some ordinary pastoral work. Islamic militants are suspected, but authorities have not been able to identify the perpetrators.

As in other countries where militant Islam operates at both collective and individual levels, there have also been various random

---

[101] Quoted in Chris Tomlinson, "Media Blames Christmas Massacre of Nigerian Christians on 'Climate Crisis,'" *European Conservative*, December 28, 2023, https://europeanconservative.com/articles /news/media-blames-christmas-massacre-of-160-nigerian-christians -on-climate-crisis/.

killings of Catholics for trumped up charges of "blasphemy." Just a few months before Fr. Igechi was murdered, a Christian student, Deborah Samuel Yakubu, was stoned to death and her body burned by igniting tires that had been piled up over her body by fellow students at the Muslim Shehu Shagari College of Education in Sokoto (the very place where the local bishop says the desire to return to a caliphate is widely shared). Her crime? Posting comments allegedly critical of some acts by the Prophet Muhammad.

Though she was an Evangelical, rumors in the city circulated claiming that the Catholic Church had put her up to the "blasphemy." As might be expected, further violence followed. The local Catholic diocese released a statement that read in part:

> During the protest, groups of youths led by some adults in the background attacked the Holy Family Catholic Cathedral at Bello Way, destroying church glass windows, those of the Bishop Lawton Secretariat, and vandalized a community bus parked within the premises. St. Kevin's Catholic Church was also attacked and partly burnt; windows of the new hospital complex under construction, in the same premises, were shattered.... The hoodlums also attacked the Bakhita Centre ... burning down a bus within the premises.[102]

No further lives were lost—fortunately. But many other Christian religious establishments in Nigeria have not been so lucky.

❖ Fr. Isaac Achi was burned to death in January 2023 when bandit terrorists set fire to his rectory in the Catholic

---

[102] Maria Lozano, "Anti-Christian Violence and Curfew Follow Killing of Girl in Sokoto, Nigeria," Aid to the Church in Need, May 17, 2022, https://acninternational.org/anti-christian-violence-in -nigeria/.

Diocese of Minna. His colleague Fr. Collins Omeh survived but was shot, though not killed, as he escaped.[103]

* A few months later, at St. Raphael Fadan Kamantan parish, seminarian Na'aman Danlami also perished in a rectory fire set by Fulani militants.
* In August 2024, seventy Christians were killed, and twenty Christian medical students were kidnapped by Islamic raiders, forcing many to take shelter in St. Joseph's Church in the state of Benue.

Boko Haram terrorism is so fanatical that female suicide bombers, one with a baby, killed eighteen people at a wedding in Gwoza in June 2024; other militants then moved on to a hospital where the wounded were being treated and later revisited the original scene, detonating another device among the mourners at the funeral for its victims.

Given all this carnage—according to Open Doors, nine out of every ten Christians killed around the world meet their end in Nigeria—it seems imperative that both the Vatican and other Christian bodies keep the plight of Nigerian Christians constantly in front of the eyes of the global community. Various international organizations, such as the United Nations and the European Union, and especially influential countries, such as the United States, need to do much more as well. If a large country that is half Christian as well as half Muslim is allowed to continue to produce so many Christian deaths without serious consequences, it is not only a grave injustice but will also send the message to the most extreme elements in the Muslim world that such things can be done year after year without repercussions.

---

[103] Courtney Mares, "Catholic Priest Burned to Death in Nigeria," Catholic News Agency, January 15, 2023, https://www.catholic-newsagency.com/news/253356/catholic-priest-burned-to-death-in-nigeria.

It's often difficult to get international bodies to reach common agreements, let alone common action. This is why it's particularly important that the United States take the lead in calling out the actions of extremists groups in Nigeria as well as the inaction—and occasional complicity—of the Nigerian government with them. A minimum first step would be to return Nigeria to the U.S. State Department's list of Countries of Particular Concern for religious liberty. America's own Commission on International Religious Freedom has encouraged the U.S. State Department—which is apparently balking for economic, political, and diplomatic reasons—to do precisely that and even to name a "special envoy" to Nigeria to monitor its behavior.[104]

The head of the International Society for Civil Liberties and the Rule of Law (Intersociety), Emeka Umeagbalasi, has made clear the urgency of those steps and much more: "The killings have been elevated to state policy in Nigeria." He cited an example of the action of the Nigerian army, allegedly in pursuit of a pair of extremists but, in fact, acting as something akin to a "jihadist force." "Three Catholic parishes, not just one, were raided. Parishioners were violently dispersed, the congregants sacked, and the church services disrupted, even in the presence of the Blessed Sacrament."[105] Fr. Moses Lorapuu, director of social communications for the Makurdi

---

[104] Elizabeth Cassady, host, *USCIRF Spotlight Podcast*, "Shortcomings of the State Department's CPC Designations," United States Commission on International Religious Freedom, January 25, 2024, https://www.uscirf.gov/news-room/uscirf-spotlight/shortcomings-state-departments-cpc-designations.

[105] Ngala Killian Chimtom, "Catholic Leader Claims Nigeria's Military Has Become 'Jihadist Force,'" *Crux*, August 24, 2024, https://cruxnow.com/church-in-africa/2024/08/catholic-leader-claims-nigerias-military-has-become-jihadist-force.

Diocese, warned Western nations about inaction: "As long as the leadership of this country remains in the hands of those who are part of the persecution, there will be no justice for Christians. Relativistic euphemisms such as 'communal clashes' are political and economic lifelines [i.e., rationalizations] for a Christian West that does not care much about the sufferings of the Christian South."[106]

Democratic Republic of the Congo

Amid so much persecution and mayhem, it's remarkable that the African continent is the place where Christianity is growing—and growing faster than in any other part of the world. In the first quarter of the twenty-first century alone, the number of Christians in Africa doubled from around one hundred million to two hundred million. This continues a long-term trend that reflects not only absolute numbers but the relative proportion of Christians in Africa as well. A century earlier, Christians made up less than 10 percent of the African population. By the early 2020s, the figure was, by some estimates, more than 60 percent. By then, for the first time, there were more Christians living in Africa than on any other continent. And most of that growth, unlike in the past, is internally generated, not the result of Western missionary efforts. It's safe to say that Christianity's future, and not only demographically, will be heavily influenced by Africa, especially given the severe decline in religious adherence in the developed nations.

The Christian—and, specifically, Catholic—presence in a country, however, is no guarantee of local tranquility. Indeed,

[106] Ngala Killian Chimtom, "Biden Administration Under Fire in Nigeria over Religious Freedom Report," *Crux*, July 2, 2024, https://cruxnow.com/church-in-africa/2024/07/biden-administration-under-fire-in-nigeria-over-religious-freedom-report.

sometimes the very opposite. The Democratic Republic of the Congo (DRC), for example, is believed to be more than 95 percent Christian, with Catholics making up over half of the population as the single largest religious group—and the most Catholics in sheer numbers of any African country. Nevertheless, attacks on Catholics are common and savage, not least because the Church usually remains with the people during troubled times and even in some of the most unsettled areas.

The DRC, unfortunately, displays all the usual atrocities against Christians by various rebel factions that can be seen in other African nations where governments are chaotic and extremist groups are uncontrolled. A double murder took place in December 2009 in the Archdiocese of Bukavu. First, a priest, Fr. Daniel Cizimya Nakamaga, was shot and killed in his rectory. Shortly after, a Trappist nun at the Monastery of Clarté-Dieu in Murhesa, Sr. Denise Kahambu Muhayirwa, was shot in the back by thugs who broke into the religious house. She bled to death when the other sisters were unable to reach her. She had been in charge of welcoming strangers to the monastery, and when she answered the door, her assailants pushed in and chased her down a hall before shooting her. In both instances, nothing was stolen, and robbery therefore appears not to have played any part in the murders. The motivation seems to have been intimidation of clergy to prevent resistance to the operations of armed gangs seeking to control the region. In any event, violence is so widespread in regions such as eastern DRC that it's a sign of heroic virtue when clergy and laity alike choose to remain and go about their business, in the full knowledge that a swift end, as happened to these two, is possible for anyone, any day.

Even by the standards of postcolonial Africa, the situation in the DRC is a rare state of conflict. The country was wracked by deep turmoil following independence in 1960, even changing its name to Zaire from 1971 to 1997 before changing it back. It suffered two civil wars, the second of which ended, in theory, in 2003. But while large-scale forces have ceased to clash, a steady stream of violence has continued. By reliable estimates, there are more than a hundred conflicting factions in the country, some seeking to control territory and the gold, cobalt (an essential mineral in the manufacture of cell phones), and other natural resources they contain. Others are seeking larger political control, and still others are engaged in sectarian religious strife. The Congolese population is almost entirely Christian, and Muslims make up less than 2 percent of the people. But that large Christian population has offered Islamic radicals, and various small groups of secular militias vying for wealth, multiple opportunities for terror. When regions are experiencing generalized violence, it is often only the Catholic churches that remain close to the people.

The situation has remained particularly violent in the eastern parts of the country, which border Uganda, Rwanda, and Sudan and where the central government — not very effective in protecting the people anyway — is weakest. As in many other conditions of disorder and generalized conflict, it is not always easy to identify perpetrators or their motives in any given instance. And it did not help an already perilous situation that armed groups from those troubled bordering nations began operating in eastern DRC. In May 2000, for example, two armed factions — the Armée Patriotique Rwandaise (APR, "Patriotic Rwandan Army") and the Uganda People's Defence Forces (UPDF) — engaged in a "Six-Day War" in the town of Kisangani and killed and destroyed indiscriminately, even doing serious damage to the Cathedral of Notre-Dame du Rosaire. At other times, the death and destruction were clearly targeted to eliminate priests and other Catholic leaders and to intimidate the general population.[107]

Rwandan forces, mostly Tutsis, had already killed the heroic archbishop of Bukavu, Christophe Munzihirwa, in 1996, when they invaded then-Zaire in pursuit of Hutu refugees. The bishop heroically defended them, even as he foresaw that it would bring his death.[108] The world remembers the attempted "genocide" of the Tutsis in Rwanda at the hands of the Hutu; at least half a million and perhaps twice that number were killed. The violent forces from Rwanda and also Uganda that pursued Hutus into Zaire were set on revenge and did not care who—even a Catholic archbishop—stood in their way. High-profile deaths like this went mostly unnoticed by the international community, but they had a powerful and continuing influence on attitudes and behavior for years after.

Among the additional factors that kept the violence going was a Ugandan Christian "insurgency"—the Lord's Resistance Army (LRA)—which professed an extremist faith that incorporated Muslim and traditional tribal elements into a militant belief system that allowed them to assault even other Christians whom they found insufficiently "Christian." In the tangled relations among the various states in the region, the LRA formed in opposition to the Ugandan government's National Resistance Army (NRA),

---

[107] United Nations Human Rights Office of the High Commissioner, *Democratic Republic of Congo, 1993–2003* (United Nations, August 2010), 190, https://www.ohchr.org/sites/default/files/Documents/Countries/CD/DRC_MAPPING_REPORT_FINAL_EN.pdf.

[108] John L. Allen Jr., *The Global War on Christians: Dispatches from the Front Lines of Anti-Christian Persecution* (New York: Image, 2013), 47, Kindle ed.

an undisciplined and brutal force that terrorized the population. People who resisted their violence were suspected of being LRA sympathizers. And the LRA itself was receiving aid from Sudan, which was oppressing its own Christian population in what would become the independent nation of South Sudan. The Ugandan government, the Sudanese believed, was encouraging the independence movement and made use of the LRA to distract it.

When the LRA moved into what was back to being the Democratic Republic of the Congo, it carried out utterly staggering slaughters. In 2008, for instance, according to reports:

> [The LRA] made the decision to wait until Christmas Eve and Christmas Day to attack civilian populations in an effort to pound them into submission. The rebels targeted people at their churches, Protestant and Catholic alike, surrounding them and killing them by crushing their skulls with axes, machetes, and large wooden bats. The victims were hacked into pieces, decapitated, or burned alive in their homes, and several people reportedly had their lips cut off as a "warning not to speak ill of the rebels." A pair of three-year-old girls reportedly suffered serious neck injuries when rebels tried to twist their heads off. More than 20,000 people were reported to have been displaced by the attacks, with as many as 225 people, including 160 children, abducted and more than 80 women raped.[109]

The situation was exacerbated when the Allied Democratic Forces (ADF)—a group that started as an insurgent movement in neighboring Uganda and spilled over into the DRC—became officially associated with ISIS in 2019. (ADF is the local name for the

---

[109] Allen, *Global War*, 51–52.

more formally designated ISIS-Democratic Republic of the Congo.) ISIS-like outrages were taking place years earlier, however. According to the National Counterterrorism Center, ADF murdered an estimated four thousand civilians between 2014 and 2020.[110]

The terrorists spared no one, not even medical personal who were obviously providing services to a people badly suffering from violence and the social dislocations it causes. Sr. Marie-Sylvie Kavuke Vakatsuraki, a member of the Congregation of the Little Sisters of the Presentation of Our Lady in the Temple and a doctor, perished in 2022 along with six of her patients in senseless violence at the hospital run by the Diocese of Butembo-Beni. ADF not only killed them, but abducted others, stole medicine and supplies, and burned the hospital down as they left. Even measured alongside the many acts of terror in the DRC, this amounted to sheer ruin and intimidation.[111]

As might be expected, armed militants who regularly carry out such raids have not spared even religious sites. The year before the attack on the hospital, the bishop of Mbujimayi, Bernard Emmanuel Kasanda, wrote a letter deploring what he described as "abominable acts of desecration in places of worship: parishes, Marian caves, altars, sanctuaries … acts going so far as to desecrate our tabernacles where the Blessed Sacrament rests."[112] The Congolese bishops also

[110] "ISIS — Democratic Republic of Congo (ISIS-DRC)," National Counterterrorism Center, February 2022, https://www.dni.gov/nctc/ftos/isis_drc_fto.html.

[111] Kevin J. Jones, "Islamist Rebels Kill Nun, Six Others at Catholic Hospital in DR Congo," Catholic News Agency, October 21, 2022, https://www.catholicnewsagency.com/news/252620/islamist-rebels-kill-nun-six-others-at-catholic-hospital-in-dr-congo.

[112] "Catholic Bishops in DR Congo 'Strongly Condemn' Attacks on Church," Catholic News Agency, August 9, 2021, https://www.catholicnewsagency.com/news/248619/catholic-bishops-in-dr-congo-strongly-condemn-attacks-on-church.

deplored the attacks on the Church by the government, including the invasion of the cardinal's residence in Kinshasa because leaders were unhappy with the Church's efforts at national unity, which the rulers regarded as "politicizing" the faith.

The violence has escalated as the century has worn on. In 2024, for example, the Allied Democratic Forces (ADF) — despite the name, an Islamist terror group allied with the Islamic State's Central African Province — carried out large-scale slaughters of Catholics. The Middle East Media Research Institute (MEMRI) has documented that 639 Christians have died at the ADF's hands in the first half of 2024 alone. The procedure is simple and repeated in almost every case. Christians are captured in large numbers. They are given the choice of converting to Islam or death. Most refuse to convert. Then things vary a bit. There are mass beheadings, and, as in the world-famous case in Libya, cell-phone videos of the slaughter are uploaded to the Internet to intimidate whole swaths of the population. Shootings and stabbings also occur, always with the same choice offered and graphic images of the carnage.

In March 2024, fifty died after capture by the ADF; they were also given the choice of conversion or death. In May, eleven died and many more taken hostage. In June, it was an additional fourteen. These were all clearly planned assaults with the common aim of killing as many Christians as possible, terrorizing others, and driving many to flee, all with the hope of establishing an Islamist beachhead in an unsettled nation.

Among the many, and perhaps one of the most egregious, ways that human dignity is being disrespected in the twenty-first century is by the targeting of humanitarian aid workers — the generous people who dedicate themselves precisely to the relief of the poor and the displaced in situations of war and persecution — by political and religious militants. Common human decency would suggest that aid workers, who typically stay out of partisan and sectarian conflicts and focus on concrete aid, should be exempt from the generalized violence in so many places in the modern world. But, according to a report by Humanitarian Outcomes, an independent group that does research on aid activities, attacks on aid workers have been escalating worldwide. In 2023, the group found that 595 such attacks occurred in thirty-three countries, resulting in 280 deaths.[113]

Among those countries, the Democratic Republic of Congo was of special concern. In the fall of 2024, for example, Dieudonné Barondezi, the director of Caritas in Congo's office in Kalonge, was murdered as he sought to pass a toll set up by Islamic militants. Caritas Internationalis is the Catholic Church's global network of relief and development services, which operates in two hundred countries and is the largest such network except for the International Red Cross. Staff who work in places such as the Congo know they are putting themselves in harm's way as competing groups seek political and economic advantage and sometimes religious dominance as well. Dieudonné Barondezi, who carried out his labors in full knowledge of what the consequences might be, was one of a series of aid workers attacked in the Congo.

The Congo seems to be a virtual machine for manufacturing the kind of "new martyrs" that St. John Paul II identified as increasingly common in the modern world.[114] They may not be killed directly

---

[113] Junno Arocho Esteves, "Caritas 'Shocked' by Murder of Director in Democratic Republic of Congo," *Catholic Review*, September 24, 2024, https://catholicreview.org/caritas-shocked-by-murder-of-director-in-democratic-republic-of-congo/.

[114] See the introduction to the present volume.

for theological differences, but they perish as a result of carrying out their responsibilities as Christians in troubled circumstances.

A noteworthy case is that of Fr. Vincent Machozi, an Assumptionist priest and a DRC native who had studied at Boston University and was killed on March 20, 2016 (Palm Sunday), by ten armed soldiers as he was working on his laptop. It happened only three days after he had published an online report on a local atrocity. He has sometimes been described as a "human rights activist." But he was more than that, much more. There had been seven earlier attempts on his life because he had been posting online in *Beni Lubero*, a publication he had started, not only accounts of attacks but the names of people who had carried them out. This clearly threatened a number of local leaders as well as higher-ups in the military and the government. To its credit, the DRC arrested some of those who had perpetrated the murder. But when the murderers were tried by a military court, they were acquitted—a verdict that shocked many local people who knew what had actually happened.[115]

Fr. Machozi carried out a brave—indeed, fearless—ministry of trying to protect people in his homeland, which borders Rwanda and Uganda, in part, he said, because no one else was trying to do anything about the atrocities. He did. Not only did he document them personally; he also organized a network of collaborators who took cell-phone videos of events. It's a sign of how difficult that mission was, however, that his superiors in the Assumptionist Order feared not only for his life but for the safety of the other 150

---

[115] "Acquittals in the Death of Fr. Machozi Dismay Local Residents," Vatican News, September 12, 2018, https://www.vaticannews.va /en/africa/news/2018-09/acquittals-in-the-death-of-fr-machozi -dismay-local-residents.html.

Assumptionists working in the DRC if his efforts were identified with the order as a whole. He was careful to issue his materials solely in his own name—avoiding any larger association that might bring trouble on his fellow priests. Shortly after he returned to the DRC in 2012, three of his fellow Assumptionists were kidnapped and never heard from again. It's no wonder that, though he was also working toward a Ph.D. at Boston University, he interrupted his studies to help protect his people. The situation was quite dire: "In many villages three-quarters of the women had been raped by soldiers, and ... women, boys, and men were forced by militia to dig for the highly prized ore coltan, which is essential for the manufacture of cell phones."[116]

Not only did Fr. Machozi serve as a parish priest in Butembo, but he set up a social center for the people and was elected president of the Nande people, a position he used to help publicize their plight. His name, Machozi, in the native language of the Nande means "son of tears." But according to his colleagues in Boston, that did not reflect the hopeful spirit he exuded. According to one, "he was such a sweet, kind, good-natured person, but there was a lot of sorrow and anger and frustration over what was going on back home." Another commented on his peaceful decision to interrupt his studies: "What surprised me when he decided to go back was how matter-of-fact he was." Perhaps most indicative of his character and spirit was a message he wrote to his Assumptionist superior in Rome: "Pray for me, because I will be murdered. I feel it ... but like Christ, for the sake of our people, I will not be silent."[117]

---

[116] Art Jahnke, "Machozi's Calling," *Bostonia* (Fall 2016), https://www.bu.edu/bostonia/fall16/vincent-machozi-congo-machozis-calling/.

[117] Jahnke, "Machozi's Calling."

It's no surprise that thirty thousand local admirers showed up at the funeral for such a brave, selfless soul.

Sudan

Sudan, like many of the African nations discussed here, became independent in the middle of the twentieth century (1956) and immediately entered into a period of disorder and multiple civil wars. But it is unique—and perhaps second only to Nigeria on the African continent—in the extent of clashes between Christians and various forces, clashes that would eventually lead to a formal division of the nation into two independent states. The first civil war—a North-South conflict—anticipated some of the worst days that were to follow. The South (with a large Christian population) would vote to secede in 2011. In the meantime, the nation endured not only political and economic turmoil but sharp religious conflict as well. Other African countries may have repressed Christians more systematically; in Sudan, the division was open and large.

In modern times, the still undivided nation was roughly 70 percent Muslim, 20 percent Christian, and 10 percent tribal religions. Four governments took power between the first days of the independence of the nation of Sudan and the separation of South Sudan. For all their differences, these governments were united in a common endeavor, but one that produced paradoxical results. As a Sudan expert put it:

> All four governments undertook violent military campaigns against the southern Sudanese people, persecuting local Christian populations and expelling missionaries. This persecution has had profound consequences for southern Sudan

because it has accelerated the growth of the indigenous churches and led to one of the largest and fastest conversion of indigenous people to Christianity in modern history.[118]

That Christian growth was, of course, an unintended byproduct of modern Islamist persecution, but, in a strange way, it mirrors the somewhat similar persecution of the early Church by the ancient Roman Empire—which also produced a large crop of both martyrs and Catholic converts.

Religious violence strikes most frequently at everyday figures— Catholic priests, religious, catechists, laypeople, business owners, local political authorities. And that was mostly the case for Sudan. But not always. It was almost to be expected that, in a place like Sudan, one of Open Doors' top persecuting nations (number eight in 2024), it would even strike at the highest level of the Church. In 2010, Hamdan Mohamed Abdurrahman stood up during the Gloria at a Mass in Khartoum and rushed the altar wielding a knife. Cardinal Gabriel Zubeir Wako, the celebrant, narrowly escaped the assassination attempt because the master of ceremonies for the Mass intervened. The assailant was clearly a Muslim and seemed to be responding to the cardinal's public criticisms of Islamic fundamentalism. The cardinal had also denounced attacks against Christians in Southern Sudan, which would become an independent state the following year.[119]

The twenty-first-century persecution in Sudan was primarily carried out by the regime of President Omar al-Bashir, the longest

---

[118] Andrew S. Natsios, *Sudan, South Sudan, and Darfur: What Everyone Needs to Know* (New York: Oxford University Press, 2012), 7.

[119] "Attempt against the Life of Card Gabriel Zubeir Wako, Archbishop of Khartoum," AsiaNews, October 13, 2010, https://www.asia news.it/news-en/Attempt-against-the-life-of-Card-Gabriel-Zubeir -Wako,-archbishop-of-Khartoum-19715.html.

The Martyrs of the New Millennium

Fr. Frans van der Lugt of
Syria was fatally shot in the
besieged city of Homs on
April 7, 2014.

The grave of Fr. Frans van der Lugt.

Fr. Ragheed Ganni of the Diocese of Mosul,
Iraq, was killed on June 3, 2007.

Eighteen-year-old seminarian Michael Nnadi was abducted from the Good Shepherd Seminary in the city of Kaduna, northern Nigeria, along with three other students on January 8, 2020, and was killed on January 28.

Shahbaz Bhatti, a Pakistan government minister who gave his life for persecuted faith groups, was assassinated on March 2, 2011.

Shahbaz Bhatti's grave, in a cemetery in Gojra, in the Diocese of Faisalabad.

Pakistani mother of five Asia Bibi was falsely accused and sentenced to death for blasphemy. She was arrested in June 2009, went on trial, and was put on death row in November 2010. She was freed in 2018 when Pakistan's Supreme Court reversed the case.

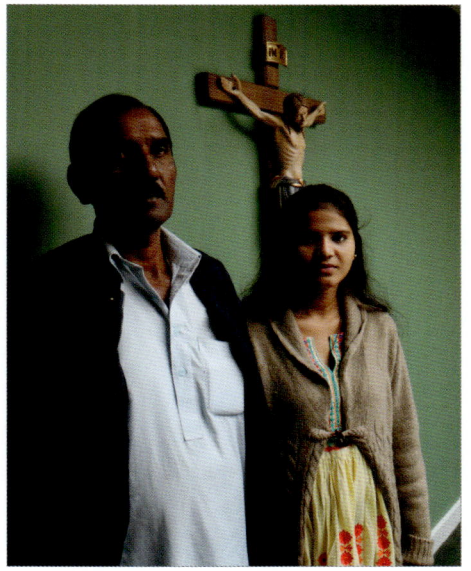

Asia Bibi's husband, Ashiq Masih,
and daughter Eisham Ashiq.

Asia Bibi in Paris on February 26, 2020,
for an interview with ACN France.

Asia Bibi's husband, Ashiq Masih, and daughter Eisham Ashiq.

Fr. Jacques Hamel was killed by Islamic radicals in his church in the town of Saint-Étienne-du-Rouvray, France, on July 26, 2016.

Mass on the sixth anniversary of the death of Fr. Jacques Hamel.

sitting ruler in the history of an independent Sudan (1989–2019). In turn, he was inspired by the popular Islamist preacher Hassan al-Turabi, whose fiery sermons sought to inspire global Islamist uprisings in Sudan and other African nations as a first step to universal Muslim world domination. Needless to say, leaders in other African nations were not necessarily pleased at the prospect of Muslim minorities or varying Islamic sects stirring up already fragile social orders and seeking to carry out a radical jihad, even against moderate Muslims. And neither was the rest of the world. As the Sudan expert cited above has explained, "The Sudanese government caught the attention of the United States and Western Europe when it invited dozens of Islamist groups that had been involved in bombings and assassination attempts to move their headquarters and training schools to Sudan, including al-Qaeda led by Osama bin Laden."[120] In 1996, Bin Laden would be expelled to continue his mischief in Afghanistan under the Taliban, but radical Islamism would remain in Sudan.

In Africa, Sudan has presented a special case of Christian persecution. Until 2011, when South Sudan seceded, northern Sudan carried out a brutal campaign in the South, where Christians and tribal religions are predominant. Historically, the North had raided the South to capture slaves, who were then sold in Egypt or the Ottoman Empire. So there were longstanding precedents for seeking to subdue Southerners. This was what happened even in more recent times under the harsh and sharia-based regime of Omar al-Bashir. Even when persecution stopped short of actual death, there were floggings and public amputations, among other punishments. Christians were also murdered, of course, and crucifixions were not unknown in both North and South for criminals as defined

---

[120] Natsios, *Sudan*, 7.

under strict sharia law, which could include religious minorities, especially Christians. Independence for the South eased its situation some, and the government that took over from al-Bashir removed sharia from the constitution and banned practices such as female genital mutilation and punishment for apostasy.

During the struggle for independence, Catholics in the South were attacked in all the usual ways—and some that were unusual. According to eyewitnesses, the government in the North would send planes to bomb Christian villages and even churches. In some places, the danger was so great that Catholics were forced to have Masses under trees so that the planes could not see what was going on. But the government planes made indiscriminate bombing runs anyway, sometimes dropping barrel bombs that would spread shrapnel and death for hundreds of yards around the bomb site.

Christians in the South were subject to attacks from other quarters as well. The Lord's Resistance Army (LRA), a group that initially arose in Uganda—and, as mentioned earlier, followed a messianic syncretism that mixed together Christian, Islamic, and traditional African elements—carried out atrocities in Southern Sudan. In 2009, just two year prior to the South's independence, bodies were discovered in Ezo, a town on the southernmost border of what was then still the united nation of Sudan; they were the bodies of persons whom locals say had been kidnapped by the LRA and that appeared to have been crucified. In other words, Christians in Sudan could even find themselves attacked by "Christians" in an armed movement that did not hesitate to use one of the holiest images of the Christian faith to torture and kill them.[121] In 2011, when U.S. President Barak Obama sent troops to resist the LRA, controversy arose in America among some uninformed

---

[121] Allen, *The Global War*, 57.

Christians who thought that the U.S. government was attacking a Christian movement. A woman who had been kidnapped by the LRA and mutilated by a bomb, however, echoed the opinion of bishops and other Christians in the region, saying that "the LRA is not Christian" and that LRA leader "Joseph Kony and his commanders could hardly be considered human."[122]

In 2023, yet another civil war broke out between the government, headed by General Abdel Fattah al-Burhan, and the so-called Rapid Support Forces (RSF), led by General Mohamed Hamdan Dagalo. The two generals had fought together to bring down the Bashir regime. And following its fall, they became president and vice president, respectively, of the new national government. Conflicts over how to integrate the two groups, however, led to the "war of the generals" and further woes for the Sudanese people.

Christians, and specifically Catholics, had long been active in Sudan. The Comboni Fathers, an Italian religious order, began work in Sudan in 1842 and became well known for running the best schools. Even in the twenty-first century, Sudanese elites (including Muslims) sent children to those institutions. Fr. Daniel Comboni, founder of the order and a tireless worker against the slave trade, was canonized by Pope John Paul II in 2003. And one of the other great African saints of modern times, canonized in 2000, is a once enslaved Sudanese woman, St. Josephine Bakhita.

This made the desperate situation of the Catholic Church in Sudan as the first quarter of the twenty-first century was ending all the more heart-wrenching. In April 2024, Aid to the Church in Need reported that because of the "Third Civil War" in Sudan,

---

[122] Ed Beavan, "LRA Is Not Christian, Says Victim," *Church Times*, October 27, 2011, https://www.churchtimes.co.uk/articles/2011 /28-october/news/uk/lra-is-not-christian-says-victim.

the Church has practically disappeared from the country and has no seminarians. Historically, the Sudanese considered the Church a place of refuge, but according to Aid to the Church in Need, the violence has forced the closing of parishes, hospitals, and schools. Religious orders have also been driven out, and many believers have escaped to South Sudan.[123]

For the immediate future, South Sudan remains the main hope for Sudanese Catholics. Unlike in the North, in the South the Church remains one of the most promising institutions. A student of modern Sudan claims:

> The three most functional indigenous institutions are the Christian churches (Roman Catholic, Anglican, Presbyterian, and Pentecostal), the SPLM [Sudan People's Liberation Movement], and the SPLA [Sudanese People's Liberation Army]. Of these, the most powerful by far are the churches. The values the churches inculcate, and the extent to which they use their influence to pursue the public good, will determine the South's future. The role of the churches should not be compared to that of the Christian churches in the current day West, where churches—however influential—make up only one of many institutions that guide the building of a modern civil society. In South Sudan, Christian churches are the central private institution, exercising a powerful influence in the development of the emerging social order.[124]

---

[123] Andrés Henríquez, "Sudan Civil War Leaves No Seminarians and Almost No Catholic Church," Catholic News Agency, April 13, 2024, https://www.catholicnewsagency.com/news/257375/sudan-civil-war-leaves-no-seminarians-and-almost-no-catholic-church.

[124] Natsios, *Sudan*, 220–221.

Other African Hotspots

While Nigeria is by far the worst offender in the whole world in terms of numbers of persecutions and martyrdom of Christians, there are several other African nations that can be regarded as somewhat worse—not in terms of absolute number, but in manner and intensity. Open Doors, which conducts yearly worldwide surveys of threats against Christians, lists Nigeria as "only" number six in its rankings. While the closed society of North Korea outstrips all other persecutors, Open Doors puts three African states—Somalia, Libya, and Eritrea right behind North Korea in the category of "extreme levels of persecution." And Sudan trails them and Nigeria only slightly. These nations are small and little known to most people in the international community, but they warrant some attention as evidence of several ways in which things may go awry in radical Islamic states when they go unchecked, even largely unobserved, by the wider world.

Somalia

Somalia was the only Muslim nation that martyred a Catholic after Benedict XVI's controversial lecture at Regensburg in 2006. As I mentioned briefly in the introduction to the present volume, Sr. Leonella Sgorbati, an Italian Consolata Sister, was a nurse and trainer of medical personnel who had worked for thirty-five years in Africa, five of them in Somalia, before she was killed. She was well aware of the risks she was running in trying to help the Somali people. In a television interview earlier in 2006, she had said, "I know there is a bullet with my name on it. I don't know when it will arrive, but as long as it does not arrive, I will stay [in Somalia]." Pope Francis declared her a martyr in 2017 and beatified her in 2018. Like those of many Christian martyrs, and Jesus

Himself, her last words were reported to have been, "I forgive, I forgive, I forgive."[125]

In several respects, her mere presence and activities in Somalia were a minor miracle. The political chaos in the country for the previous seventeen years meant that Islamic radicals had been free to attack Christian individuals and institutions and even those they regarded as not sufficiently pure Muslim. She was nonetheless determined to make a difference for the people in Somalia. After decades of experience in Kenya, she took a sabbatical and studied how to open a school for training nurses in Mogadishu that would operate in conjunction with a hospital of SOS Children's Village. She succeeded and became its first head. It's hard to imagine a more selfless—and thankless—task in the circumstances under which she had to work. By the time she died, she was said to be fluent in Somali, testimony to the fact that she went out of her way to engage the Somalis and was not in the country as a Western "colonizer," nor even primarily as carrying out missionary rather than medical work. But as in other areas terrorized by militant Islam, all that counted for nothing. She was a Christian. In Rome, her pope had criticized a conversation that had taken place in the fourteenth century—or at least some said that he had. Sheikh Abubakar Hassan Malin called for Muslims to seek and eliminate anyone "offending" the Prophet. Several Western aid workers died, including Sr. Leonella Sgorbati.

Tellingly, most Muslims in Somalia—the many not radicalized—were moved to denounce her murder as well.

[125] Francis Njuguna, "Italian Nun Murdered in Somalia to Be Beatified in Italy," *Crux*, May 25, 2018, https://cruxnow.com/global-church/2018/05/italian-nun-murdered-in-somalia-to-be-beatified-in-italy.

Somalia went into a period of chaos in 1991, when the government was effectively destroyed by civil warfare among various factions. The country briefly gained international attention when, in 1993, as UN forces were under attack, the United States attempted to open up relief corridors for about a quarter million people. In an ill-advised U.S. military action, which later became famous as "Black Hawk Down" (the title of both an illuminating book and a popular film), eighteen American soldiers died, a pair of Black Hawk helicopters were shot down, and hundreds of Somalis were killed. Chaos continued in many parts of the country. By the early 2000s, the Islamic Courts Union, a network of local sharia-based groups, came together in the capital, Mogadishu, with the aim of establishing order and fighting the violence of competing warlords.

Earlier in the year in which Sr. Sgorbati was killed, a Tanzanian invasion backed by the United States established a Transitional Federal Government in Somalia. Many of the leaders of the Islamic Courts Union fled to Eritrea, which would itself become a radical Islamic state (see below). But militants of the Islamic Courts Union remained in Somalia and became a radical Islamic terrorist organization, Al-Shabaab (Party of Youth). Some leaders of the Islamic Courts Union merged with the Transitional Federal Government, and in 2012 a new Islamic government practicing sharia law was formed. Despite the state's official designation as Islamic, it clashed repeatedly with the more extremist Al-Shabaab, which had members who had trained with the mujahideen in Afghanistan and embraced a pure form of Salafist Islam. It's no surprise that they also had ties to al-Qaeda and regarded themselves as the Islamic Emirate of Somalia. They have carried out bomb attacks on the government, which they regard as made up of apostates, and have murdered Sufi mystics (in theory, fellow Muslims).

The Martyrs of the New Millennium

Christianity has existed in Somalia since the second century A.D., though, over the course of history, it has come to be concentrated in certain areas. Bantus, evangelized by the Italians early in the twentieth century, formed a large part of what was once a community of nearly ten thousand. As recently as 1928, a Catholic cathedral was built in Mogadishu. But it was damaged in later civil unrest and is no longer in use. Other than that, there is no Christian church in the country. Al-Shabaab is especially vigilant over Somalis who have visited Kenya or do not show up regularly at mosques. There have been several instances of beheadings of Evangelicals on the merest suspicion of being Christian. A single Diocese of Mogadishu exists for the entire country, with one priest and perhaps a hundred Catholics, and it seems to survive because the federal government offers protections where it controls the territory.

But even the Somali federal government was not able to protect Sr. Leonella Sgorbati and many others in the nation's capital city.

Libya

Because of its proximity to several Christian nations, Libya—though more than 90 percent Sunni Muslim—is also home to tens of thousands of Christians. There are about fifty thousand Roman Catholics divided between dioceses in Tripoli—where they are often Italian—and in Benghazi—where many are Maltese. In addition, there are about an equal number of Coptic Orthodox of Egyptian origin and a small number of Anglicans. The world pays little attention to the country, it seems, except insofar as it is a departure point for Africans seeking to migrate to Europe. But when twenty-one Coptic Orthodox were beheaded by ISIS on a Libyan beach in 2015, and the terror group broadcast videos of the event, it was difficult for the international community not to take notice. Pope Francis declared them Christian martyrs and took the extraordinary ecumenical step of adding them to the Roman Martyrology, the official listing of those the Catholic Church regards as martyrs, which means that they may also be remembered during liturgies. On February 15, 2024, at a ceremony in St. Peter's Basilica, where Coptic Orthodox leaders were also present, Cardinal Kurt Koch, who heads the Dicastery for Promoting Christian Unity, recalled the words of Pope Francis that in martyrdom there is a "ecumenism of blood." And he added: "If the enemy unites us in death, who are we to divide ourselves in life?"[126]

Libya's 2011constitution professes to guarantee freedom of religion, nondiscrimination on the basis of faith, and other such basic protections. It also declares Libya to be an Islamic state and sharia to be the basis of its legal system. Since the overthrow of longtime ruler Muammar al-Gaadhafi in 2011, there has been a temporary government that lacks the ability to control much of the nation, even the capital. Armed militant groups, therefore, are able to operate everywhere as a kind of "morality police" throughout the country—though the government is able, at times, to mount countermeasures if it finds them a problem. But it can also take steps, including violence, against anyone it regards as publicly flouting sharia by "unIslamic behavior." Some militants seem to be affiliated with the government, and others, particularly in the east, have ties with the Libyan army.

Though churches remain open in several cities for foreigners, anti-Christian pressures make all religious activity other than Islamic worship potentially precarious. Christians often do not feel safe

---

[126] Joseph Tulloch, "Vatican Marks First Feast of Coptic Martyrs," Vatican News, February 16, 2024, https://www.vaticannews.va /en/vatican-city/news/2024-02/vatican-coptic-martyrs-feast-first -ecumenical-prayer.html.

traveling in the country, and Christians from points further south who transit the country hoping to cross the Mediterranean into Europe are particularly in danger of being kidnapped or trafficked. The Catholic cathedral in Tripoli was damaged during clashes in 2015 and has still not been made accessible for worship again.

Eritrea

The tiny nation of Eritrea—with a small landmass and a population of only three to ten million people (reliable figures are difficult to obtain)—nevertheless bulks large in terms of persecution of Christians, right behind the worst offenders (North Korea, Somalia, and Libya) and merits brief attention here.

The Eritrean constitution—honored more often in the breach than in observance—officially recognizes four religions: Islam and three small Christian denominations (Catholics, Orthodox, and Lutherans). Though the law prohibits discrimination on the basis of religion, the government routinely arrests, tortures (pressuring conversion to Islam), and "disappears" people—especially those outside the approved groups—on religious grounds. In 2023, by estimates of some human rights groups—one thousand Christians were being held prisoners for infractions of sharia law or unspecified reasons.

It's noteworthy that the persecution of individuals and groups is being carried out by the Eritrean *government*. Eritreans of various religious backgrounds seem to get along reasonably well in everyday life. The U.S. government's *2023 Report on International Religious Freedom*, for instance, noted:

> The government's lack of transparency and intimidation of civil society and religious communities continued to make it difficult to obtain information on the status of societal respect for religious freedom. International observers,

however, continued to state that religious tolerance appeared to be widespread between different groups within society. Churches and mosques were near each other, and most citizens congratulated members of other religious groups on religious holidays and other events. There were no reports of sectarian violence, and most towns and ethnic groups included members from all the major religious groups.[127]

Though the Catholic Church in Eritrea is "officially recognized," its activities are sharply curtailed. Catholic schools, along with those of other non-Sunni religious groups, were taken over by the government in 1995, and the Church is not allowed to carry out any of the usual civil-society activities that are an integral part of its social mission. In 2019, Catholic hospitals were taken over, and in 2020, there was anti-Catholic violence, a spillover from Ethiopia, owing to the usual mixture of lawlessness, competing factions among generalized poverty, and Islamist militancy. Though there have not been instances of outright martyrdom, it's emblematic of the whole religious oppression of the country that a Catholic bishop, Fikremariam Hagos Tsalim of Segheneity, was arrested by the government in October 2022. That same month, two Catholic priests — Fr. Mihratab Stefanos, pastor of the St. Michael's Church in the same diocese, and Capuchin Abbot Abraham — were also detained, without explanation.[128] Religious figures are known to

---

[127] "Eritrea," in U.S. Department of State, 2023 *Report on International Religious Freedom*, "Executive Summary," https://www.state.gov /reports/2023-report-on-international-religious-freedom/eritrea/.

[128] Fredrick Nzwili, "Eritrean Authorities Detain Catholic Bishop, but Won't Say Why," Catholic News Service, October 18, 2022, https://angelusnews.com/news/world/eritrean-authorities-detain -catholic-bishop-but-wont-say-why/.

have been detained for more than a decade, with little information about their whereabouts or condition. Eritrean sources have speculated that the bishop may have been apprehended for calling for peace during Eritrea's war against Ethiopia in the Tigray Province. (The previous month, the government rounded up teenagers during Mass at a church in the bishop's diocese to send them to the battlefront.) But in such repressive conditions, that or almost anything the government may perceive as opposition or budding Catholic activity could be "grounds" for imprisonment.

The situation of the Church, like that of all non-governmental-approved activities in Eritrea, is precarious in the extreme and subject to almost any violation, even by African standards.

4

Asia

Shall my eyes always turn to the west
As thine toward the east?
Can a love that found its spring in the west
Die in the glaring east?
Shall we each find comfort where we be
With never a thought for over the sea?

Shade that lieth equally,
On Western sea and Eastern sea,
Who can tell what the end can be?

            —Kipling

They of the west are appalled at his day,
and horror seizes them of the east.

          —Job 18:20

India

As previous chapters have made clear, some of the most spectacu-
lar instances of the martyrdom of Christians in the twenty-first

century have been the result of militant Islam seeking to expel or eliminate non-Muslims by force. But in a less-noticed way—at least for most people in Western nations—India has witnessed some large-scale persecutions and martyrdoms for a somewhat different but also somewhat similar cause. There have been several cases of Indian Muslims attacking Christians in India, to be sure. But Christians have more often been victims of Hindu nationalists, religious believers who, like other believers in modern and post-modern nations, have felt threatened by the militant secularism and attendant rootlessness spreading around the world, often with the financial and ideological support of the formerly Christian nations. The resulting resentments often add to long-standing local differences—and erupt, often enough, in violence.

A noteworthy instance occurred in 2008 in Kandhamal, a rural district remote from the larger Indian population centers, in which thirty-six Catholics were killed. In 2023, the Dicastery for the Causes of Saints decreed that a process of beatification could begin for "the Servant of God Kantheswar Digal [Bernard] and companions, martyrs of Kandhamal." The Dicastery documented that thirty-five of the thirty-six were killed *in odium fidei*; the Vatican had used the intervening fifteen years to make an official determination of the basic facts of the case. And the most basic fact of all was that anti-Christian violence—drawing on anti-Christian sentiments already existing in some Hindu communities—erupted after the unexplained murder in a Kandhamal monastery of a Hindu nationalist monk, Swami Laxmanananda Saraswati.

The sequel was as horrible as it was predictable. Hindu nationalist groups claimed, implausibly, that the murder was perpetrated inside a Hindu monastery by a Christian conspiracy, though there was no evidence of any such thing. In fact, a local Maoist group claimed to have carried out the assassination. The swami's body was paraded around the region for days by the Hindu nationalists, who, despite the Maoist admission, chose instead to ban Christianity in the region and stir up popular emotions against the Christians. The Hindu groups demanded that Catholics enter Hindu temples and apostatize. Many heroically resisted. As one news report summarized what followed: "Valiant Christians who defied the order were burned alive, buried alive, and chopped into pieces. Nearly 100 Christians were killed, and over 300 churches and 6,000 houses were plundered in unabated violence that rendered 56,000 people homeless."[129]

Among the thirty-five approved to enter the process of beatification, all but one were laypeople. The one priest, Fr. Bernard Digal, died owing to a series of seemingly random but significant circumstances.[130] At the time of his death, he was serving as the procurator of the Archdiocese of Cuttack Bhubaneswar. He was in the Kandhamal area, his place of birth, because he wanted to check on the building of a new church in his native parish. When the Hindu swami was murdered, Fr. Digal was staying nearby with a priest in his seventies, Fr. Alexander Charalankunnel, and chose not to leave him because he suspected trouble was brewing.

At one point, the procession with the swami's body approached the church, and both priests, along with three nuns and the parish

---

[129] Anto Akkara, "Vatican Puts 35 Catholic 'Martyrs of Kandhamal' in India on Road to Sainthood," Catholic News Agency, October 26, 2023, https://www.catholicnewsagency.com/news/255826/vatican-puts-35-catholic-martyrs-of-kandhamal-in-india-on-road-to-sainthood.

[130] Anto Akkara, "Meet the Only Priest Among Indian's 35 'Martyrs of Kandhamal,'" National Catholic Register, November 16, 2023, https://www.ncregister.com/news/meet-the-only-priest-among-indian-s-35-martyrs-of-kandhamal.

staff were forced to flee into the jungle. It was a prudent move. The mob burned down the church and a convent, along with Fr. Digal's van. Fr. Digal went out looking for a way to convey Fr. Charalankunnel, who had trouble walking, to safety. But Fr. Digal was captured, beaten to a pulp, and left for dead. He survived as best he could in the jungle and was even forced to drink his own urine to stay alive. Eventually, he was found and transferred to a nearby hospital, then flown to a larger hospital in Mumbai. Though both his legs were broken and he had suffered brain damage, he held on to life for several weeks. But when he had been transferred to a monastery to recuperate, he succumbed to a brain clot. His was a common story. Of the thirty-five killed, fourteen died immediately; the rest—like the priest—died later from injuries suffered during the mob violence.

With more than 1.4 billion people, India is the most populous nation on earth and among the largest in land mass. Its Christian population (about 30 million), only a little more than 2 percent of the total population, is dwarfed among the 80 percent who are Hindu, and more than 200 million Muslims. But the Christians who are native to the subcontinent belong to one of the most ancient Christian communities in the world. According to legends—or perhaps a true history—the apostle Thomas arrived in what is modern-day Kerala in A.D. 52 and was killed and buried in Chennai in the southern India state of Tamil Nadu. Records are sparse until more than five hundred years later. Portuguese traders and missionaries who arrived in the sixteenth century found the tomb of the apostle, mostly forgotten, and built a church there. St. Francis Xavier is known to have spent time there on his way to Formosa. And the Santhome Basilica, a late-nineteenth-century structure, presently marks the site, which was designated a national shrine in 2004.

In modern India, however, that long history notwithstanding, Christians have been threatened and harassed by what Western sources sometimes call "Hindu supremacists" and a "growing anti-Christian hysteria." As the *New York Times* summed up the situation in a lengthy 2021 article:

> Anti-Christian vigilantes are sweeping through villages, storming churches, burning Christian literature, attacking schools and assaulting worshippers. In many cases, the police and members of India's governing party are helping them, government documents and dozens of interviews revealed. In church after church, the very act of worship has become dangerous despite constitutional protections for freedom of religion.[131]

This is quite a sweeping indictment of a country that considers itself "the world's largest democracy."

India became an independent state and a secular democracy in 1947, partly at the insistence of Mahatma Gandhi, widely considered the father of his country, and the firm stance of the first prime minister, Jawaharlal Nehru. So these offenses against Christians run directly contrary to India's basic laws.

The growth of anti-Christian violence in recent decades is not easy to explain; many Indian Christians themselves wonder what they've done to deserve such rough treatment. But at least part of the problem has arisen because of government policies aimed at inspiring the people to create a nation that is purely Hindu. Narendra Modi, leader of the Bharatiya Janata Party (BJP) and president of India for more than a decade (beginning in 2014), has been widely regarded as pushing a radical interpretation of Hindutva (i.e.,

---

[131] Jeffrey Gettleman and Suhasini Raj, "Arrests, Beatings and Secret Prayers: Inside the Persecution of India's Christians," *New York Times*, December 23, 2021, https://www.nytimes.com/2021/12/22/world/asia/india-christians-attacked.html.

"Hindu nationalism"). It is not, to be sure, the pluralist human-ism that once was the party's official political philosophy, but, by legislation and manipulation of institutions, it now seeks to limit Islam in India and also Christianity. The U.S. Commission on International Religious Freedom recommended in its 2024 report that the American government "designate India as a 'country of particular concern,' or CPC, for engaging in systematic, ongoing, and egregious violations of religious freedom, as defined by the International Religious Freedom Act (IRFA)."

Specifically, the report noted:

> In 2023, NGOs reported 687 incidents of violence against Christians, who continued to be detained under various state-level anti-conversion laws. In January, Hindu mobs attacked Christians in Chhattisgarh in eastern India, destroying and vandalizing churches and attempting to "re-convert" individuals to Hinduism. An estimated 30 people were beaten for refusing to renounce their faith. The same month, two Christians were detained without bail, accused of forcibly converting individuals of Scheduled Tribes and Scheduled Castes.[132]

Converting Hindus to other religions seems to have become some-thing considered a serious offense under current policies, an attitude that the government has transmitted and reinforced via lawyers, officials, and community leaders among the general population. Ironically, leaders of the political opposition have responded that

---

[132] "India," in United States Commission on International Religious Freedom, *Annual Report 2024: Recommended for Countries of Particular Concern* (CPC), 30, https://www.uscirf.gov/sites/default/files/2024-05/India.pdf.

this militant—and violent—Hinduism is "not Hindu."[133] Mahatma Gandhi, the prominent promoter of nonviolent public actions, would certainly have agreed. Historical Christian states in India usually do not have these anti-conversion laws or the generalized anti-Christian attitudes. It's in the places where Christians are minorities, and often at a distance from the cities, that the greatest militancy arises. The scale of the violence has increased as the twenty-first century has progressed, but anti-Christian violence in India is not entirely new in the third Christian millennium.

At the very threshold of the twenty-first century, an Indian priest, Arul Das, was murdered, on September 1, 1999, by a militant Hindu group in the Mayurbhanj district of Odisha. His church was set on fire, and, as he was trying to escape the flames, he was cut down by an arrow. Almost two dozen people were indicted by Indian officials as being implicated in the arson and the killing. Seventeen were dismissed for lack of evidence—though their involvement seems reasonably certain. And four were convicted, the guilt for the actual murder being attributed to Dara Singh, the leader of the vigilante mob and a member of the Hindu nationalist movement Bajrang Dal, which takes its orientation from the militant interpretation of Hindutva.[134] More specifically, he was active—and became something of a local celebrity—in the "cow

---

[133] "Religious Persecution Takes Center Stage in Indian Parliament," International Christian Concern, July 2, 2024, https:// www.persecution.org/2024/07/02/religious-persecution-takes -center-stage-in-indian-parliament/.

[134] "Dara Singh Gets Life Term for Killing Priest in 1999," *Mumbai Mirror*, updated September 23, 2007, https://mumbaimirror.india times.com/news/india/dara-singh-gets-life-term-for-killing -priest-in-1999/articleshow/15743541.cms?utm_source= contentofinterest&utm_medium=text&utm_campaign=cppst.

protection" movement, cows being sacred to Hindus. He was earlier indicted for beating a Muslim cattle trader to death but was released on "insufficient evidence." He received a life sentence for the murder of Fr. Das, but many others who perpetrated religious violence against non-Hindus escaped without paying any price.

Among the many other cases that might be mentioned, a spate of violence in 2004 shows the continuing problem. Within a matter of a week, three incidents occurred. On August 22, two priests were stabbed by a mob of masked men who invaded their rectory in the eastern state of Jharkhand. Fortunately, neighbors who heard noise from the attack came to the rescue. Frs. John Sundar and Albanus Tirkey had to be hospitalized, but they survived. On August 26, the church of Our Lady of Charity in the state of Odisha was desecrated. Two days later, in the state of Kerala, Fr. Job Chittilappilly was stabbed to death while he was sitting outside his rectory by someone who clearly knew his daily routine. The perpetrator, twenty-five-year-old Panthalkoottam Raghukumar, was apprehended a few weeks later and told police that he had killed the priest because he was performing "anti-Hindu" acts of charity for Hindu families. A local bishop remarked that one Hindu family had, as a result of the priest's kindness, removed Hindu idols from their home. The president of the Catholic Bishops' Conference of India, Cardinal Telesphore Toppo, noted, accurately at the time, "It is very unfortunate that such things are happening all over the country."[135]

All these events transpired while Indian officials were trying to cultivate relations with Western Christians, especially those in

---

[135] Anto Akkara, "Catholic Priest Murdered in India as Violence Continues," *National Catholic Register*, September 19, 2004, https://www.ncregister.com/news/catholic-priest-murdered-in-india-as-violence-continues.

the United States. The Indians seem to have believed that, just as Christians are feeling pressured from "woke," often anti-Christian, elements in Western culture, also operating on a global scale, Hindus could portray themselves as being embattled as well. As Ram Madhav, one of the leading voices of the BJP, told a conservative audience in Washington, D.C., in mid-2024, "We share most of the ideas that you ... consider dear—God, religion, tradition, family, patriotism, nationalism." He also claimed that religious liberty was sacrosanct in India, even as that nation seeks to maintain its own Hindu identity.[136]

As a sales pitch to Western Christian ears, Madhav's speech was well crafted—in theory. But as is easy to document, in practice, maintaining Hindu identity by keeping globalist values at bay—to say nothing of courting Christians to help with tensions with Muslim nations—often means repressing Christianity in India as a part of, and maybe even the source of, the "globalist" threat. Some reports indicate that Christians are even denied rights that are accorded to Dalits, the Hindu cast often characterized as the "untouchables" in the West. That ideological stance only further exacerbates the usual interreligious resentments at a popular level to produce a potent and poisonous brew.[137]

Pakistan

The situation in parts of India remains quite bad, but the status of Christians in nearby Pakistan is, if anything, even worse.

---

[136] Bethel McGrew, "Is Hindu Nationalism Friendly to Christianity?," *First Things*, August 1, 2024, https://www.firstthings.com/web-exclusives/2024/08/is-hindu-nationalism-friendly-to-christianity.

[137] McGrew, "Is Hindu Nationalism Friendly?"

In fact, one of the clearest indications of the problems in the region is that, in 2011, Shahbaz Bhatti, a Catholic then serving as Pakistan's federal minister of minorities affairs—an office charged with the protection of religious and ethnic minorities, including both Christians and other small religious groups—was himself murdered. He had been a brave figure for his entire life. As a teenager, he was one of the leaders of protests against a law requiring Christians to carry special identity cards. In 1985, when he was an undergraduate at the University of Punjab and eighteen years old, he founded the Christian Liberation Front. In the early 2000s, he went on to head the All Pakistan Minorities Alliance.

Given that personal history, he was the logical choice to serve as the minister for minorities when that office became a cabinet-level position. Death threats, however, started to arrive almost immediately after his appointment. And his enemies delivered on them when, while he was on his way to work, his car was sprayed with machine-gun fire. Though police were uncertain as to which of several radical Islamic groups had carried out the murder, a leader of the Pakistani Taliban told a BBC journalist that Bhatti was killed because he was a "known blasphemer."

Laws against "blasphemy" are a common cause of persecution and even martyrdom in multiple Islamic nations. Typically, they are written in such vague terms that, even when the legal guidelines of such countries are properly followed (which is far from always being the case), it's possible to prosecute someone for virtually anything a government decides to define as "blasphemy." In addition, radical Islamic groups, unconcerned in any case about satisfying the niceties of local laws, often make independent judgments of their own, without waiting for official action. Estimates are that sixty-five Christians have been killed in Pakistan since 1990 for alleged blasphemy.[138] These were murders by private individuals and groups, not legal executions. The government has not yet executed anyone for blasphemy, but neither has it been very vigorous in controlling anti-Christian violence. And that figure of sixty-five does not take into account the hundreds more who have been arrested, harassed, beaten, tortured, and driven into exile because of their Christian faith.

In one of the most notorious modern cases of a prejudicial application of "blasphemy law," Asia Bibi — a Pakistani Catholic women — was sentenced to death by hanging and held on death row from 2010, the year before Bhatti's murder, until 2018. Shahbaz Bhatti's advocacy for her appears to have been one of the main reasons he was killed just a few months after her death sentence. Partly in response to international pressures — including written petitions and pleas from Popes Benedict XVI and Francis — Pakistan's Supreme Court reversed the case for "insufficient evidence."

As well it might because, as in so many similar cases, the evidence for the charges was slender, to say the least. Bibi, a poor agricultural worker, had long been harassed by her fellow workers, who pressured her to convert to Islam. She resisted. Matters came to a head when a neighbor with whom she was having a property dispute confronted her for having drunk water from a cup used by Muslims — something forbidden, since some Muslims in the area regarded Christians as unclean. Angry words were exchanged. And, at a certain point, Bibi was reported to have replied, "I believe in my religion and in Jesus Christ, who died on the cross for the sins of mankind. What did your Prophet Mohammed ever do to

---

[138] "Asia Bibi: Imran Khan Attacks Hardliners over Court Case," BBC, October 31, 2018, https://www.bbc.com/news/world-asia -46048433.

save mankind? And why should it be me that converts instead of you?"[139] She later apologized for this angry—though relatively harmless—outburst.

But as often happens with "blasphemy" charges, local Muslims began to claim that she said far more insulting things, which does not seem plausible, given the lack of evidence of anything remotely resembling what she was charged with. Local mosques used loudspeakers to encourage mobs to form. She was beaten near her home, taken into police custody, and remained in prison for over a year before the case was even heard, all of which only allowed things to become inflamed further. She became a central bone of contention for Muslim militants in Pakistan. And slanted reports in the nation's press only further stirred up popular hatred.

At one point during her detention, she said, "After the newspaper reports ... 10 million Pakistanis are ready to kill me by their own hands."[140] And she described the moment of her death sentence:

> I cried alone, putting my head in my hands. I can no longer bear the sight of people full of hatred, applauding the killing of a poor farm worker. I no longer see them, but I still hear them, the crowd who gave the judge a standing ovation, saying: "Kill her, kill her! Allahu Akbar!" The courthouse is invaded by a euphoric horde who break down the doors, chanting: "Vengeance for the holy prophet. Allah

[139] Rakesh Krishnan Simha, "Blasphemy of Aasia Bibi: How Pakistan's Christians Went from Cheerleaders of Partition to Its Victims," IndiaFacts, May 13, 2019, https://www.indiafacts.org.in/blasphemy-of-aasia-bibi-how-pakistans-christians-went-from-cheerleaders-of-partition-to-its-victims/.

[140] Hal St John, "Ten Million People Now Want to Kill Me," *Catholic Herald*, June 14, 2012, https://catholicherald.co.uk/ten-million-people-now-want-to-kill-me/.

is great!" I was then thrown like an old rubbish sack into the van.... I had lost all humanity in their eyes.[141]

Campaigns in her defense kept the sentence from being carried out. And when she was finally exonerated, she was whisked away to Canada.

This was the case for which, in part, Shahbaz Bhatti was given a death sentence—by fundamentalist Islamic forces. He was, of course, quite aware of the threats he faced—he had faced them since he was a teenager. His parents were both Christians—his father was a British army officer and later a teacher—and they had instilled in him a fearless adherence to the truth. In fact, their son had recorded a moving video a few months before his assassination in case his enemies were successful in eliminating him. In it, he spoke with an almost unbelievable courage and faith: "I believe in Jesus Christ, who has given his own life for us. I know what the Cross means, and what it means to follow the Cross. And I'm ready to die for the cause of my suffering community, and I will die to defend their rights.... I prefer to die for justice and for the rights of my community than compromise with these threats."[142] It's no wonder that a score of nations protested his death, and voices within the Church immediately proclaimed him a martyr.

The "community" he was defending was, in the first instance, Catholics and other Christians in Pakistan. But already, as founder of the All Pakistan Minorities Alliance, Bhatti had seen it as his duty as a Christian to defend the basic rights of other minorities in Pakistan, such as Hindus, Sikhs, and even Muslims who protested

---

[141] St John, "Ten Million People."

[142] Austen Ivereigh, "Shahbaz Bhatti, Martyr," *America*, March 4, 2011, https://www.americamagazine.org/content/all-things/shahbaz -bhatti-martyr.

against the blasphemy laws or found themselves at odds with militants for other reasons. After Shahbaz's murder, his brother Paul Bhatti—a surgeon—returned to Pakistan from Rome, where he had been practicing medicine, and took up his work on behalf of religious tolerance as the Pakistan government's minister of national harmony.

Harmonizing multiple interests in such a country is by no means easy. The very name Pakistan is a modern invention. It was coined in 1933 by a Muslim activist to incorporate the first letters of several regions where large Muslim percentages of the population, it could be argued, might be brought together as constituting a single people—though this was at least as much myth as reality. In addition, *pak* in Pashto means "pure." And so, at its very conception, the nation was—among other matters—making a claim to be the land of the "pure."

Whatever that might mean in other cultural contexts, for the modern nation of Pakistan it has often meant rough treatment of those thought to be *impure*, both non-Muslims and "bad" Muslims. These tendencies were only heightened when Britain gave up colonial rule in 1947 and allowed India to be partitioned. Hundreds of thousands, perhaps even a few million, died in the chaos that followed. Millions of Muslims moved from the newly independent India into what had now become independent Pakistan, and millions of Hindus took the reverse route. Some scholars believe it was the largest migration of peoples in human history. When it was all over, Pakistan was a more purely Muslim land than it had previously been—and it intended to keep things that way.

The preamble to the Pakistan constitution specifies that "sovereignty over the entire Universe belongs to Allah Almighty alone and the authority which He has delegated to the state of Pakistan, through its people for being exercised within the limits prescribed by Him is a sacred trust."[143] A superficial reading might suggest that this is merely a general statement of principle — and some both in and outside Pakistan do read it that way. But it also prohibits non-Muslims from occupying government offices, such as president and prime minister, though there have been efforts to change those restrictions. As the Bhatti case and that of Salman Taseer — a Muslim governor of Punjab who was slain months before Bhatti because he opposed blasphemy laws and defended Asia Bibi — indicate, however, there are both Muslims and non-Muslims in Pakistan who see room for religious tolerance even within a Muslim confessional state. There are twenty-three officially Muslim states in the world,[144] exactly half of the forty-six where Muslims predominate, several of which are relatively tolerant of Christians.

The most worrisome and terrorizing elements in Pakistan's political system are the blasphemy laws, which many international human rights organizations have argued should be repealed, both for what they are in themselves and for the abuses that they foster in extremists. Observers of Pakistan have noted a strange pattern in these cases. Because of the severity of punishments against "blasphemy," Muslims in dispute with Christians, even over minor secular matters, often use the threat to accuse them of blasphemy as a trump card. That is already bad enough. But frequently, when such a charge is made, extreme elements among the mosques stir up local passions — one way to keep ordinary Muslim believers

---

[143] Constitution of the Islamic Republic of Pakistan, National Assembly of Pakistan, as modified up to February 28, 2012, https://na.gov.pk/uploads/documents/1333523681_951.pdf.

[144] Afghanistan, Algeria, Bahrain, Bangladesh, Brunei, Egypt, Iran, Iraq, Jordan, Kuwait, Libya, Malaysia, Maldives, Mauritania, Morocco, Oman, Pakistan, Qatar, Saudi Arabia, Somalia, Tunisia, United Arab Emirates, and Yemen.

convinced that the leaders are dedicated defenders of Islam. A good number of Muslim Pakistanis, however, believe such "defenses" are not really Islamic behavior.

The police play along with what they typically know are fraudulent charges as a way to calm the mobs. They then arrest the persons accused. The first trial will find people guilty—often just as a way of maintaining social peace. And then, after a shorter or longer period (though sometimes several years), when the initial outrage has dissipated and is perhaps even forgotten, an appellate court, the Supreme Court—especially if Pakistan comes under international pressure—will dismiss the initial guilty verdict for a "lack of evidence." This process has occurred so often that it's clear that this charade is one way that authorities employ to diffuse explosive situations—without, however, seeking to resolve the underlying legal and social problem.

In 2014, Pakistan's Supreme Court itself issued a public statement that "the majority of blasphemy cases are based on false accusations stemming from property issues or other personal or family vendettas rather than genuine instances of blasphemy and they inevitably lead to mob violence against the entire community."[145] The contrast between the legal protection and popular persecution of Christians, however, is large and not narrowing. Besides the injustice dealt out to those falsely accused of blasphemy, the failure of police and the courts to hold the perpetrators of violence against Christians to account has only encouraged further false charges and attacks from Islamic extremists. Pakistan's anti-Christian offenses might best be characterized as often the result

---

[145] "Pakistan: Mob Attacks Christian Settlement," Human Rights Watch, August 22, 2023, https://www.hrw.org/news/2023/08/22/pakistan-mob-attacks-christian-settlement.

of local religious leaders and their emotion-prone followers taking advantage of the effective impunity they enjoy under official government agencies—a situation that presents enormous challenges to efforts to protect the rights and the very lives of Christians and other religious minorities in Pakistan.

Despite multiple condemnations of such incidents, going back decades, in the twenty-first century, they continue and, in some ways, have grown even worse. The penal code has outlawed offenses against any religion. But, in fact, sections 295A–C, which deal with different types of blasphemy are the ones most often actively adjudicated: section 295A prescribes up to ten years and a fine for insulting religion (i.e., Islam, as is clear from the next two sections); section B states, "Whoever willfully defiles, damages or desecrates a copy of the Holy Quran or of an extract therefrom or uses it in any derogatory manner or for any unlawful purpose shall be punishable with imprisonment for life"; and section C goes even further:

> Whoever by words, either spoken or written, or by visible representation, or by any imputation, innuendo, or insinuation, directly or indirectly, defiles the sacred name of the Holy Prophet Muhammad (peace be upon him) shall be punished with death, or imprisonment for life, and shall also be liable to fine.[146]

It's no surprise that this has led to dozens of cases being brought.

One of the most notorious was the charge that Ayub Masih, a poor bricklayer, had offended against section 295C by

---

[146] "Pakistan's Anti-Blasphemy Laws," World Watch Monitor, accessed December 13, 2024, https://www.worldwatchmonitor.org/pakistans-anti-blasphemy-laws/.

recommending Salman Rushdie's controversial novel *The Satanic Verses* to a Muslim neighbor. The book was banned in Pakistan for casting Muhammad in a bad light, and thousands of Pakistanis protested its appearance. As mentioned earlier in the present book, Iran's ayatollah Khomeini issued a *fatwa* against the author, and in 2022 Rushdie eventually was attacked in New York, stabbed multiple times, and blinded in one eye. But that Ayub Masih, a simple and barely literate man, would have known anything about the book or its author is highly unlikely—let alone that he would have recommended the book or any book to a Muslim neighbor. The Muslim who brought the charge was at the time trying to take over land from Masih and was using this notorious book against him, and it led to his arrest and to the flight of fourteen Christian families from the neighborhood. Masih was attacked in prison, shot inside the very court where his case was being heard, and sentenced to death. The usual Supreme Court review overturned the case in 2002, after six years of unjust detention and abuse.

But in a sense, Masih was lucky. In the end, he survived and was set free. Over the next two decades, dozens of similar cases, some resulting in death, arose. One of the worst came in 2009, around the same time as Asia Bibi's arrest. Eight Christians died when riots erupted in Gojra, a city in the Punjab state, over rumors that pages of a Quran had been desecrated at a Christian wedding. Shahbaz Bhatti pronounced the charges false and ordered the police to protect the Christians, but he was ignored. Instead, the usual prejudice and blind violence ensued, as did similar events year after year, increasing in frequency and even scope.

In August 2023, for example, a mob of twelve hundred, mostly young Muslim men, rampaged through a Christian community in Jaranwala. According to a report by Pakistan's own National

Commission for Human Rights, loudspeakers at local mosques spurred on the riot, and twenty-two churches and eighty homes were burned.[147] Sadly, this had been a region where Christians and Muslims had mostly lived peacefully with one another until several small incidents touched off the larger frictions that exist everywhere in Pakistan.

The report specified: "According to the local residents, the issue of blasphemy that had sparked the violence was rooted in a financial dispute between two Christian youths and a Muslim businessman/travel agent." To its credit, this time the government sent in thirty-five hundred police to keep order and arrested more than a hundred people suspected of participating in the rampage. The charges of blasphemy were implausible on their face. The initial claim was that pages of the Quran had been found in the street with derogatory comments about Islam. But there was more—more that put the whole charge, like many earlier ones, in serious doubt. As one outlet commented:

> The police claims that the desecrated pages of the Quran carry the names, addresses, and even identity card numbers of two Christian brothers, who have been arrested and charged with blasphemy. Why blasphemers should sign their blasphemy, supply even the numbers of their identity cards. and literally ask to be arrested and charged with a capital offense was not explained.[148]

[147] National Commission for Human Rights, Pakistan, *Jaranwala: Incident Report* (2023), https://www.nchr.gov.pk/wp-content/uploads/2023/10/Jaranwala-Report.pdf.

[148] Massimo Introvigne, "Pakistan: Mob Burned Churches, Police Arrests —Christians," *Bitter Winter*, August 25, 2023, https://bitterwinter.org/pakistan-mob-burned-churches-police-arrests-christians/.

Whether this was a fabrication of the Muslim businessman, the local religious leadership, or the police themselves to justify the arrests remains undetermined, but that it was a ridiculously clumsy fabrication is clear.

And as has all too often been the case in Pakistan, after almost a year had passed, virtually no one had been held to account for the violence. As Bishop Indrias Rehmat of Faisalabad commented: "More than 300 people were arrested [following the atrocity] but it is unlikely that they will face justice. Slowly, they have started releasing them. Nobody has been charged." Further, while the government pledged assistance in restoring the churches that had been destroyed, they were still unsafe to enter and unusable a year later. In fact, the bishop asked the government to stop work: "They wanted to show the media that everything was OK but they had just whitewashed the walls."[149]

Whitewashing the walls is a fitting epithet. Less than a year later, in May 2024, similar mob violence erupted in Punjab over an alleged desecration of the Quran. Nazir Gil Masih, the alleged Christian desecrator, was lynched by a mob. Popular passions had been raised to such an absurd level over the rumors that the following month—June 2024—a *Muslim* tourist, Mohammad Ismail, from Punjab was lynched when someone claimed to see pages of the Quran burning and accused the unfamiliar figure. A crowd began to beat him. As a report described the horrifying sequel: "Police managed to take him to the Madyan police station but had to succumb to hundreds of people that set fire to a police vehicle and started burning the police station itself as well. Mohammed

---

[149] John Pontifex, "PAKISTAN: Still No Justice for Jaranwala Victims—Bishop," Aid to the Church in Need, April 9, 2024, https://acnuk.org/news/pakistan-still-no-justice-for-jaranwala -victims-bishop/.

Ismail was taken out of the police station by the mob, lynched, and burned."[150]

Such outrages are unlikely to stop anytime soon—unless anti-blasphemy laws are repealed, and Pakistani officials undertake to bring about a vast shift in public attitudes.[151] International leadership is crucial in this battle. When your own Supreme Court recognizes that many of the blasphemy cases brought before it are bogus, there can be no respect for a nation's legal system or its government without serious effort to change. In its most recent report, the U.S. Commission on International Religious Freedom, recommended sanctions against Pakistani officials in order to put pressure on them to change laws. And it spelled out two changes that could immediately help with the remedies described in the preceding pages:

❖ Repeal blasphemy and anti-Ahmadiyya laws; until such repeal, enact reforms to make blasphemy a bailable offense, require evidence by accusers, ensure proper investigation by senior police officials, allow authorities to dismiss unfounded accusations, and enforce existing penal code articles criminalizing perjury and false accusations; and

❖ Hold accountable individuals who incite or participate in vigilante violence, targeted killings, forced conversions, and other religiously based crimes.

---

[150] Massimo Introvigne, "Pakistan, Tourist Lynched and Burned Alive for Alleged Blasphemy," *Bitter Winter*, June 24, 2024, https://bitterwinter.org/pakistan-tourist-lynched-and-burned-alive-for-alleged-blasphemy/.

[151] Babar Dogar, "A Mob in Pakistan Burns Down a House and Beats a Christian over Alleged Desecration of Quran," Associated Press, May 25, 2024, https://apnews.com/article/pakistan-blasphemy-mob-christians-60362eafebbd9ef76ea1f5b97b3e66b3.

Reasonable, modest enough reforms, to be sure, but they could go a long way at least as a beginning toward preventing some of the worst abuses of Christians and other minorities, not only in Pakistan but in Muslim nations with similar laws.

In the inscrutable ways of Divine Providence, however, the mayhem in Pakistan may lead to the proclamation of the nation's first Catholic saint. On March 15, 2015—the middle of Lent that year—suicide bombers attempted to enter two Christian Churches during a Sunday Mass in Lahore. One church was penetrated, resulting in multiple deaths. The other—St. John's Catholic Church—was mostly spared because of the heroic intervention of Akash Bashir, who sacrificed himself to stop the attackers. Manifesting what I described earlier as Pope Francis's notion of *oblatio vitae*—the spontaneous offering of one's life—the twenty-one-year-old Bashir promptly stepped forward and forfeited his young life when he saw the bombers coming. He died at the entrance of the church along with about fifteen others, and another seventy or so were wounded. But without his swift action, the body count could have easily run into the hundreds.

In 2022, Pope Francis announced that Akash Bashir could be referred to as "Servant of God," the first step on the way to canonization as a martyr and a saint. Lahore's archbishop said of the news, "Akash Bashir, a young man, sacrificed his life for his brothers and sisters who prayed in church. He discovered that there is something much greater than this earthly life. And he understood it without studying theology or philosophy. He lived a simple life, following Jesus every day, every moment, even when his hour was not expected."[152] In a place such as Pakistan, to be sure, violence against Christians is quite common. But to step up boldly on the

---

[152] Kamran Chaudhry, "Honoring Akash Bashir, the First Servant of God in Pakistan," Aid to the Church in Need, March 24, 2022,

spur of the moment, as Bashir did, is a kind of revelation of a deep life of faith that persists, almost miraculously, in circumstances that, by all human reckoning, should have been snuffed out long ago.

East Asia

As recorded at the very beginning of the present volume, one of the deadliest attacks on Catholics in the twenty-first century occurred in Sri Lanka, an island just south of India. Several churches were struck by suicide bombers simultaneously on Easter Sunday 2019; 171 perished, and many more were wounded. This was doubly tragic: in addition to the lives lost or maimed, it showed a level of Islamist violence that, in an earlier time, was thought to be mostly confined to the Middle East among Arab and Persian populations, or to places such as Pakistan, with its special history of partition from India and movement toward becoming a purely Islamic state. Islamist ideology spread to Africa during the rise of ISIS for several reasons, as we discussed in the previous chapter. But just a few decades ago, many people believed that Islam in East Asia was, broadly speaking, a gentler, more tolerant form of that faith.

Dennis Ignatius, a former Malaysian diplomat, described the situation just a few years before the Sri Lanka attack:

Traditionally, Islam in countries like Indonesia, Brunei, Malaysia, was always moderate, open, very tolerant of other cultures and other faiths. I remember as a kid in Malaysia hanging out with friends who were Muslim, Hindu, Buddhist, Christian, and there was never any problem. Today,

https://www.churchinneed.org/honoring-akash-bashir-the-first -servant-of-god-in-pakistan/.

however, after years of Wahhabi infiltration, after hundreds of Wahhabi-trained teachers, preachers, religious scholars spreading their extremist ideology, we find ourselves in a very different region now.[153]

Many experts in Islamic thought have pointed to Wahhabism—a strict movement for the "purification" of Islam by a reform of sharia law and reconfiguration of Islamic societies in line with what they believe to have been the practices of Muhammad and his first three successors—as the main culprit behind radicalization and violence worldwide. And the critics blame Saudi Arabia for the oil-fueled financial and moral support that has helped it to spread not only to the Middle East, Africa, and the Far East but to the whole world. The same Malaysian diplomat added:

> The Saudi Wahhabis have also invested massively in building mosques, Islamic centers, establishing Muslim university student associations, prison outreaches, etc., in the United States. Saudi Arabia has funded or partially funded Islamic centers in several major cities, and of course these are all promoting Wahhabi extremism. And then add to that the thousands upon thousands of students from all over the world who attend a network of Saudi-supported and Saudi-funded religious universities and schools where they are influenced to adopt the Wahhabi worldview and then sent back to their own countries to propagate it—it's spreading hate and extremism on a global scale.[154]

[153] John Burger, "Want to Stop Islamic Terrorism? Talk to Saudi Arabia, Malaysian Diplomat Urges," Aleteia, April 15, 2015, https://aleteia.org/2015/04/15/want-to-stop-islamic-terrorism-talk-to-saudi-arabia-malaysian-diplomat-urges.
[154] Burger, "Want to Stop Islamic Terrorism?"

In Malaysia, for instance, as in much of Southeast Asia, Catholics and other Christians are theoretically free but are practically subjected to narrow social restrictions—and increasingly to violent outbursts by radical Muslim groups. Early in the new millennium, for instance, two Catholic churches—Christ the King in Sungai Petani, in the northern state of Kedah and St. Philip's Catholic Church in Segamat—were firebombed. In the latter case, a Molotov cocktail was thrown at the tabernacle but fortunately did not explode. Investigators speculated that these attacks were distant protests against the U.S. incursions into Afghanistan in 2001, prompted by the attack on the World Trade Center in New York. But whatever the motive, similar church attacks—which identify Christianity with the actions of secular Western governments—would continue to take place in Malaysia in the years that followed.

One of the reasons for such attacks unique to Malaysia arose in 2009, when the Malaysian government ruled that a Catholic publication could use the name Allah in translations of the Bible and other Church materials to refer to God. The Catholic Church and various Christian groups had argued that *Allah* was the only word in Malaysian languages that adequately conveyed what both Muslims and Christians mean when they refer to the Deity. A string of attacks against Christian churches, a school, and other institutions followed.

In 2013, when the papal nuncio Archbishop Joseph Marino tried to defend the use of the word *Allah* in Church documents, he was met with various threats. Radical Islamic groups even went so far as to say: "If he does not retract his statement in seven days, we will have ... to ask the prime minister ... to close the Vatican office and ask that the ambassador be sent back to the Vatican."[155] They

---

[155] "Malaysia 'Galloping' Towards Islamization, Says Christian Bishop," International Christian Concern, July 15, 2013, https://www

regarded the mere use of the term as an attempt at "Christianization." By contrast, another Catholic bishop described similar measures by the government as evidence of "galloping Islamization."

Malaysia is almost two-thirds Muslim, maybe 9 percent Christian, and only half of the latter are Catholic. But pressures from increasingly radical groups have made Malaysia a bit of a center for Islamic State recruiting. According to the International Centre for Political Violence and Terrorism Research, one reason for this is that Malaysia is conveniently located for contacts with Mindanao in the Philippines, Rakhine in Myanmar, and the southern provinces of Thailand—three areas where Islamic extremism is particularly active. According to the center, there are now thousands of Islamic State members or sympathizers in Malaysia—so many, in fact, that the report characterizes them as a "virtual caliphate." Most Malay Christians are unaware of this growth and underestimate the threat, not only to themselves but to the whole region.[156]

Indonesia

Indonesia may once have been, as the Malaysian diplomat described it, among the more easygoing, tolerant countries where Muslim and Christian children played with one another. But in the twenty-first century, it has also been the scene of repeated attacks on Christian churches and individuals. On Christmas Eve 2000, the first in what would become a series of church bombings occurred at multiple sites

---

.persecution.org/2013/07/15/malaysia-galloping-towards -islamization-says-christian-bishop/.

[156] Zam Yusa, "Report: IS Sympathisers Pose Threat to Malaysia, Region," *Free Malaysia Today*, January 24, 2018, https://www.free malaysiatoday.com/category/nation/2018/01/24/terrorist -sympathisers-pose-threat-to-malaysia-warns-research-centre/.

in the capital and in eight other cities. The Jakarta Cathedral of Our Lady of the Assumption was among the targets. Fortunately, because of heightened security around Christmas, only eighteen people died, though many more were injured. Nurjaman Riduan Isamuddin and Mohamad Iqbal Abdurrahman were later identified by Indonesian and American authorities as among the leaders of Jemaah Islamiyah (JI) "an al-Qaida linked terrorist group with cells operating in several countries in Southeast Asia,"[157] responsible for the attacks.

There had been unrest in Indonesia in the late 1990s and early 2000s over a series of violent clashes—the Poso riots—between Muslims and Christians in a central part of the country that had resulted in thousands of deaths on both sides. Indonesia is more than 85 percent Muslim and about 10 percent Christian (only 3 percent Catholic). With a population of around 285 million, it's the largest Muslim country in the world. And only India, China, and the United States have larger overall populations. But religious clashes arose around the turn of the century because there is a large concentration of vulnerable Christians in Poso.

The causes of the clashes there were mixed and murky, and many polarizing events were simply made up, on both sides. One story that a Christian man had raped a Muslim girl set off widespread violence, for example, but violence was going on anyway for the more usual sectarian reasons. Another story, this one true, was that three young Christian girls were beheaded on their way to a Christian school in the area. In any event, the result was that, for the first decades of the twenty-first century and beyond, the region

---

[157] Office of Public Affairs, "Statement by the Treasury Department Regarding Today's Designation of Two Leaders of Jemaah Islamiyah," press release, January 24, 2003, https://home.treasury.gov /news/press-releases/kd3796.

became a center of militant Islam where JI and the mujahideen of Eastern Indonesia (also sometimes called Mujahidin Indonesia Timur [MIT]) were strong.

The latter group even declared its allegiance in 2021 to the Islamic State, less out of an exact adherence to that Middle Eastern group's ideology than as a kind of general statement of its participation in the global Islamist movement. Though the Indonesian government took serious steps to tamp down the militants, a report by the Institute for Policy Analysis of Conflict noted in 2023:

> The police and military operations in the area for the last seven years have resulted in many deaths and arrests, creating potential new recruits from angry family members. The district (kabupaten) of Poso has one of the largest concentration of released terrorism offenders in the country and more will be released from prison in 2023 and 2024. Some of the deradicalization programs have created new grievances.

The report highlighted ongoing "attacks on police and Christians that included beheadings" and "an ongoing jihad against the Christian community."[158]

The bad blood in the Poso region, however, did not remain there but spilled over into the rest of the nation. Besides the church attacks in 2000, Catholics and other Christians were targeted by militants everywhere and also at times by the government. In 2006, for example, three Catholic men—Fabianus Tibo, Marinus

---

[158] Institute for Policy Analysis of Conflict, "Militant Groups in Poso: Down but Not Out," IPAC Report No. 86, June 27, 2023, https:// understandingconflict.sgp1.digitaloceanspaces.com/dashboard /a50d83c4f6838767106103f4f94e044a.pdf.

Riwu, and Dominggus da Silva—were found guilty and executed for involvement in the Poso Riots, "which killed 224 people, and burned about 5,000 buildings, including homes. The statement [from their legal defenders] notes that there was no legal action resulting from the naming of 16 other people believed to be the masterminds." Capital punishment is considered impermissible in much of the world, but beyond the legal technicalities—a former Indonesian president and the pope asked for clemency—the seemingly one-sided application of justice further stirred up animosity. It didn't help that the government did not allow the three to have a funeral at St. Mary Church, as they requested, and interfered with a Christian burial.[159]

And other factors also came to the fore. For much of the twentieth century, Portuguese interests—which extend back to the centuries of the great missionary efforts—had been strong in East Timor, which became independent from Indonesia in 2002. Because of its history (St. Francis Xavier landed there in 1546), East Timor is 98 percent Catholic—its Charter recognizes the importance of the Catholic faith—with small percentages of Protestants, Muslims, and others. In 1975, Indonesia invaded and treated the population, which was taking steps toward independence, with considerable violence until the withdrawal of Indonesian forces in 1999. Catholic priests and women religious stayed with the people and died trying to protect them. The bishop of Baucau was wounded in one attack; native priests, seminarians, catechists, and nuns as well as foreign missionaries perished in what was another repetition

---

[159] "Lawyers to Take Case of Catholics' Executions to International Court," Catholic News Agency, October 5, 2006, https://www.catholic-newsagency.com/news/7772/lawyers-to-take-case-of-catholics-executions-to-international-court.

of religious commitment suffering deadly consequences, which perpetuated tensions between the Church and a Muslim regime.[160]

Though Indonesia shares many characteristics with other predominantly Muslim nations, blasphemy charges against Christians are not as frequent there. They do occur, however, and sometimes stick, and not only for poor people who get involved in controversies beyond their everyday circumstances. Sometimes they even touch people with considerable social standing. Basuki Tjahaja Purnama, a former governor of Jakarta and a Chinese Christian, was convicted after he left office in a murky case involving a technical interpretation of some verses in the Quran and was sentenced to two years in prison. Indonesia's criminal code prohibits anyone from denigrating any religion, but, in point of fact, when it's applied, it's usually applied to alleged offenses against Islam—which often enough also include charges against Muslims who are practicing a "wrong" form of the faith.

Still, Christians are a conspicuous target. So widespread has the threat of violence against Christians in Indonesia become that in 2017 the government planned to deploy 250,000 security personnel to protect 5,000 churches for the Christmas holidays. (The province of East Nusa Tenggara alone, where Catholics predominate, had well over 4,000 troops guarding churches.) In 2018, the national deployment went down to 90,000. The following year, it increased again to 160,000—despite the fact that security forces have been known at times to persecute and even kill religious workers. One hopeful sign amid such numbers, however, is that young Christians

---

[160] "Asia/East Timor—Stories of Faith and Martyrdom in the Church of East Timor," Agenzia Fides, September 11, 2024, https://www.fides.org/en/news/75399-ASIA_EAST_TIMOR_Stories_of_faith_and_martyrdom_in_the_Church_of_East_Timor.

and Muslims volunteer for these security services. It's certainly not a full return to the days of peaceful coexistence that the former Malaysian diplomat recalled. But it's also no small thing that at least some elements of the different religious groups in a larger country like Indonesia are actively seeking a way to live together.

As might be expected, the terror groups have gone after the Catholic hierarchy as well, perhaps precisely because of efforts like these. Archbishop Petrus Canisius Mandagi of the Merauke Diocese on the Indonesian island of Papua New Guinea revealed in 2023 that Islamist militants had tried twice to assassinate him, once at his home and once at the Cathedral of St. Francis Xavier. He had only just become bishop of the region—which is majority Christian—the previous year. The terrorists were so eager to get him that the first bomber showed up on January 1, the very day he arrived in the diocese: "A terrorist was waiting for me at the bishop's house, but he only spoke to the archbishop's secretary. He had a backpack full of explosives and was pretending to look for a boarding house." The second attempt failed because it was planned for a Mass, but the archbishop happened to be traveling elsewhere that Sunday. Sadly, that's not likely to be the end of the attempts against bishops or many other Christians in Indonesia.

A joint 2017 Christmas message from the Indonesian Catholic Bishops' Conference and Protestant church leaders in Jakarta urged recognition of how urgent such efforts were:

At the moment we are worried. Our unity as an Indonesian nation is in danger of breaking. Restlessness and worry have been felt more and more in recent years. There are those who, vaguely or shamelessly, are tempted to follow different paths and ways of the Charter at the base of our nation, the Pancasila. This was seen in many acts and events: in an unhealthy political competition that justifies any means; in the restricted fanaticism that exploits religion and in many other ways. Under such conditions, the desire of our nation to create coexistence and peace becomes difficult to achieve.[161]

The Church and tolerant Muslim elements in the nation carry on.

Philippines

The Philippines have been described as the only Christian nation in Asia—though, since the independence of East Timor, there are now two. But the Philippines' claim of being a Christian nation is almost 100 percent true. Catholics account for around 85 percent of the population, and many Protestant groups make up nearly all the rest, with just 4 percent Muslims, concentrated mostly in the south. But among that 4 percent are some quite active terrorist groups that have carried out numerous attacks. Abu Sayyaf has been the most prominent and deadly of the terrorist organizations, largely operating in the southwest of the Philippines, close to Malaysia and Brunei, and with ties to Jemaah Islamiyah (JI), which is active in several Southeast Asia countries with headquarters in Indonesia.

In a way, the overwhelming Catholicity of the Philippine nation contributes to attacks on Catholic sites by offering many targets of opportunity. In December 2023, on the first Sunday of Advent, for

---

[161] "Asia/Indonesia—Christian Leaders: 'Indonesia Risks Division,'" Agenzia Fides, December 12, 2017, https://www.fides.org/en/news/63384-ASIA_INDONESIA_Christian_Bishops_Indonesia_risks_division.

example, four people—Junrey Barbante, Janine Arenas, Evangeline Aromin, and Riza Ramos Daniel—died when a bomb exploded during Mass at the Catholic chapel on the campus of the Mindanao State University. More than forty others were wounded. The attack was the work of an Islamic State group. But there was no reason to attack a chapel of no more than ordinary importance except that it provided an opportunity to strike simultaneously at three of the institutions such groups violently oppose: the Philippine state, Western-style higher education, and the Catholic Church.

The attack came as government military forces were cracking down on the three major Islamic State groups in the region: Dawlah Islamiyah, Abu Sayyaf, and Maute. Local police suspected that it was probably intended as retaliation.[162] Although Muslims make up a small percentage of the overall population in the Philippines, Mindanao has a large concentration of them, perhaps as many as six million. That mere fact—and the existence of Islamist movements in Asia—makes some tensions inevitable. As traumatic as this event was, however, it was also something of a consolation that most Muslims in the region expressed solidarity with the victims and the Church. That may have had something to do with the work of Silsilah, a movement for Islamic-Christian dialogue that has existed in the southern Philippines since the 1980s. It was founded by PIME missionary Fr. Sebastiano D'Ambra and has sought to maintain good relations between the two faiths through several initiatives, including schools in which Christians and Muslims study together and often overcome mutual suspicions.

[162] "Asia/Philippines—Reopening of the University Affected by the Attack in Marawi: Prayer and Memory of the Victims," Agenzia Fides, December 11, 2023, https://fides.org/en/news/74493 -ASIA_PHILIPPINES_Reopening_of_the_university_affected _by_the_attack_in_Marawi_prayer_and_memory_of_the_victims.

The main obstacle to mutual coexistence, however, remains the violent nature of Islamist movements. At the start of the new millennium Abu Sayyaf perpetrated what has become an all-too-common act against innocents. The group raided a school run by Claretian missionaries in Basilan, burned it, and took staff and male and female students hostage. Fr. Rhoel Gallardo, a Claretian priest, tried to protect the girls from rape and led the hostages in the Rosary to keep up their spirits. He was shot along with eight others at close range. When their bodies were discovered, the priest's fingernails were found to have been torn out—a sign that he had been tortured and refused to apostatize and become a Muslim. In 2021, the Claretians started the process of declaring him a martyr.

In the Philippines, as in nations in Latin America and Africa, there have also been cases of Catholics killed over social-justice concerns. One noteworthy case is that of Fr. Fausto Tentorio, an Italian PIME missionary who was murdered in 2011. Fr. Tentorio worked for thirty years in the Philippines, especially in the Arakan valley, and defended the human rights of the Manobo, a small tribe in the region. His activities might be viewed from one angle as political—tribal rights and environmental concerns, as opposed to big-business interests—but in another sense, he fit into the category of "new martyrs" that Pope John Paul II has made current. He certainly might be called a "martyr for justice," the title of an Italian book written about him.[163]

His end was brutal; he was hit by ten shots on the grounds of the Mother of Perpetual Help parish in Arakan. The perpetrators seem to have been a paramilitary group, "Bagani"—connected to the army—which didn't like the priest's efforts to preserve the

---

[163] Giorgio Bernardelli, *Fausto Tentorio, martire per la giustizia* (Milan: Edizioni San Paolo, 2015).

ecosystem of Manobo. A large network of shadowy economic interests was involved; at least eleven people were arrested in connection with the murder. Some who were willing to talk about the perpetrators went into a witness-protection program, and that led to further investigations by police. But the accused have been under protection of another kind. And while Fr. Tentorio's work continues in the people he catechized and protected, no one has been brought to trial for the crime.

Ironically, some orders of religious women who work with poor indigenous communities in the Philippines and defend people from human rights abuses have been charged with "financing terrorism" even though they explicitly preach nonviolence and express a willingness to "work in poor and remote areas, even those affected by armed conflicts, even when these areas are subjected to militarization."[164] Meanwhile, they and other conspicuous Catholic religious have been subject to violent attacks, and not only in the Muslim-dominated South. In December 2017, Islamists shot and killed Fr. Marcelito "Tito" Paez in the town of Jaen. His murder was followed by similar attacks. In April 2018, Fr. Mark Ventura was killed after saying Mass; in June, Fr. Rey Urmeneta was shot but survived; that same month, Fr. Richmond Nilo was shot and killed in the northern city of Zaragoza, as he was vesting for Mass. And these are just some of the ongoing cases among many more.[165]

---

[164] "Asia/Philippines—Missionaries Accused of Supporting Terrorism: Civil Society Takes the Field alongside Them," Agenzia Fides, September 8, 2022, https://www.fides.org/en/news/72766 -ASIA_PHILIPPINES_Missionaries_accused_of_supporting _terrorism_civil_society_takes_the_field_alongside_them.

[165] 'Third Catholic Priest Is Murdered in Philippines," Archdiocese of Malta, June 14, 2018, https://church.mt/third-catholic-priest -is-murdered-in-philippines/.

Other Asian Trouble Spots

In addition to the Islamist-inspired anti-Christian violence in Asia, there are several communist nations—North Korea, Vietnam, Laos, China (more on China in the next chapter)—that visit persecution and death on their Christian populations. Vietnam and Laos allow officially recognized religions, such as the Catholic Church, to operate within strict limits—which means not doing anything that might directly challenge or stir up popular resistance against the regime. North Korea, however, is brutally tyrannical, combining the paranoid dictatorship of one ruling family with harshly applied Marxist principles. Practicing the Christian faith is thus regarded as a political crime against both the atheist state and Kim Jong Un personally. Open Doors ranks North Korea as the single most anti-religious regime on earth. While the regime is careful not to perpetrate anti-Christian repression too openly, it conducts limitless, thorough repression over individuals, families, communities, and churches.

Figures about numbers of believers and religious practice in North Korea are virtually nonexistent. Interviews with defectors suggest that there are maybe 800 Catholics and 12,000 Protestants in a country with a population of more than 26 million, but these are mere guesses. (By way of comparison, South Korea, with about twice the population, has almost 6 million Catholics and 10 million Protestants—and has elected three Catholics as president.) It seems certain that, in the North, there are no Catholic priests recognized as such by the Vatican. During the Korean War (1950–1953), the North's army was told to eliminate "reactionary forces" as they retreated from the South; this means, according to a report finally issued in 2022, that they killed 450 Christians, including 119 Catholics. In the North, all native Korean priests were killed and foreign priests were expelled. Among those "disappeared" and presumed dead was the then-bishop of Pyongyang, Francis Hong Yong-ho. The Vatican has begun the canonization process for him and about eighty of his companions from the same period.

The punishments still being inflicted on Christians in North Korea are the equal of anything that was carried out in the prison camps of Nazi Germany, the Soviet gulag, or truly demonic tortures like the Pitesti Experiment in Romania. The numbers of Catholics are so small that it's difficult to say how they are treated, but, from the stories of the Protestant defectors, it seems that all religious believers — including non-Christians — are subjected to the same inhuman degradations. According to Korea Future, which monitors human rights abuses in North Korea:

> The adherents of two religions, North Korean Shamanism and Christianity, have experienced arbitrary arrest and detention; forced labour; torture and cruel, inhuman, or degrading treatment; the denial of fair trial rights; the denial of the principle of non-refoulement; the denial of the right to life; and sexual violence. Spanning the years 1987–2019, these violations were neither arbitrary nor random. They have been a part of systematic and targeted attacks directed at religious minorities.[166]

And the cases have shown a significant uptick, beginning in about 2012, the time when Kim Jong Un succeeded his father to the supreme power.

Christianity has existed in Korea for hundreds of years, but the Korea Future report notes that "it has become the most severely

---

[166] Korea Future, *Persecuting Faith: Documenting Religious Freedom Violations in North Korea*, vol. 2 (2021), 5, https://www.koreafuture.org /news/report-persecuting-faith-volume-2.

persecuted religious tradition within North Korea." Whole families have been arrested under the merest suspicions. Their treatment in detention is often hellish: "Evidence demonstrates that victims were subjected to physical beatings with objects, fists, and feet.... Furthermore, the broader experience of detention was one where cruel and inhuman treatment was enabled by poor conditions of detention that incited further harm, including overcrowded cells."[167] A report by the Office of International Religious Freedom goes into greater detail describing prisoners' treatment:

> being forced to hang on steel bars while being beaten with a wooden club; being hung by their legs; having their body tightly bound with sticks; being forced to perform "squat-jumps" and to sit and stand hundreds or thousands of times each day; having a liquid made with red pepper powder forcibly poured into their nostrils; being forced to kneel with a wooden bar inserted between their knee hollows; strangulation; being forced to witness the execution or torture of other prisoners; starvation; being forced to ingest polluted food; being forced into solitary confinement; being deprived of sleep; and being forced to remain seated and still for up to and beyond 12 hours a day.[168]

When it wasn't sheer sadism, sometimes the goal was to force "confessions" of being Christian. Even foreigners have been arrested and subjected to similar treatment for alleged religious practice or even mere belief.

[167] Korea Future, *Persecuting Faith*, 41.
[168] Office of International Religious Freedom, 2021 Report on International Religious Freedom: North Korea, U.S. Department of State, sect. 2, https://www.state.gov/reports/2021-report-on-international-religious-freedom/north-korea/.

In 2024, *Forbes* magazine wondered whether the persecution of Christians in North Korea might properly be called a kind of genocide.[169] International institutions have condemned North Korea and tried to impose sanctions in order to shift behavior. The UN Commission of Inquiry has said that the "the gravity, scale and nature" of the North's human rights violations "reveal a state that does not have any parallel in the contemporary world."[170] But short of a change in regime, all such external efforts have very limited effect in such a tightly controlled communist system.

Vietnam

Almost all religions in Vietnam are "foreign" imports, including Buddhism, Confucianism, and Taoism, but the Asian origin of these three and their longer existence in Vietnam means that they are more integrated into the society as a whole than is Christianity. Still, Christian missionaries of the Jesuit, Dominican, and Franciscan Orders, the Paris Foreign Missions Society (MEP), and the Augustinians had, haltingly and despite some conflicts with one another, managed to establish a continuous Catholic presence in Vietnam since the sixteenth century, even though various regimes sometimes took up anti-Western attitudes, including opposition to the Church. In the early nineteenth century, a period of intense anti-Catholic persecution resulted in the deaths of perhaps as many as three hundred

---

[169] Olivia Enos, "Are North Korea's Christians Facing Genocide?," *Forbes*, May 17, 2024, https://www.forbes.com/sites/oliviaenos /2024/05/01/are-north-koreas-christians-facing-genocide/.

[170] United Nations General Assembly, *Report of the Commission of Inquiry on Human Rights in the Democratic People's Republic of Korea*, February 2014, https://www.ohchr.org/en/hr-bodies/hrc/co -idprk/reportofthe-commissionof-inquiry-dprk.

thousand. More than a hundred of the victims—among many who are unknown by name—have been formally declared saints by the Church. In the later nineteenth century, France established a "protectorate" that lasted until French forces were famously defeated in 1954 by the Vietminh army at Dien Bien Phu.

The defeat led to the partitioning of the nation: North Vietnam was ceded to the communists under leader Ho Chi Minh while Ngo Dinh Diem, a Catholic, became the leader in the South. Though Catholics were a minority—perhaps only 10 percent—even in the South, Diem placed many of them in key positions in government and the military. The division was to be only temporary. The 1954 Geneva Conference specified that there were to be nationwide elections in 1956 to choose a government for the whole country. In the event, Vietnam became one of the "proxy wars" within the larger Cold War. And communist nations such as the USSR and China supported the North, while the United States and other Western nations backed the South. The proposed elections never happened. Instead, open war occurred that, despite America's massive military efforts, resulted in another Western defeat. U.S. troops withdrew in 1973, and communist forces eventually took over the entire country.

It's difficult to characterize the religious situation in Vietnam since then; almost half of the population practices what surveys vaguely call "folk religions." About another 30 percent have no religion at all, but whether these correspond to what in the West would be categorized as atheists or "Nones" is not clear. The communist state is formally atheist, but close to 15 percent of the people are Buddhist and about half that number are Catholics, with tiny percentages of Protestants and other faiths.

Perhaps the single thread that serves to explain the situation in Communist Vietnam is the usual one with totalitarian and authoritarian states: the regime carefully monitors, quickly re-presses, and ruthlessly eliminates—when necessary—any resistance, even any serious criticism. There are frequent reports of Catholic institutions, especially those that are seen as opposing human rights violations, being shut down or dispersed. The government is not above a kind of religious cleansing in some places and using both police and criminal elements to prevent Masses from being offered. After one such incident in which several Massgoers were injured and a statue of the Virgin defaced, a priest—Fr. J. B. Nguyen Dinh Thuc—was beaten. He later bravely offered remarkable Christian witness, "To die on the altar would be such a blessing to me."[171]

That might indeed be the motto of bishops, priests, religious, and laypeople all over East Asia. And no place more so than in China, which is our next subject.

---

[171] Allen, *The Global War*, 89.

5

White (and Red) Martyrs
in Red China

Fr. Chrysostom Chang
A *flowering of wire*
Binds the bare wrists behind;
The opened skin a fire
He suffers to remind
Of one before who wore a crown of briar.

—James Matthew Wilson,
"Stanzas for the Chinese Martyrs"

The twentieth century was a uniquely violent period, even outside of the two great World Wars. Scholars estimate that something on the order of two hundred million *of their own people* were killed by various regimes during that century. And among those regimes, which were typically totalitarian in differing forms and to one degree or another, the bloodiest of all in terms of overall repressiveness and sheer numbers of people murdered was the regime that emerged in 1949 after China's Communist Revolution with the establishment of the People's Republic of China.

The Martyrs of the New Millennium

After the triumph of the Communist Party, China—which is to say, in effect, its leader, Chairman Mao Zedong—followed a path first explored by Lenin and Stalin but with even greater scope and mayhem. It chose an ideological reign of terror involving widespread persecution, imprisonment, and slaughter of Christian believers and others seen as threats to the state's total dominance of Chinese society.

The numbers of those killed—which range from seventy million to more than one hundred million—do not simply reflect China's great size. Those figures also represent a deliberate effort to eliminate any and all possible pockets of resistance or dissent. Further, they reflect Mao's determination to intimidate those whom he did not kill into accepting not merely the ideology but the everyday decisions of the Chinese Communist Party, which, in practice, meant Mao himself. Tens of millions are thought to have also perished in a forced famine, though statistics on this and other matters in a society that closely limits information are hard to verify. And some Catholic scholars would add that hundreds of millions of unborn Chinese perished in the womb as a result of "population control" via the one-child policy (1980–2016), which, ironically, has produced a demographic crisis for the Chinese people. In any event, the body count—all categories of victims considered—is probably the largest in all of human history, and over just a few decades.

The Chinese leadership took a less crudely violent approach to social control after Mao's death in 1976. For almost three decades, stretching into the early years of the twenty-first century, there was something of a "respite," at least as far as the most openly violent measures were concerned. Hundreds of thousands imprisoned in the mid-1950s, for example, and given life sentences as enemies of the regime—including the great confessor Cardinal Ignatius

Kung Pin-Mei[172] and hundreds of Catholic priests—were granted amnesty in 1979 after more than two decades of detention. They were released from the prisons and laogai, the Chinese equivalent of the Nazi *lager* and Soviet gulag with this difference: the Chinese prison camps did not merely confine and exploit the labor of prisoners but engaged in elaborate brainwashing in an attempt to condition prisoners to accept Marxist ideology and the day-to-day leadership of the Chinese Communist Party (CCP).

From the first, it was clear that the aim was not only to eliminate opposition but to "convert" Christians and other believers to a different faith, a process that continues in various ways in the twenty-first century. There is no better example of what this means than the experience of Fr. Robert Juinger of the MEP. He had the great misfortune to have been captured by the Nazis and sent to a detention camp during World War II. Then he was arrested again, this time as a missionary in China, in 1952. During his Chinese detention, he was subjected to intense brainwashing: four hours of "instruction" in Marxism-Leninism every day; in the evenings, for two hours, he and his fellow prisoners were forced in "struggle sessions" to make "confessions" and "self-accusations" of past "errors." He told his captors: "I was a prisoner in the hands of the Germans for eighteen months. But they never treated me like this, and above all they did not try to make me believe in Nazism. You, on the other hand, want to convert us all to Communism by force."[173]

Happily, he was eventually "punished" by being expelled to then-independent Hong Kong.[174] But his case reveals, via concrete

---

[172] See Paul P. Mariani, *Church Militant: Bishop Kung and Catholic Resistance in Communist Shanghai* (Cambridge, MA: Harvard University Press, 2011).

[173] Royal, *Catholic Martyrs of the Twentieth Century*, 329–330.

[174] Royal, *Catholic Martyrs of the Twentieth Century*, 330.

experience, that the Chinese Communists were even more fanatical than the Nazis about their ideology.

Mao's war on Christianity—indeed, on all religion and everything that might oppose the total triumph of his rule—proceeded in several phases. In the first, until the mid-1950s, there was a direct assault. When the Communist Party finally took control of the country, foreign Christians, both Catholic and Protestant, were simply branded as agents of their home nations and treated as such in ways that included imprisonment, torture, and death. Christian organizations made up of ordinary laypeople were branded in similar fashion as enemies of the CCP. In an especially ridiculous instance—for anyone who knows anything about the group—the Legion of Mary was accused of being a "paramilitary organization."[175] It's no surprise, then, that the Vatican itself was simply designated as a foreign power and an enemy whose influence in China had to be eliminated.

But direct action against the Christian churches, as has happened throughout history, did not destroy them, though it damaged them severely. Christians accepted martyrdom, went underground, both individually and in groups, making it difficult to identify them and root them out. This called for more nuanced tactics. As he had with other opponents, Mao set up a "front group," the Catholic Patriotic Association, which might mimic some of the characteristics of the churches loyal to Rome but was ultimately intended to control the real believers. Laypeople themselves were not deceived, and quite a few refused any engagement with the "official" Church. It was these persons and communities, many of whom for years had resisted at great personal cost, who would

---

[175] Stephen P. Mosher, *The Devil and Communist China: From Mao Down to Xi* (Gastonia NC: TAN Books, 2024), 270.

feel puzzled by the Vatican's 2018 Secret Accord with the Chinese government—which they regarded as far too trusting of a regime that had proven itself unworthy of trust.

Things took an even worse turn when, toward the end of his life, Mao launched the Cultural Revolution in the mid-1960s, lasting more than a decade. All subtleties were now abandoned against both secular and religious organizations not subservient to the regime. Control was the goal, and even the front groups such as the Catholic Patriotic Association were shuttered for a time, seemingly because religion per se was regarded as a threat. Despite the persecutions, arrests, imprisonments, and murders, miraculously the Chinese Catholic Church—an underground Church of martyrs—survived what may very well have been the bloodiest regime in all of the sad, violent history of the human race. Numbers are uncertain, but it's safe to say that there are at least ten to twelve million Catholics in China, despite all the persecution and mayhem.

Mao died in 1976, and the harshest period of persecution passed with him. But it did not end. While China hands speak of a "respite" until 2005, the Church remained under constant pressure, nonetheless. With the 1979 amnesty, the repression of independent social groups such as the Catholic Church shifted under the "reforms" of Deng Xiaoping from what might be termed "red martyrdom" to "white martyrdom"—for the most part; that is to say, continued persecution, imprisonment, intimidation, and mistreatment that (usually) stopped short of death. Or at least that's the impression Chinese authorities have tried to give—because bishops, priests, and other figures still disappeared, often for years, sometimes with fates unknown. Some died in custody; others died soon after release, owing to long periods of mistreatment. The post-Mao Chinese leadership wanted to save face with the international community—by shrewdly avoiding producing more martyrs. Still, as Communism was collapsing in Eastern Europe and the Soviet Union in 1989, the Chinese regime was quite willing to use tanks to mow down thousands of its own democracy protesters in Tiananmen Square—and to deny that it had occurred, even arresting protesters on later anniversaries of the event.

The Chinese leadership also still believed, however—and with renewed vigor after the rise of Xi Jinping in 2012—that they needed to exert total control over all sectors of the nation. They began doing so with greater and greater emphasis on the need for the "Sinicization" of religion in China, which has often been presented to people willing to suspend disbelief (which includes some high officials in the Vatican) as merely a kind of "inculturation," similar to the old Catholic way of describing how the faith finds a way to become part of a new culture and society.

President Xi himself, in a 2021 CCP conference on religion, however, made clear that Sinicization has far greater ambitions than that. The five approved religious groups—Catholic, Protestant, Taoist, Islam, and Buddhist—should all be developing a "religious theory of socialism with Chinese characteristics." In other words, they should adapt their religious activities to support the political ideology of the state. Observers of the conference noted that Xi called for increased surveillance and punishment of religious groups that questioned government policies and the Communist Party itself, or, as one put it, "Religion must support the party, the state, and its leaders.... Sinicization of religion means that all religious communities should be led by the Party, controlled by the Party, and support the Party."[176]

---

[176] Hu Zimo, "China: First CCP National Conference on Religion Held Since 2016," *Bitter Winter*, December 8, 2021, https://bitterwinter.org/china-ccp-national-conference-on-religion/.

White (and Red) Martyrs in Red China

This has been a constant note to one degree or another since communism came to China. Even though brute force and subtle manipulation have not succeeded in subjugating the faithful, they have not stopped the regime. As the twenty-first century has progressed, it has kept up with change by implementing ever new measures. In 2024, for instance, the office regulating the Internet banned the Catholic prayer app Hallow presumably because its relatively harmless instructions in prayer are independent and not under the control of the regime.

It's necessary to keep all this history in mind in assessing China's varying attitudes and acts toward Catholics and other Christians in the twenty-first century. For example, the Patriotic Association is often referred to as the "official" church, as distinguished from the "underground" Church in communion with Rome. But despite the machinations of the Communist Party inside and outside the official group, the lines of loyalty—and the success of the ploy—are not exactly what Mao intended when he created the Patriotic Association.

On the one hand, there are obviously compromised figures—including some bishops—in the official church. And in the case of "official bishops" consecrated without Rome's approval, the Vatican has tried to resist regularizing them if they have shown themselves to be overly submissive to the Communist Party. Since the Vatican "Secret Accord" (2018) with the regime, however, the situation has become more confused. In theory, under the agreement—which is "secret" in the sense that it's known to exist but hasn't been made public—the pope has the power to veto candidates for bishop proposed by the Patriotic Association, in effect with state approval. In practice, China has not only gone ahead with the consecration of bishops without consulting Rome on a few occasions; in 2024, the Chinese even created a new diocese without consulting the Vatican; Pope Francis was forced to accept the move after the fact.[177]

On the other hand, even as staunch and uncompromising an anti-Communist figure as Cardinal Joseph Zen, the former archbishop of Hong Kong, has experienced a more hopeful reality. The cardinal taught for several years in both official and unofficial seminaries in China. And without weakening in the least in his criticisms of the pressure put on both groups by the state, he has noted:

> Teaching in seminaries, of the official Church, of course, gave me the opportunity of learning about many things that I could not imagine before, good things and less good things. The "less good things" include the terrible control by the Communist government. The "good things" include the fact that there was faithfulness not only within the underground Church, but also among most people in the official Church. We came to realize that our categories were too sharply divisive, when in reality there were so many healthy forces.[178]

Many questions remain about the relative status in any given context of the officially recognized Patriotic church in China and the unofficial, unrecognized Catholics who remain loyal to Rome and independent of the Chinese government. As Zen stated, it's

---

[177] Courtney Mares, "Pope Francis Creates 'New' Diocese in China, Accepting Borders Drawn by Beijing," Catholic News Agency, January 29, 2024, https://www.catholicnewsagency.com/news/256669/pope-francis-creates-new-diocese-in-china-accepting-borders-drawn-by-beijing.

[178] Joseph Zen, *For Love of My People I Will Not Remain Silent: On the Situation of the Church in China* (San Francisco: Ignatius Press, 2019), 15.

not always easy to draw a clear dividing line between the two. The official church—especially in terms of leadership—is controlled to a significant degree by the Communist Party. Still, as Cardinal Zen has carefully put it—the Chinese regime monitors and pressures both groups of Catholics:

> Although the systematic, large-scale persecutions of the Maoist period are a thing of the past, the suffering of the Church has not entirely ended. The communities and bishops of the official "Patriotic" Church, which is recognized by the government, are subjected to constant surveillance, interference, mistreatment, and harassment. Hence the communities of the official Church and its leaders are not entirely free, although it may seem so to the casual observer. The so-called clandestine or underground communities, which refuse (with good reason) to submit to the religious policy of the government, are continually subjected to abuse and even violence, so it would not be an exaggeration to speak, in these cases, of persecution.[179]

What this means is that the one-party Chinese system is wary even of its own creature—the Catholic Patriotic Association—since it seems to regard all real religious activity as a potential source of opposition. It may no longer operate with quite as much brutality as in the early days of the Communist takeover, but it seeks and practices as far as possible total control over Chinese society nonetheless.

In spite of continuing repression and persecution, the relative softening of the Chinese regime in the 1980s and 1990s gave the Vatican some hope that dialogue might be possible. Pope John Paul II, who had experienced both Nazi and Soviet totalitarianism

---

[179] Zen, *For Love of My People*, 14–15.

in his native Poland, nevertheless hoped to open up relations that would be helpful to Chinese Catholics and, at the same time, was realistic about the perilous nature of the situation. He took several steps in that direction.

In 1996, as part of the preparations of the Jubilee 2000 celebrations, the pope laid out his vision for a possible future in a Message to the Catholic Church in China:

> The civil authorities of the People's Republic of China should rest assured: a disciple of Christ can live his faith in any political system, provided that there is respect for his right to act according to the dictates of his own conscience and his own faith. For this reason I repeat to the governing authorities ... that they should have no fear of God or of his Church. Indeed, I respectfully ask them in deference to the authentic freedom which is the innate right of every man and woman, to ensure that those ... who believe in Christ may increasingly contribute their energies and talents to the development of their country.[180]

Almost needless to say, the Chinese Communists were not persuaded. As the twenty-first century was dawning, China itself was also looking for a very different kind of change in relations with the Vatican. On January 6, 2000, the Catholic Patriotic Association and China's Office for Religious Affairs planned to consecrate a dozen bishops in Beijing's cathedral. The number was chosen deliberately to reflect a similar event scheduled for the same day in Rome, in which Pope John Paul II was also to consecrate a group of

---

[180] John Paul II, "Be United to Christ and Peter's Successor" (December 3, 1996), no. 7, EWTN, https://www.ewtn.com/catholicism/library/be-united-to-christ-and-peters-successor-8839.

twelve bishops. All this came in the midst of negotiations between China and the Vatican over various matters.

John Paul II had published precisely two months earlier a "post-synodal exhortation" on the Church in Asia, *Ecclesia in Asia*, which addressed Asia in general but also had some specific things to say about China. It was post-synodal in that it was the result of a special assembly for Asia of the synod of bishops in the spring of 1998. (The synod of bishops is an advisory body instituted by Paul VI to help the pope in dealing with various questions concerning the Church and the world.) The Vatican hoped to organize a papal trip to Hong Kong to present the document at a location in Asia. The Communist Chinese government was obviously not pleased at the prospect of the Polish pope, who had helped bring down communism in the former Soviet Union and Eastern Europe, issuing a major document on its doorstep.

Ecclesia in Asia, however, is a sober document, looking to a better future for the Catholic Church in several parts of Asia. Its few references to China per se are truthful but restrained. For example, it expresses "a sense of sadness at the fact that Bishops from Mainland China could not be present" at the synod. But the desire not to worsen relations is carefully balanced with a certain candor: "The Synod Fathers remembered in a special way the people of China and expressed the fervent hope that all their Chinese Catholic brothers and sisters would one day be able to exercise their religion in freedom and visibly profess their full communion with the See of Peter."[181]

That was the same note that Pope John Paul II had struck in dealing with Communism in Eastern Europe, against the advice

---

[181] John Paul II, post-synodal apostolic exhortation *Ecclesia in Asia* (November 6, 1999), nos. 3, 8.

of many in the Vatican who wanted him to pursue the softer *Ostpolitik* that his predecessors had followed toward the Communist bloc. The proof of the right approach, however, was in the results that his stronger stance helped to produce. And it's no surprise that the Chinese did not wish to see another round of stout John Paul II *Ostpolitik* aimed at Asia.

One way it sought to express its displeasure was via the parallel consecrations of bishops in that very first week of the twenty-first century and the third Christian millennium. This tactic did not quite work out as planned, however. Seven of the twelve "official" candidates, selected by the government, displaying the loyalty to Rome that Cardinal Zen had noted even outside of the underground Church, chose not to participate in the ceremony. According to reports, 120 seminarians who were also slated to attend refused as well. Repercussions followed—among them, the seminarians and their instructors at the seminary who encouraged their resistance were expelled and the institution "reformed."[182]

John Paul II was not finished, however, with putting diplomatic pressures on the Chinese. When they mounted a powerful media campaign to counter his intention to make a proclamation about the Catholic martyrs in China over the centuries, he nevertheless chose to canonize 120 of them. He did so, in the very first year of the new century, on October 1, 2000, the feast of St. Thérèse of Lisieux. But the date was also the anniversary of the creation of the People's Republic, which the Communist Chinese took to be a deliberate provocation.[183] Whether that was the case or whether it was a mere coincidence is difficult to say. But given the Polish

---

[182] Gerolamo Fazzini, *The Red Book of Chinese Martyrs*, trans. Michael Miller (San Francisco: Ignatius Press, 2009), 327.
[183] Fazzini, *Red Book*, 238.

pope's cleverness in dealing with Communist regimes, it may not have been deliberate, but it was at the very least a sign that Rome was not going to be intimidated by the powers in Beijing. John Paul II had been seeking an opening with China since the early 1980s—which is to say, just a few years into his papacy—even writing a personal letter to Deng Xiaoping in 1983, but he had been mostly ignored.[184] Nonetheless, as was his custom, he did not give up. At various points, he expressed his admiration for Chinese culture. And while he was not willing to take a conciliatory approach to the regime, he and several of his advisers in the Vatican were conscious of the fact that when Rome had condemned "ancestor worship" during the Chinese Rites controversy in the eighteenth century, it had partly misunderstood the situation and thus missed a chance at evangelizing one of the oldest and largest cultures in the world. Communism, of course, lies much further outside a Catholic worldview than the honoring of ancestors, a practice that could have been interpreted as filial piety or akin to devotion to saints and heroes of the past. In any event, Rome and the pope were prepared to take a new approach to China, an approach they hoped could be more successful.

As might be expected of two such different human entities, relations between the Catholic Church and various governments of China have been marked, from the very beginning, by multiple religious and secular complications. Clashes were inevitable—physical clashes as well as intellectual and spiritual ones. The status of Christians and Christianity itself in China underwent multiple changes, depending on the regime in power, even prior to modern times. It is estimated that during the Boxer Rebellion (1899–1901), for example, more than thirty thousand Christians perished along

---

[184] Weigel, *Witness to Hope*, 596.

with several dozen Catholic priests in the Boxers' effort to stamp out the influence of a "foreign" religion, though many of the victims were native Chinese.[185] The attack didn't work very well, a testimony to an affinity between the Church and some elements in Chinese culture.

Missionary efforts in China, despite the Boxer persecution, returned with near miraculous vigor. About 886 missionaries were working in China in 1900. When the Communists came to power in 1949, there were 4,415, nearly five times as many. There were similar developments among women religious. Their communities increased five- and sixfold, and there were 6,927 native Chinese members among them. China's Catholic population, in line with the other figures, increased from about three-quarters of a million to nearly four million.[186] And contrary to the claims of propagandists, most missionaries worked in poor, rural areas, where destitution was endemic, building infrastructure, starting schools, even as they evangelized — not seeking to advance Western "imperialism" and influence in the country as a whole. It's no wonder, then, that a communist government, hell-bent on controlling the people, portrayed the missionaries as agents of foreign powers and took vigorous steps to keep the Church in check, resulting in dozens of martyrdoms.[187]

But the two institutions have also displayed no little mutual curiosity over more than five centuries. The high point in those

---

[185] Mariagrazia Zambon, *Crimson Seeds: Eighteen PIME Martyrs*, trans. Steve Baumbusch (Detroit: PIME World Press, 1997), 37.

[186] J. Krahl, "Martyrs of China," in *The New Catholic Encyclopedia* (1967), 3:597.

[187] For a detailed account of these martyrs see the chapter "Chinese Carnage" in Royal, *The Catholic Martyrs of the Twentieth Century*, 317–338.

relations probably came in the early 1600s, when the scholar and polymath Matteo Ricci, a Jesuit, arrived in China. And while Westerners have occupied a precarious position in China for the past century and a half, it was the advent of the Chinese Communist takeover of a vast and ancient nation that began the bloodiest period in a long history and a fresh crop of Christian martyrs.

An often-quoted saying by Confucius helps to specify the heart of the problem: "Just as there are not two suns in the sky, so there cannot be two emperors on earth."[188] As in most non-Christian societies, in China there is no "Caesar's coin" separation of spheres (Mark 12:14–17). Jesus Christ's reference to Caesar's coin was His way of indicating that it is right to render unto Caesar the things that belong to Caesar—primarily the administration of practical matters on earth—but there are more important matters that belong to God. In the biblical understanding, as even the Old Testament documents, kings exercised legitimate authority only when their actions were congruent with God's ultimate goodness and truth. Chinese tradition also speaks of obeying the "orders of Heaven," a Confucian concept that has been both exploited and distorted by various leaders, including the Communists, even as they deny that there is any natural order other than the one pursued by the CCP.

But when that deep cultural vision of the unity and the harmony of the cosmos was shattered and replaced with a debased Western import (Marxist materialism), the change brought in the same absolutizing of the political (the Communist Party itself) that produced such slaughters in the twentieth century, only on an even larger scale in China.

---

[188] From the *Li Ji* (*The Book of Rites*), quoted in Mosher, *The Devil and Communist China*, chap. 7.

The historical irony, of course, was that, in various ways, Chinese communism—though, like all communism, it was deeply marked by Western thinkers such as Marx and Hegel—was also driven by a desire to throw off Western imperialism and affirm China's unique identity and status in the world. Yet somehow in the course of the Chinese Revolution, Marxism—for all its Western baggage—came to be regarded as a tool for affirming national independence, while Christianity and, in particular Catholicism, did not. It was a further irony that Chinese communism not only went to work eliminating the hated "foreign religions" but saw it as a necessity to repudiate China's own cultural past to achieve its Great Leap Forward.

In a sense, then, John Paul II's expressions of regard for traditional Chinese culture and his claims that Catholicism was compatible with various regimes and could help build them up rang two alarm bells among the Chinese leadership. Mao's Cultural Revolution had sought to abolish the "four olds": old thought, old culture, old customs, old habits. The pope's openness to writing another chapter in the history of China and the Church that respected both past and present was not reciprocated. Relations remained frosty. In 2005, just weeks before John Paul II died, AsiaNews—an agency of the Pontifical Institute for Foreign Missions (PIME)—published a "List of Bishops and Priests in Prison, Isolation or Labor Camps."[189] The document compared those missing in China to the *desaparecidos*—the "disappeared" persons, a term that arose during the Cold War in several Latin America

---

[189] "List of Bishops and Priests in Prison, Isolation or Labour Camps," AsiaNews, March 5, 2005, https://www.asianews.it/news-en/ (East-Asia,China)-List-of-bishops-and-priests-in-prison,-isolation-or-labour-camps-2705.html.

countries. Noting that the list was probably incomplete given the difficulty of obtaining information in totalitarian societies, AsiaNews named six bishops who had been arrested:

1. Mgr James Su Zhimin (diocese of Baoding, Hebei), 72, was arrested in 1996. Since then no one has heard anything about him except once when he was seen in a Baoding hospital under police escort receiving medical treatment for a heart condition and eye ailment. He was never seen again.

2. Mgr Francis An Shuxin (auxiliary bishop of the diocese of Baoding, Hebei), 54, was arrested in 1997. No one has heard from him since.

3. Mgr Han Dingxian (diocese of Yongnian/Handan, Hebei), 66, was arrested in December 1999. He previously spent a total of 20 years in prison. Since his detention he has been in isolation, unable to see anyone, whether a parishioner or a relative.

4. Mgr Cosma Shi Enxiang (diocese of Yixian, Hebei), 83, was arrested on April 13, 2001. Mgr Shi was ordained bishop in 1982. Previously he had spent 30 years in prison. The last time he was arrested was in December 1990. He was later released in 1993. Thereafter he was under forced isolation.

5. Mgr Philip Zhao Zhendong, (diocese of Xuanhua, Hebei), 84, was arrested in late December 2004.

6. Fr Paul Huo Junlong, administrator of the diocese of Baoding, about 50, was ordained in 1987. Arrested in August 2004, he has been detained in an undisclosed location without trial or charges brought against him.[190]

---

[190] "List of Bishops," AsiaNews.

These were only the most prominent and best-known cases. In addition, according to PIME sources, dozens of "unofficial" bishops had been harassed to the point where they could not carry out their duties. The regime especially targeted older bishops who might be sick and carefully monitored who visited them, when they were allowed to be visited at all. Typically, these bishops would be arrested and detained for a certain period, then allowed to go back to their churches but kept under close surveillance and sometimes subjected to brainwashing. AsiaNews made a point of offering the names of thirteen bishops being given such treatment in 2005:

1. Li Side, 78, unofficial bishop of Tianjin, is interned and cannot perform his pastoral duties. He was previously arrested in December 1989 and released in June 1991.

2. Mgr Julius Jia Zhiguo (diocese of Zhengding, Hebei), 68, has been arrested and released in quick succession several times. This year he has already been arrested twice. The Holy See has publicly appealed for his liberation on more than one occasion. Every month he undergoes forced indoctrination about government policies for weeks on end.

3. Mgr Zhang Weizhu (diocese of Xinxiang, Henan), 45, is an active pastor and the founder of two religious orders. He is prevented from visiting his diocese and is kept under surveillance in Hebei province.

4. Mgr Bartholomew Cengti, 74, is bishop of Hanzhong (Shaanxi). Since December 2001 he has been under house arrest. He lives in isolation with his priests unable to meet him. He is ill and cannot perform his pastoral work.

5. Mgr Li Hongye (diocese of Luoyang, Henan), 83, was arrested in 1997. He is also ill.

6. Mgr Liu Guandong (diocese of Yixian, Hebei), 84, is not free to move. He cannot exercise his ministry anymore because of illness.

7. Mgr Joseph Fan Zhongliang (diocese of Shanghai), 85, is ill. He is always under surveillance but has some freedom.

8. Mgr Han Jingtao (diocese of Sipin, Jilin), 82, is under police surveillance despite being ill and cannot work in public.

9. Mgr John Yang Shudao (diocese of Fuzhou, Fujian), 84, is archbishop. Altogether he has spent 30 years in prison. He was arrested in 1955 for refusing to join the Patriotic Association. Released in 1981after 26 years, he was rearrested in 1988 and spent another three years behind bars. He is regularly arrested and under surveillance. He, too, is very ill.

10. Mgr Thomas Zeng Jingmu (diocese of Yujiang, Jiangxi) is 83.

11. Mgr Xie Shiguang (diocese of Mingdong, Fujian), 86, was arrested in October 1999. In taking him into custody the police told him that he was being invited to a talk with government representatives. He was brought to an undisclosed location. He had always refused to register his underground church in Mindong with the authorities. He was released soon thereafter but has remained under surveillance.

12. Mgr James Lin Xili (diocese of Wenzhou, Zhejiang), 84, was arrested in September 1999 and freed in 2002. He is still under surveillance and is not free. Catholics from his diocese say that his arrest and that of several priests was due to a campaign launched by the local Patriotic Association to force the bishop and his clergy to join the

association. Usually, such campaigns include violence and blackmail. In the bishop's diocese, the unofficial church is permanently under threat, its personnel risking arrest and its property, destruction. In April 1999 three churches were blown up in Wenzhou; in mid-December 1999, another two received the same treatment. In the village of Linjiayuan the local church was built three times and destroyed three times, the last time in October 2001.

13. Shi Hongzhen, 75, is coadjutor bishop of Tianjin. This year he celebrates 50 years since his priestly ordination. He cannot work, especially since he is ill, but he is not interned.[191]

Given that the number of Catholics in the underground Church at the time must have been approaching ten million, the absence or neutralizing of so many bishops could not help but significantly hobble their ecclesial life.

But the communist regime hardly stopped there. If they could exercise such repression on leaders who were at least known, they could do as much or more against individual priests. AsiaNews gave a mere snapshot of some of the things that had happened in the years immediately before the report was issued — and occurred often in the years after, a period in which around eighteen priests had been arrested and as many seminarians, though the latter were later released:

❖ Zhang Zhenquan and Ma Wuyong (diocese of Baoding, Hebei) were arrested in July-August 2004 during a ceremony celebrating the anniversary of their ordination along with Fr Huo Junlong, administrator of the diocese of Baoding.

[191] "List of Bishops," AsiaNews.

❖ Fr Li Wenfeng, Fr Liu Heng, and Fr Dou Shengxia (diocese of Shijiazhuang, Hebei) were arrested on October 20, 2003, with some seminarians, attending a spiritual retreat in Gaocheng.

❖ Fr Chi Huitian (diocese of Baoding, Hebei) was arrested on August 9, 2003, whilst celebrating mass at a youth summer catechism camp.

❖ Fr Kang Fuliang, Chen Guozhen, Pang Guangzhao, Yin Ruose, and Li Shujun (diocese of Baoding, Hebei) were arrested on July 1, 2003, because they were visiting Fr Lu Genjun, who had just been released after spending three years in a labour camp for "evangelization".

❖ Fr Lu Xiaozhou (diocese of Wenzhou, Zhejiang) was arrested on June 16, 2003, as he was giving a dying person the last rites.

❖ Fr Lin Daoming (diocese of Fuzhou, Fujian) was arrested on May 3, 2003, on a visit to his mother, who had just been released from prison where she had been sent for being the cook of an underground seminary in Ch'angle.

❖ Fr Zheng Ruipin (diocese of Fuzhou, Fujian) was arrested on April 12, 2003, with 18 seminarians. The latter were all released but Father Zheng remains in prison at an undisclosed location.

❖ Fr Pang Yongxing, Fr Ma Shunbao, and Fr Wang Limao (diocese of Baoding, Hebei) were arrested respectively in December 2001, and March 24 and March 31, 2002 (Palm and Easter Sunday). On July 7, 2003, all three were sentenced to forced labour.

❖ Fr Li Jianbo (diocese of Baoding, Hebei) was arrested on April 19, 2001, in Xilinhot (Inner Mongolia) and

sentenced to a labour camp to be re-educated. He is said
to be very ill.[192]

Similar lists could have been produced periodically in the years
that followed.

Though all this—and much more—is well known and documented, the Vatican Secretariat of State decided to open up direct
negotiations with Beijing in 2005 and tried to get Beijing to sign
a written agreement that might help protect Catholics in China.
There had been precedents for such arrangements in Catholic history—several of which might have served as a caution. In that same
year, Cardinal Joseph Ratzinger was elected pope with the name
Benedict XVI. It is hard to understand how a German pope—who
was well aware of what happened after the Vatican signed a concordat with the Nazi regime—allowed the process to continue.
(The answer may be that he was unable to control some of the
higher officials in the Vatican.) History had shown that a paper
barrier with an even more murderous and totalitarian system like
China's couldn't possibly turn out well. Perhaps the 1930s Vatican
was naive enough to believe that the law-abiding Germans would
follow whatever legal rules it could get put in place. The China
case was much less likely. Fortunately, for Rome and the pope,
the Chinese government had no intention of tying its own hands
in however cynical an agreement and refused to put anything in
writing. For the moment, the proposal was off the table, though
dialogue continued.

While people talked about an agreement, those persecuted
by the regime found themselves in an ambiguous situation in
which the regime claimed that the pope wanted the underground
Church to come out of the catacombs. Few believed these claims,

---

[192] "List of Bishops," AsiaNews.

and fewer, even under great pressures, disavowed their commitment to Rome. But not all. A rather typical—if extreme—example of how this sometimes turned out occurred in 2012, when the auxiliary bishop of Shanghai, Thaddeus Ma Daqin, was consecrated with the rare approval of both the official church and the underground Church (i.e., with papal approval). His consecration might have been a bit of a watershed in relations between the Vatican and the Chinese regime if things had gone properly. In the nature of things, they could not and did not. The government insisted that a bishop not recognized by Rome participate in the ceremony—a subtle way of suggesting that the new bishop was in unity with the Catholic Patriotic Association. According to reports, Thaddeus Ma Daqin refused to allow that official bishop to lay hands on him and instead stood up and embraced him. After the ceremony he also announced he was leaving the Patriotic Association. Chinese officials—correctly—interpreted this as a kind of declaration of independence from political submission.

In short order, he was arrested and put in a seminary building that had been converted into a prison, where he had little contact with the outside world for a year and a half. According to reports by both the BBC and Reuters, he was subjected to harsh interrogations and "political lessons," that is, ideological indoctrination.[193] In a sense, he was given relatively mild treatment. For years, ordinary priests in China have been routinely arrested and tortured while in custody to compel them to join the

---

[193] Sui-Lee Wee, "Special Report: The Bishop Who Stood Up to China," Reuters, March 31, 2014, https://www.reuters.com/article/world/special-report-the-bishop-who-stood-up-to-china-idUS BREA30018/.

Patriotic Association. The Chinese usually began with offering benefits with such membership but could turn sharply to more direct methods if that failed.

Tragically in Ma's case, he recanted four years later and said, "For a certain time, I have been deceived by others and made certain wrong words and deeds about the CPA."[194] He added that this was "extremely unwise in hindsight." Whether this was a reversal owing to brainwashing, a sincere change of mind, or a tactic to gain the best for all Catholics in Shanghai—members of both the official as well as the underground church—is impossible to determine. It's also worth noting that the negotiations leading to the 2018 "secret accord" with Rome were well advanced by this point. But whatever the case, the government's actions resulted in precisely what its various pressures on all Catholics seek: submission to the regime, as well as to the tenets and policies of the CCP.

Cardinal Zen, who was deeply involved in the Vatican's negotiations with the Chinese at the time, has written in detail about the safeguards Pope Benedict tried to keep in place. Many of the Curia officials involved, he observes, were Italians who had not had direct experience with totalitarian regimes—fortunate for them but unfortunate in that their approach to China was somewhat "naive and optimistic," though well-intentioned. The pope organized several private consultations that included bishops from Hong Kong, Macau, and Taiwan as well as experienced China experts to help draft a letter to China, which would both show doctrinal clarity about the official and underground churches and take into account

---

[194] Carey Lodge, "China: Bishop Under House Arrest Who 'Stood Up to China' Alludes to Shock Turnaround," *Christian Today*, June 16, 2016, https://www.christiantoday.com/article/china.bishop.under.house.arrest.who.stood.up.to.china.alludes.to.shock.turnaround/88497.htm.

the situation of Catholics in China. The letter appeared in 2007 on Pentecost and called for an annual World Day of Prayer for China. The main point was a theological one: "Communion and unity ... are essential and integral elements of the Catholic Church: therefore the proposal for a Church that is 'independent' of the Holy See in the religious sphere, is incompatible with Catholic doctrine."[195]

Benedict later also set up a formal commission to follow China. Again, the invited participants were sound, but the agenda was set by the Curia, which wanted to avoid confrontation almost at all costs. Zen worried about this resurgent soft *Ostpolitik*: "Their strategy was wrong, all about compromise and surrender. Since the Church in China still had so many healthy forces, why commit suicide? Many Bishops, priests, and faithful are courageous. The officials of the Curia make them appear to be in error. The Curia has always tried to please the Chinese government." In his judgment, even the pope suffered some from a similar attitude: "Pope Benedict is a saint, a great theologian, but he has a weakness: he is too good, too humble, too tolerant."[196]

One of the most sensitive points had to do with the underground Church coming out into the open, which would be desirable if it didn't mean reprisals against its leadership and members, or a requirement that they subordinate doctrine to communist ideology or forsake principles such as loyalty to Rome. The regime almost always pressed for such things. In the event, Benedict was content to leave the decision to bishops in China within their own dioceses. But Zen cautioned: "Reconciliation is the most important issue today. Only after a long journey can we hope to reach unity. If the government does not recognize the rights of the Church, where will unity be achieved?"

---

[195] Quote in Mariani, *Church Militant*, 224.
[196] Zen, *For Love of My People*, 46.

Reconciliation is an attitude of the mind, he stated. Reunification is a more ambitious and—for the moment—more dangerous change in structures that might make all Catholics even more vulnerable to the state.

The relationship between the Vatican and the Communist Chinese took another major turn when the leadership of both institutions changed. Jorge Mario Bergoglio, the cardinal archbishop of Buenos Aires, was elected to the papacy, taking the name Francis, after Benedict XVI resigned the office in March 2013. Just a few months earlier, in 2012, Xi Jinping had come to power in Beijing and displayed a hostility to Christianity reminiscent of Chairman Mao's. Top Roman officials seem not to have fully appreciated the ferocity of anti-religious sentiment that had reappeared in China. Indeed, as was his practice of promoting peace in other situations of conflict, Pope Francis immediately began to seek ways to overcome historical divisions and reach an agreement that would not only open up relations between Rome and Beijing but would also allow for a reunification of the Patriotic church with the underground Church in China.

That was already a tall order, but it was also somewhat compromised from the start. Cardinal Theodore McCarrick, a former archbishop of Washington, D.C., who had ended his active career in disgrace when his sexual abuse of multiple seminarians and others came to light, insinuated himself into the negotiations. Pope Benedict XVI had ordered McCarrick to cease his travels and devote himself to prayer and repentance. But McCarrick had ignored those instructions and continued involving himself in various international missions on a private basis. Indeed, one of his assistants reported that McCarrick wrote to Pope Francis:

When you greeted me so cheerfully in Washington as an adjunct member of the foreign service, I received this as a challenge to continue as an amateur in the very noble work of the foreign relations of the Holy See. I have maintained on a quiet level our relationship with China and have been developing new relationships with the Arab countries of the Middle East.... With God's help, before He calls me home, I will help to bring you China and the great dream of Matteo Ricci will begin to be realized once again.[197]

This was a clever ploy on McCarrick's part. Invoking the name of the great Jesuit missionary Matteo Ricci in this context must have sparked some hopes on the part of the first and only Jesuit pope, who, in his youth, had himself dreamt of missionary work in some far-off exotic setting. Ricci's brilliance in various disciplines, including astronomy, mathematics, and the Chinese language itself, had made him the first Westerner to impress the leader of that ancient culture as a kind of Western mandarin. Indeed, so revered was he by the Chinese that, when he died, they allowed his body to be buried in a Buddhist Temple in Beijing at a time when the law specified that all foreigners who died in China had to be buried in Macau.[198]

But Matteo Ricci was a scholar and probably a saint. McCarrick was a smooth operator and certainly no saint. Yet he worked his way into the very complicated negotiations with a hostile communist government beginning in 2014, just a year into Francis's papacy. Since the accord with the Chinese remains "secret"—as explained earlier, meaning the text has not been published but its existence has been acknowledged—it's difficult to say what is in it. But it's not difficult to speculate that McCarrick, and perhaps others involved

---

[197] Quoted in Mosher, *The Devil and Communist China*, 268.
[198] For a rich account of his life see, Jonathan D. Spence, *The Memory Palace of Matteo Ricci* (New York: Viking, 1984).

in the negotiations, knew that Pope Francis wanted an agreement in order to promote peace, and they may have considered it essential to their remaining in his good graces that they come up with one.

China had earlier balked over two main issues. According to Stephen Mosher, an experienced China hand, they were as follows:

> First, the Holy Father must, without exception, consecrate all the patriotic bishops that he and Pope Benedict, for very good reasons, had previously rejected.
>
> Second, he must eliminate the underground church, starting with its bishops. Elderly underground bishops must be forcibly retired and replaced with patriotic bishops of Beijing's choosing, while younger underground bishops must be reassigned to subordinate roles in the patriotic church. This process must continue until the last of the thirty or so underground bishops have been sidelined and silenced, one way or another.[199]

It seems that Rome compromised on both points while agreeing to a complex process of appointing future bishops whereby the Chinese would propose a candidate and Rome could approve or not. Obviously, this situation favors the more relentless partner, and the Chinese clearly placed a limit on how many candidates could be refused before they would go ahead on their own—which they have done in the years since the accord.

Another sign of the kind of attitudes toward China that existed in the Vatican—perhaps not widespread, but seemingly plausible enough to some figures—appeared around the time that the accord was being finalized. In February 2018, Archbishop Marcelo Sánchez Sorondo was interviewed about his recent trip to China.

---

[199] Mosher, *The Devil and Communist China*, 270.

An Argentinian, like Pope Francis, he had been appointed chancellor of the Pontifical Academy for the Social Sciences. In his view, "at this moment, those who best realize the social doctrine of the Church are the Chinese." Given his position, his voice carried some weight, to be sure. But he also aroused criticism with his further contentions: "They [the Chinese] seek the common good, subordinate things to the general good."

Even that was not enough praise. He added:

> I found an extraordinary China; what people do not know is that the central Chinese principle is 'work, work, work.' ... As Paul said: "he who does not work, who does not eat." You do not have shantytowns, you do not have drugs, young people do not have drugs. There is a positive national consciousness, they want to show that they have changed, they already accept private property.... [The People's Republic of China] has defended the dignity of the human person, [and, in the area of climate change is] assuming a moral leadership that others have abandoned.[200]

Critics were astonished that the head of the Pontifical Academy for the Social Sciences naively took Chinese claims at face value, ignored reports of China's extensive human rights violations, of its building coal-fired power plants at a furious pace, and the existence of some of the most openly polluted cities on earth. The archbishop's remarks concluded with what he saw as the contrast with the poor environmental and social record of the West.

---

[200] "Vatican Official Praises China for Witness to Catholic Social Teaching," Catholic News Agency, February 6, 2018, https://www.catholicnewsagency.com/news/37694/vatican-official-praises-china-for-witness-to-catholic-social-teaching.

It was in the midst of all this turmoil that in September 2018 the Holy See signed the "secret" accord with China. Though "secret," it is very well known and spoken of by both sides as a breakthrough agreement. The Chinese government now has the prerogative of suggesting a slate of bishops when a diocesan see lies open, and the Vatican can choose among the candidates—who, not surprisingly, are friendly toward the communist regime and the Patriotic church, the Chinese Catholic church licensed by the regime. For even that minor concession, Rome has then encouraged members of the underground Church to regularize their situations.

That is all to the good in theory, to be sure. In practice, troubling signs emerged quite soon after the September 2018 agreement. To begin with, some observers thought the date of the signing to be particularly inopportune because China was then implementing what one scholar writing in *Foreign Policy* magazine called "the worst crackdown on religion since the Cultural Revolution."[201] Both official and unofficial churches had been required to install surveillance cameras connected to police computers the previous year, and many places of worship were under constant police supervision.

Even the implementation seemed to be lopsided—in favor of the Chinese regime. Priests and bishops detained before the agreement was signed should have been released—as a precondition—but were not. By contrast, the pope agreed to acknowledge officially six bishops of the Patriotic church who had been appointed without his approval, which he duly did on September 22,

---

[201] Benedict Rogers, "China Is Already Breaking Its Vatican Deal," *Foreign Policy*, September 17, 2020, https://foreignpolicy.com/2020/09/17/china-francis-vatican/.

2018.[202] His fidelity to the agreement, however, was not matched by similar steps on the part of the Chinese.

Among many unknown repressive measures, in November of the same year (which is to say, just two months into the agreement), two shrines to the Virgin Mary were torn down—one because it displayed "too many crosses," the other because it lacked the proper "building permits."[203] These lame rationalizations, all too familiar from the operations of other communist regimes, were really intended to implement "Sinicization" of all religious bodies, when not to suppress them outright. Chinese authorities seemed impervious to charges that they were violating both the spirit and letter of agreements when such facts came to light. Indeed, their attitudes were so brazen that even as the agreement was coming up for renewal in September 2020, it was reported that "in Jiangxi province, dissenting Catholic priests have been placed under house arrest, in breach of an agreement to protect clergy from coercion. Priests from Yujiang diocese, under surveillance, have been forbidden from 'engaging in any religious activity in the capacity of clergy' after they refused to join the regime's so-called 'patriotic church,' and Bishop Lu Xinping was barred from celebrating Mass."[204]

In that same year, prior to the renewal of the accord, Hong Kong businessman and human rights activist Jimmy Lai, a Catholic

---

[202] Holy See Press Office, "Briefing Note about the Catholic Church in China, 22.09.2018," Vatican website, https://press.vatican.va/content/salastampa/en/bollettino/pubblico/2018/09/22/180922g.html.

[203] "China-Vatican Accord Followed by the Destruction of Two Shrines in Shanxi and Guizhou," AsiaNews, October 25, 2018, https://www.asianews.it/news-en/China-Vatican-accord-followed-by-the-destruction-of-two-shrines-in-Shanxi-and-Guizhou-%28videos%29-45306.html#google_vignette.

[204] Rogers, "China Is Already Breaking Its Vatican Deal."

convert, was arrested in Hong Kong for "organizing unauthorized assemblies." He has been kept in jail by various legal maneuvers. In 2022, as the accord was coming up for renewal again, Cardinal Zen was arrested—though released shortly thereafter—for "colluding with foreign forces." In reality, the cardinal had participated in the creation of a human rights advocacy group.

As in many totalitarian systems, Catholics persecuted under Chinese communism have left interesting memoirs of their experiences. But they have been reluctant to publish them, not only for the further troubles it might bring to the authors but also for the harm it might cause to fellow believers. In the 2016 preface to Gerolamo Fazzini's *Red Book of Chinese Martyrs*, however, Cardinal Zen, shortly after being made a cardinal by Benedict XVI, wrote:

> To continue today on the path of silence would be an incomprehensible and unpardonable error. As John Paul II often reminded us, we have the duty to remember without further reticence all the martyrs under any regime whatsoever, particularly the martyrs of the twentieth century. The confessors and martyrs of the Church of China belong to Christianity as a whole, and it is our duty, as well as our right, to present their testimonies so that they might nourish the faith of Christians throughout the world.[205]

Telling unpleasant truths about brutal acts when all too many in the global community prefer to avert their eyes, says Cardinal Zen, is a mandatory "harvest of memory."

By 2022, however, even the Vatican was openly complaining about violations. When the Chinese appointed a bishop to a see not recognized by Rome, the Vatican, "with surprise and regret,"

---

[205] Fazzini, *Red Book*, 8.

asked for an explanation, adding that the move did not "conform to the spirit of dialogue" and that they hoped that "similar episodes are not repeated"—but of course they were.[206] In 2023, for example, the Vatican stated that China had "unilaterally" appointed bishops to Shanghai, and Pope Francis was forced to accept that a few months after the fact for the "greater good" of the faithful.[207]

As late as the spring of 2024, as the time for another renewal of the accord approached, many of the old practices continued, if, in ways, less open than in the past. Priests and bishops who have refused to follow the Vatican's encouragement that they join the Patriotic church are still subjected to lawlessness. In May 2024, two "conscientious objectors"—Fr. Chi Huitian and Prof. Chen Hekun—in the Diocese of Baoding, not far from Beijing, were "disappeared" and not heard from again. Other conscientious objectors were jailed at the same time and subjected to heavy ideological indoctrination. Impatient with the pace of "Sinicization," in August 2024, the United Front Work Department prescribed "Patriotic Education" for Catholic priests.[208]

At the very time that the accord was up for approval again in October 2024, Nina Shea, a longtime student of religious liberty worldwide, published a report on ten bishops who had suffered

[206] Philip Pullella, "Vatican Says China Violated Pact on Bishops, Wants Explanation," Reuters, November 26, 2022, https://www.reuters.com/world/vatican-says-china-violated-pact-bishops-expresses-regret-2022-11-26/.

[207] Nicole Winfield, "Pope Recognizes China's Unilateral Appointment of Shanghai Bishop, Three Months after the Fact," Associated Press, July 15, 2023, https://apnews.com/article/vatican-china-bishop-pope-shanghai-8883e3dba4716aaa430f331094decb21.

[208] Wu Xiuying, "China, Catholic Clergy Starts Receiving 'Patriotic Education,'" Bitter Winter, August 23, 2024, https://bitterwinter.org/china-catholic-clergy-starts-receiving-patriotic-education/.

since the accord went into effect.[209] In the report, Shea presents evidence that "religious repression of the Catholic Church in China has intensified since the 2018 China-Vatican agreement on the appointment of bishops." Like the 2005 report by AsiaNews cited earlier, Shea's report goes into detail about each of the bishops she names. She sums up her general findings:

> The CCP has subjected the 10 bishops in the report to indefinite detention without due process, disappearances, open-ended security police investigations, banishments from their dioceses, or other impediments to their episcopal ministries including threats, surveillance, interrogation, and so-called reeducation. Seven of these bishops have been detained without due process, with some of them having been under continuous detention for years or decades, while others have been detained repeatedly, up to six times since the agreement's signing. This report does not include persecuted bishops who have died over the last six years or bishops on whom there is little information. Other persecuted Catholics, including priests, other religious leaders, and laity, are also not covered.[210]

Even without those additions, the picture is quite brutal.

Shea believes that the Vatican signed the agreement hoping to be able to appoint around thirty bishops that the Communist Chinese were either holding up or blocking. Chinese Catholics needed dozens more bishops, as was clear from Pope Francis's initial message when he signed the accord and explained that it

---

[209] Nina Shea, *Ten Persecuted Catholic Bishops in China* (Washington D.C.: Hudson Institute, 2024), 9.
[210] Shea, *Ten Persecuted Catholic Bishops*, 10.

intended "to support and advance the preaching of the Gospel, and to reestablish and preserve the full and visible unity of the Catholic community in China." One of the safeguards for the Church would be that individual priests and bishops could practice a kind of conscientious objection and not join the official church if they believed that, if they did so, they could not still remain in communicn with the universal Catholic Church and Rome. Some tried: "Specifically, the Vatican suggested that clergy who were conscientious objectors could take the CPCA pledge while rejecting the 'independence' provision. In Mindong, for four days police tortured one priest who followed this advice."[211]

All the bishops cited also refused to join the official church, with the usual results. Shea highlights the fate of one in particular who may serve as an example for what may be happening to many other unknown resisters:

> The Chinese government has uniquely persecuted Bishop Vincent Guo Xijin of Mindong Diocese in Fujian Province. Directly due to China's precondition for the agreement, in 2018 Pope Francis demoted Bishop Guo from serving as the ordinary bishop of Mindong, a position he had held for two years, and replaced him with the government-appointed Bishop Zhan Silu, one of the seven Chinese bishops for whom the pope had lifted excommunication. Bishop Guo obediently served as Zhan's auxiliary bishop but found himself thwarted from carrying out his pastoral ministry and eventually forced from his home. The authorities first served him an eviction notice, which forced him to sleep on the street in wintertime, then cut off his water,

---

[211] Shea, *Ten Persecuted Catholic Bishops*, 18.

heat, and electricity. In 2020, after two years of nonstop government pressure on him and his priests and left with no autonomy, he resigned. His current whereabouts and well-being are unknown.[212]

The future for Catholic clergy and laypeople deemed insufficiently receptive to "Sinicization" and incorporation into the official church is uncertain, but the clear trend in China since the arrival of Communism makes it likely that little will change for the better—much more likely that they will grow worse. As Phil Lawler noted in the final days of 2024, despite hopes that the secret accord would allow the appointment of many more bishops by the pope, only four were appointed in 2024 under the agreement. Seventy dioceses in China were still without leaders; six of the Chinese bishops in place are over eighty, and four of those are over ninety.[213] The regime's squeezing of the Church remains powerful. And the crop of white martyrs—and doubtless not a few red martyrs—seems destined to grow.

---

[212] Shea, *Ten Persecuted Catholic Bishops*, 16.

[213] Phil Lawler, "The Manifest Failure of the Vatican Deal with China," Catholic Culture, December 30, 2024, https://www.catholic culture.org/commentary/manifest-failure-vatican-deal-with-china/.

6

Martyrs and Persecution in the West

O God of earth and altar,
Bow down and hear our cry,
Our earthly rulers falter,
Our people drift and die;
The walls of gold entomb us,
The swords of scorn divide,
Take not thy thunder from us,
But take away our pride.

—G. K. Chesterton

Though the stories previously described in the present volume occur in lands and cultures quite distant from the historical homelands of Christianity—Europe and North America in particular, along with other Western outposts, such as Australia and New Zealand—it would be leaving a false, an incomplete, indeed even a misleading picture of anti-Christian threats in the twenty-first century to omit the attacks, threats, and growing prejudice against traditional Christianity on several fronts, even in the so-called developed world.

Indeed, one reason anti-Christian persecution and death — by orders of magnitude larger than that perpetrated against any other faith group — goes largely ignored in national and international bodies is that many among the affluent and elite of the world mistakenly believe it is not that big a problem or, if it is, it is sometimes merited because of Christianity's strict moral and social positions. But anti-Christian prejudices *are* a problem, in the West as well as elsewhere, and, by basic Western standards, not ever remotely merited. I've already noted that something on the order of three hundred million Christians all over the world are under threat. But it's worth also taking a look here at the tens of millions of Christians — just to take Europe and America — who are also increasingly threatened in their own societies.

Sometimes the threats are from Islamists, sometimes by various Western educational and cultural institutions, and sometimes even from their own governments, which have lately been persuaded to regard Christian teachings such as "male and female He created them" or moral teachings about homosexuality or abortion as the "teaching of hate." And this has had demonstrable effects that few people recognize as a kind of discrimination, even incipient persecution, perhaps portending even harsher measures in the near future. But if anything, what happens in more obvious places of persecution should make us more sensitive to what can happen among us as well.

The Observatory on Intolerance and Discrimination against Christians in Europe (OIDAC), an organization that operates out of Vienna, Austria, tracks anti-Christian hate crimes and other indicators of anti-Christian bias. In its annual report for 2023, OIDAC recorded an uptick in anti-Christian hate crimes from a variety of groups.[214] There is the usual Muslim-Christian friction in many parts of Europe, to be sure. But as the first quarter of the twenty-first century was coming to a close, that problem had been largely recognized, if not resolved—since the root cause of the problem is a religious clash involving large numbers of recent Muslim migrants with very different social mores from those in their new home nations.

OIDAC lists some other groups of serious concern, however:

> Our research shows that one of the main sources of aggression are radicalized members of extreme political groups, with a majority of cases coming from far-left political groups, such as Antifa, radical feminists, or LGBTIQ groups. Furthermore, we have documented attacks by radical individuals from far-right groups, satanist groups, and radical Islamist groups. These different groups might perceive Christianity or the church as an establishment that contradicts their worldview on social and moral issues, while other groups might consider Christianity simply to be wrong or unworthy of respect. While everyone should have the freedom to hold the belief that Christianity is wrong or even negative, when this prejudice translates into violent acts, it can develop into dangerous trends, particularly as attacks by extremist groups tend to be more severe.[215]

It's telling that, despite data like these, the European Union has "coordinators" for combating hate crimes against Jews and Muslims but no one for Christians—again, perhaps reflecting an assumption

---

[214] OIDAC Europe, *2022/23 Annual Report* (Vienna: OIDAC Europe, 2023), https://www.intoleranceagainstchristians.eu/file admin/user_upload/publications/files/Annual_Report_2023_ -_ONLINE_Version.pdf.

[215] OIDAC Europe, *2022/23 Annual Report*, 13.

that such attacks don't often occur or aren't important. But they do occur, they are important, and they aren't rare. Over the Christmas season in 2024 alone, there were multiple incidents involving mostly Muslim attacks on Christmas markets, New Year celebrations, and police and other forces of order in Germany, Italy, Belgium, Netherlands, and other European nations. In spite of the fact that such things occur during the year as well, it's telling that it took OIDAC, a private group, to point out what should have been obvious in ordinary news reports and by governments formally committed to protection of religious liberty.

Because the raw figures are quite startling, OIDAC carefully distinguishes between religious intolerance, discrimination, and what it calls "secular intolerance." It also recognizes when it is hard to identify clear motives in instances of prejudice or outright attacks. Yet, even allowing for all those qualifiers, it is quite surprising that, in 2022, 30 European nations were the site of 749 anti-Christian hate crimes. (OIDAC uses the European Union's criteria for hate crimes in those cases.) There were also 38 physical assaults and 3 murders attributed to anti-Christian motives. These numbers, which include arson, show a sharp rise from the previous year. In that same year, France decided to allot four million Euros to protect places of worship. Other national and regional governments have tracked similar increases, mostly Muslim-on-Christian crimes. In 2023, OIDAC found an even more alarming trend: there were 2,111 anti-Christian hate crimes—again, using Europe's definitions—in just Austria, Finland, France, Germany, and the United Kingdom—the only countries from which police statistics were available. France had the most with 950, the UK had 702, and Germany had 277.[216]

---

[216] OIDAC Europe, *Intolerance and Discrimination against Christians in Europe Report 2024*, 8, https://www.intoleranceagainstchristians

The most conspicuous attacks on Christians in Europe still come from radicalized Islamists. Even people who aren't Catholic or are Catholic but don't usually follow news about modern martyrs, for instance, are often familiar with what must be the most notorious slaying of a Catholic priest in twenty-first-century Europe. Fr. Jacques Hamel was eighty-six when, in July 2016, two nineteen-year-old Muslim radicals, who claimed ties with ISIS, entered his church in Saint-Étienne-du-Rouvray, a small town in Normandy, wielding knives. It was a tense period for violence in France. Seven months earlier, in November 2015, Islamic radicals had broken into the Bataclan Theatre in Paris during a performance and killed ninety people, in addition to wounding more than four hundred. Another forty people were killed at the same time in coordinated attacks on the Stade de France and Jewish sites. Earlier in 2015, seventeen staff of the satirical magazine *Charlie Hebdo* had been murdered because of cartoons that some Muslims found insulting to the prophet Muhammad.

Fr. Hamel had a friendly relationship with the local imam who headed the regional Muslim council, and it's unclear why the two teenagers decided to attack the priest, who was formally retired and was helping out that morning in the small parish. But they did. Brutally. They broke in as he was saying Mass and took him hostage along with five others, two laypeople and three religious sisters, eventually cutting his throat. His last words were reported to be *"Va-t'en, Satan!"* — "Go away, Satan!" Pope Francis immediately proclaimed him a martyr — though in what way was not entirely clear — and said during a Mass commemorating him: "This man accepted his martyrdom next to the martyrdom of

.eu/fileadmin/user_upload/publications/files/OIDAC_Report _2024_-_Online_Version.pdf.

Christ, on the altar.... He was beheaded on the Cross, as he was celebrating the sacrifice of Christ's cross [the Mass]." The pope also gave instructions that pictures of Hamel were to be put up in public places.

Police killed the two perpetrators—Abdel Malik Petitjean and Adel Kermiche—as they were attempting to leave the scene. Six years after the event, four other men were convicted of collaborating with the killers. But an odd spirit seemed to permeate this whole episode. There was an immediate outpouring of grief and solidarity for the elderly priest among both Christians and Muslims in France, and worldwide horror. At the trial, the four collaborators begged for forgiveness for the role they had played. One of the laypersons who was wounded did indeed publicly forgive them. And family members of the victims held hands with the defendants.

Whether this was naivete on their part or some unanticipated grace from Fr. Hamel's death at a time when French society was bitterly troubled over Islamic violence is an open question, of course. But whatever the answer, something unusual seems to have resulted from this horrifying act. Fr. Hamel's life had been quiet and peaceful except for one incident. When he was doing his mandatory military duty in Algeria in the 1950s—he was a seminarian at the time—his entire platoon was wiped out in an ambush, except for him. It affected him greatly, and he was heard to say many times that he didn't know why God had spared him.[217] Perhaps it was for this ultimate witness and spur to a small measure of reconciliation. Pope Francis immediately lifted the usual five-year waiting period before starting the process toward canonization, which is continuing.

---

[217] See Jon De Volder, *Martyr: Vie et mort du père Jacques Hamel* (Paris: Cerf, 2016).

In many places in Europe, from England to Germany to Greece, knife attacks are carried out against Christians—guns and other weapons are more difficult to acquire in Europe than in places such as America. In one such incident in Nice, in the South of France, three Catholics, while they were attending Mass, were killed by an Islamist shouting "Allahu Akbar" and wielding a knife. A Tunisian radical, who had reached France by the very common point of entry to Europe—the Italian island of Lampedusa—essentially decapitated a man and a woman. Another woman fled the scene with a deep gash to her neck and later died. At the time, the murders seemed "random," but they were actually part of a much larger series of events all around Europe whereby direct threats were carried out on practicing Catholics in the very act of worship.

It's not only in Muslim nations that Christians now have to be careful about appearing in public. There are increasing attacks on Christians—and Catholics in particular—in several European countries as well. France has been the worst of all, partly because of the relatively large number of Muslims who now live within its borders. Crucifixes are torn down, Hosts desecrated at altars, church buildings ransacked. There are, of course, in places such as France, anti-Catholics who are not Muslim and engage in such deliberate profanation—partly with a desire to intimidate Christians about safety in places of worship. It's often difficult to identify the perpetrators with any degree of confidence. But from reports that come from Muslims themselves, it's probable that the majority of such acts are by Islamic individuals and groups who adopt a certain militancy toward what remains of Christianity in their new lands of residence. Cases of a similar kind have cropped up in Germany, England, Belgium, the Netherlands, and elsewhere. Such acts serve a double purpose: they frighten both Christians and any Muslims intending to convert to a faith attacked by members of their own communities.

In March 2024, the French police tasked with internal security arrested an Egyptian man and five of his collaborators, all Egyptian jihadists, who were intending to attack the already damaged Cathedral of Notre Dame in Paris. Thanks to intelligence sources, the police were able to forestall the efforts, which also seems to have targeted other structures around Notre Dame and the population of the center of the city. French officials say such plots are not unusual, and they stop about two per month on average.[218] Naturally, attacks on a site such as Notre Dame are both religious and political, two categories that are distinguished in Western mentalities but not so much in a certain type of Islam. However the motives are parsed, though, the results are essentially the same.

People around the world were appalled when Paris's iconic Cathedral of Notre Dame caught fire in 2019 and was nearly destroyed. The cause of that blaze seems to have been carelessness by workmen doing repairs on the roof, and that carelessness allowed the "forest"—the extremely dry and flammable beams of the ancient edifice—to burst into uncontrollable flame. But in recent decades, there have many fires of highly suspicious origin all over France. The Observatoire du Patrimoine Religieux (Observatory of Religious Heritage) in Paris has estimated that France loses one religious building every two weeks—sometimes the result of neglect, but two-thirds of those lost to fire are the result of arson. And these figures do not even take into account that two

[218] Geoffroy Antoine, "Attentat manqué contre Notre-Dame de Paris, un Égyptien interpellé," *Le Journal du Dimanche*, March 30, 2024, https://www.lejdd.fr/societe/info-jdd-attentat-manque-contre-notre-dame-de-paris-un-egyptien-interpelle-143562.

additional Christian edifices are the targets of theft or desecration every day in France. According to the French central intelligence unit, there were 877 such incidents all over the country in 2018 alone. Some of those fires have hit major cathedrals in cities such as Rouen, Nantes, and Rennes.[219] The motives for so many attacks are not always easy to determine in any individual case—unless a perpetrator is caught and confesses. It's clear, however, that the vast majority of the fires result from anti-Catholic animus or Muslim militancy.

Attacks on Christian individuals and Christian sites are already an outrage. But it's remarkable that in Europe there are also open attacks on public celebrations of the faith, even in some of the most famous venues. A 2022 Holy Thursday procession (Nuestro Cristo de la Pasión y Nuestra Señora de La Estrella) in the Spanish city of Granada, for example, was blocked by young illegal migrants at several points. The procession was further disrupted by what were described as large quantities of stones being thrown from windows in an area where illegal migrants were located. There seems to have been a clear religious motive behind the attacks.[220] Five days earlier, on Palm Sunday, a group of Maghreb Islamists residing in El Vendrell, Catalonia, tried to stop a procession by harassing people in the streets.[221] In both cases, Spanish police

[219] Solène Tadié, "Why France Is Losing One Religious Building Every Two Weeks," Catholic News Agency, May 4, 2021, https://www.catholicnewsagency.com/news/247514/why-france-is-losing-one-religious-building-every-two-weeks.

[220] Borja Jiménez, "Indignación total en Granada: Boicotean una procesión lanzando objetos," OK Diario de Andalucia, April 4, 2022, https://okdiario.com/andalucia/indignacion-total-granada-grupo-menas-boicotea-procesion-lanzando-objetos-8918341.

[221] "El islamismo avanza en Cataluña: Cinco magrebíes intentan boicotear una procesión en Tarragona," La Gaceta, April 11, 2022.

moved quickly and prevented casualties and arrested some of the perpetrators.

Similarly, during the July 7, 2024, festival of San Fermín in Pamplona—a feast familiar to many people for the "running of the bulls" and because it is the setting for part of Ernest Hemingway's novel *The Sun Also Rises*—a band of radical Basque nationalists attacked the procession as it was carrying the relics of the saint back to the church. As has often been the case in such attacks, what might have been legitimate political protest in another context was expressed in violence and abuse of religious believers—while they were conducting a time-honored public function. Fortunately, as in Granada, the local police recognized the threats early in the procession, and there were sufficient numbers who took the situation in hand and prevented even greater disorder. Three police officers had to be hospitalized, however, from injuries received while protecting a religious event that should never have been attacked over political disagreements, except for the fact that certain groups believe they are justified in such attacks because the Church, in their view, hinders their political goals.[222]

For the moment, such attacks have been relatively small, though a challenge for authorities. But as immigration numbers swell in various European countries and the direct clash—it should be said candidly—between Christian and Jewish traditions on the one hand and militant Islamists on the other hand become larger and more frequent, it bodes ill for future religious relations. In addition, Western media sources are mostly unwilling to report

---

[222] "Agresión de la izquierda radical en la procesión de San Fermín en Pamplona: 3 policías heridos," Religion en Libertad, July 7, 2022, https://www.religionenlibertad.com/espana/796103657 /agresion-izquierda-radical-procesion-san-fermin-pamplona-policias -heridos.html.

on such incidents for fear of being accused of Islamophobia, xenophobia, and other ills — and of stirring up tensions by reporting on the tensions that already exist, which sometimes break out into clashes such as these. Such avoidance of the truth does no good either to indigenous citizens merely wishing to live safely in their streets and homes or to the newly arrived immigrants who have to be integrated into society and learn to live and let live in the new social circumstances.

In the twenty-first century, Christians are discriminated against in many ways that often go unnoticed, as has been repeatedly confirmed in the present volume. But one way that is particularly ignored is how Muslims who convert to Christianity are then subject to ostracization by family, attacks from other Muslims, and, at times, even death. The European Centre for Law and Justice (ECLJ) did a special study of such conversions in France and Europe and discovered some interesting facts.[223] The most salient of all is that, in nearly two dozen personal interviews they conducted in person with such converts, not one was willing to be identified by name — not even those who had moved away from their families of origin and the communities in which they had lived. The risks of violent reprisals were simply too great.

Nor is this a small problem. Given the nature of these conversions, it's difficult to say how many occur. The French Catholic Bishops' Conference, however, estimates that there are about three hundred converts from Islam to Christianity per year in France. Other sources claim, with some plausibility, that there are more, as

---

[223] European Centre for Law and Justice (ECLJ), *The Persecution of Ex-Muslim Christians in France and Europe: Testimonies*, 2022, http:// media.aclj.org/pdf/The-Persecution-of-ex-muslim-christian-in -France-and-in-Europe.pdf.

many as a few thousand annually. And given that these conversions have been increasing in frequency in recent years, it's highly likely that there are tens of thousands of formerly Muslim Catholics and other Christians in France and in other European nations who go in fear of their livelihoods and their very lives because of their embrace of Christianity.

Leaving Islam is regarded by most Muslims as not an individual act of conscience or belief. As the ECLJ puts it:

> All witnesses [interviewed personally for their report on conversion] agreed that the communitarian aspect of the Muslim religion is fundamental. The communitarian perception of Islam, of the "Ummah" implies that any departure, any conversion to another religion is necessarily a defection, a betrayal. It is inconceivable for most Muslims that a person of North African origin, even a French person, be not a Muslim. Many Muslims on the road to conversion believe, for a time, that they are the only ones in the Muslim community who are considering conversion and wonder whether it is even possible to convert. There is an identification between "Arab culture" and "Islam."[224]

Though this communitarian understanding is common within Islamic history—which is why apostates may often also be described as "traitors" going all the way back to episodes in the Quran—national and international bodies operate under very different principles. ECLJ rightly observes:

> At present, France and other European countries do not adequately guarantee the rights and freedoms of those who

---

[224] ECLJ, *Persecution of Ex-Muslim Christians*, 4.

wish to leave the Muslim religion, including the right to change their religion. For the ECLJ, the appropriate response to these testimonies must be firm and lawful: these rights and freedoms must be effectively guaranteed and protected. The Universal Declaration of Human Rights, the International Covenant on Civil and Political Rights, the Charter of Fundamental Rights of the European Union, and the European Convention for the Protection of Human Rights and Fundamental Freedoms are clear sources of international law guaranteeing this right, and France has committed itself by ratifying them.[225]

This is already bad enough. But it is even more distressing that many Christian churches and other religious bodies have also been slow to understand how to welcome converts who are taking very big risks in leaving a community in which mosque and society and state are all considered as one and are stepping out into unfamiliar religious and social relationships. Who knows how many more converts there would be in the "free" democratic nations if both states and churches would fulfill their responsibilities toward these highly vulnerable individuals?

Such fears are well founded, not only because of lived experience but because of common interpretations of sharia law in many Muslim countries. Saudi Arabia and Iran prescribe the death penalty for apostates to Christianity. Even where conversion is not subject to penalties under civil law, sharia courts—which, in many nations, rule over a whole range of everyday matters for believers in Islam—generally regard conversion to Christianity as apostasy and potentially a case for harsh penalties, including death. In 2006, for

[225] ECLJ, *Persecution of Ex-Muslim Christians*, 19.

example, Abdul Rahman was sentenced to death in Afghanistan for "apostasy," that is, converting to Christianity. As often happens in such cases, international pressure prevented the sentence from being applied. And Rahman was eventually allowed to flee to Italy. But similar cases have been brought in Jordan, Egypt, and Kuwait.

Most nations don't want the international attention and pressure that these death sentences bring, for obvious reasons. This makes international efforts all the more important. But what governments themselves may refrain from doing—owing to a desire to retain international status—militants, vigilantes, and religious enthusiasts may carry out on their own.[226] And given the best estimates that there are thousands of such conversions worldwide year after year—which are kept very quiet both in Muslim countries and in Muslim communities outside those nations—the results are all but inevitable.

There are some quite notable converts to Christianity from Islam in modern times, even saints: St. Josephine Bakhita, the human rights activist Nonie Darwish, former president of Argentina Carlos Menem, Egyptian queen Nazli Sabri, and, in 2023, Ayaan Hirsi Ali—a Somali-born writer and feminist. Even Mehmet Ali Agca, the Turkish gunmen who attempted to kill John Paul II in 1981 professed Christianity after a prison encounter with the pope, who forgave him, though there are doubts this was a formal conversion.[227] These persons are protected by status and location in the West, in ways that the ordinary convert from Islam is not. Indeed, Christian converts

---

[226] Lionel Beehner, "Religious Conversion and Sharia Law," Council on Foreign Relations Backgrounders, June 6, 2007, https://www.cfr.org/backgrounder/religious-conversion-and-sharia-law.

[227] Tom McFeely, "Mehmet Ali Agca Converts?," National Catholic Register, May 1, 2009, https://www.ncregister.com/blog/mehmet-ali-agca-converts.

have become adept at concealing their identities in even the most repressive regimes. Iran, for instance, which has been dominated by a theocratic regime for decades, is estimated by reliable sources to have around one million very quiet Christian converts.[228]

Converts who go to the police to report being physically attacked often get little relief. If the police or other official agencies begin an investigation, it usually serves only to heighten the visibility of a convert—which attracts further opposition in a self-perpetuating process.

Reactions are particularly harsh against women who convert. Not only does the same sense of apostasy and betrayal surface—again, there isn't a strong distinction between what Westerners would call "religion" and membership in a community—but in migrants from many nations, a sense of family "honor" also arises. This is especially the case when a young Muslim woman who has converted or is thinking of converting refuses to marry a Muslim man or is dating someone outside the Muslim community. As one father said, expressing what is certainly the attitude of many others, "The honour of the family is more important than my life or yours."[229] Actual "honor killings," fortunately, remain relatively rare, but it's clear that the cultural gap in such matters between Western and other cultures is wide—and is likely to lead to increased incidents without increased political and social protections of some kind.

In this regard, the Christian churches themselves bear a serious responsibility—one they have not often fulfilled—for the immediate protection and longer-term social integration of such

---

[228] Lela Gilbert, "Good News from Iran: A Million New Christian Believers," *Washington Stand*, June 15, 2023, https://www.hudson.org/religious-freedom/good-news-iran-million-new-christian-believers-lela-gilbert.

[229] ECLJ, *Persecution of Ex-Muslim Christians*, 15.

converts from Islam. Other institutions of civil society, such as hotlines and shelters, should play a role as well. In most Western countries and in international agreements, the choice to belong to any religion or none, to change religion freely, are guaranteed—in theory. Guaranteeing these rights, in fact, is a different matter, and it needs to take into account that many cases involve threats or outright violence from a convert's family members. French law, for instance, is quite clear that cases of this kind:

> are punishable by one year's imprisonment and a fine of 15,000 euros [for] those who, either by threats against an individual, or by making him fear losing his job or exposing his person, his family or his fortune to harm, have acted with a view to determining him to exercise or refrain from exercising a cult, to be part of or cease to be part of a cult association, to contribute or refrain from contributing to the expenses of a cult. The penalties are increased to three years' imprisonment and a fine of 45,000 euros when the perpetrator acts by assault or violence.[230]

Clearly, however, a sincere convert to Christianity may, all the same, feel reluctant to accuse a family member of violations of the law that incur such penalties.

Though it is little reported on, the conversions of Muslims to Christianity worldwide have become quite substantial. According to reliable observers, something on the order of several million Muslims have become Christians in the twenty-first century[231]—a

---

[230] ECLJ, *Persecution of Ex-Muslim Christians*, 19.

[231] Solène Tadié, "Boom in Muslim Conversions to Christianity in France: How Is the Church Responding?," *The National Catholic Register*, March 29, 2024, https://www.ncregister.com/news/muslim-conversion-boom.

small slice of the estimated 1.3 billion Muslims worldwide, but a significant figure, nonetheless.

Criminality

Among the many European martyrs who died in the twentieth century but are only being recognized in the new century as having been slain *in odium fidei* is Rosario Angelo Livatino (1952–1990), to whom Pope Francis has given the title "martyr of justice." His story, though hardly typical, is truly heartbreaking. By normal human standards, he was heroic—as he would have to be to work, first, for most of the 1980s as a prosecutor of organized crime. Later, at the age of thirty-seven, he became a judge in the ancient Sicilian city of Agrigento. In most places in the world, that would be a remarkable enough legal career for a talented young Catholic. Needless to say, to have chosen that path in Sicily required not only extraordinary courage but a certain spiritual fortitude as well.

The details of his death are all too familiar from what we have seen of the way Christians who oppose ruthless criminal gangs in places such as Mexico and Colombia are dealt with. The perpetrators of his murder were identified by an eyewitness and were brought to justice in three sets of proceedings. Livatino met his end through a mob hit. In 1990, he was driving to the courthouse in Agrigento. Another car forced him off the road into a field. He got out, began to flee, and was shot in the back. From the condition of the body, it's clear that he survived that as well and was ultimately given the coup de grâce, execution style, with shots fired at close range.

Two other prosecutors—Paolo Borsellino and Giovanni Falcone—were killed by Mafia car bombs in 1992 in separate incidents. Both were Catholics whose beliefs kept them at their tasks but with not as open a connection between religion and work as there was with Livatino. His writings show a conscientious and dedicated Catholic who saw his efforts to bring criminals to justice as a part of his Christian vocation—almost a textbook case of what Pope John Paul II called a "new martyr." He often wrote of having put himself under God's protection in his labors, and he made some explicit remarks about how he saw the larger context of that work. Four years before he died, he remarked in a lecture: "To render justice is a fulfillment of oneself, it is a prayer, it is a dedication of oneself to God."[232] And commenting on an even broader perspective, he wrote:

> The purpose of the magistrate is to practice justice, not as an objective closed in on itself, but as a way to the greater purpose of love for God and all humanity, especially that which navigates in the shadows of crime, also capable of recovering from a life that is once again full and happy only if it escapes the poison of selfishness.[233]

It's fitting, then, that he has become something of a patron saint of lawyers, judges, professors, and magistrates in Italy. And his inspiration lives on in the activities of the Rosario Livatino Study Center, which not only brings together people from various disciplines and walks of life, to implement a Catholic-inspired justice

---

[232] Courtney Mares, "Rosario Livatino's Postulator: Christians Urgently Need 'Credible Witnesses,'" Catholic New Agency, January 12, 2021, https://www.catholicnewsagency.com/news/246053/rosario-livatinos-postulator-christians-urgently-need-credible-witnesses.

[233] "How a Martyr Killed by the Mafia Inspired a Generation of Catholic Lawyers," Catholic News Agency, January 8, 2021, https://www.catholicnewsagency.com/news/246006/how-a-martyr-killed-by-the-mafia-inspired-a-generation-of-catholic-lawyers.

system but has also broadened into "the study, development and promotion of academic and legal studies concerning the right to life from conception to natural death and the family founded between one man and one woman within the framework of natural law."[234]

Livatino was a native of Canicattì, a small town twenty-five miles distant from the large urban center of Agrigento. It is just one mark among many of the esteem in which he was held, not only by people at a national and international level but by his fellow citizens, that, when his body was moved from the local cemetery to the cathedral in Agrigento—which officials seem to have thought a more fitting place of rest for a local martyr—it raised such a furor that his mortal remains had to be returned to their original resting place in his home town.

Priests, too, have been the targets of criminal gangs. In February 2024, organized criminals in the Southern Italian region of Calabria, the toe of the peninsula's boot, Fr. Felice Palamara barely escaped a murder plot. He was attacked during Mass by a novel method. When he poured the water into the wine in the chalice on the altar, he noticed that it had an odd smell. The primary criminal organization in that region is called the 'Ndrangheta, a network composed of traditional clans of criminals, which is suspected of having put bleach into the cruets of water and wine. Fr. Palamara halted the Mass and called the police, who put him into protective custody. In a remark characteristic of the priest—probably one of the reasons they wanted him eliminated—he told the media, "I'm calm, even if in addition to forgiveness and mercy, I hope that the justice system succeeds in bringing these criminal

[234] "Rosario Livatino: La Vita," Centro Studi Rosario Livatino, accessed December 23, 2024, https://www.centrostudilivatino.it/rosario-livatino/.

episodes to light."[235] Fr. Francesco Pontoriero, a priest of the same diocese, received multiple death threats around the same time for his similar efforts to resist the mobsters.

Wokeness and Blasphemy

Christian churches—primarily the Catholic Church, despite all her current wavering on gender ideology and many other matters—still retain enough members and social presence to be specially targeted as pockets of resistance against a new, emerging "orthodoxy." It is only a residual sense that Christians who believe in traditional faith and morals are the majority—an assumption disproved by the large numbers of people who have left and become "Nones"—that makes it possible to believe that statutes against "hate" are protecting minorities from majorities. In fact, any honest survey of the major cultural and social institutions in developed societies—universities, the media, popular entertainment, and most governmental agencies—reveals that the truth is precisely the opposite. What the old Marxists used to call the "commanding heights" of the economy and the culture—even former bastions of society, such as business, medicine, and the military—have almost entirely capitulated to the new "blasphemy" regime under what many call being "woke."

This is of little concern, of course, to those Christian churches and the elements within Catholicism that have themselves adopted progressive notions about gender ideology and even abortion.

---

[235] Crux Staff, "In Possible Mob Attack, Priest Discovers Chalice Poisoned with Bleach at Mass," *Crux*, February 26, 2024, https://cruxnow.com/church-in-europe/2024/02/in-possible-mob-attack-priest-discovers-chalice-poisoned-with-bleach-at-mass.

But for the rest, it presents literally incredible threats, perils once thought impossible.

A case in point that may seem a mere culture clash but actually has much wider implications: Matthew Grech, a native of Malta, an island nation long regarded as a stronghold of Christian orthodoxy, especially for its resistance to pressures to legalize abortion, was the target of a lawsuit in 2024. His crime: he had been an active homosexual during his early adulthood; he became a Christian, however, and, as a result, ceased same-sex activity.[236] As might be expected, this was not a story that the generally gay-friendly Western media were eager to follow. But one journalist did. Her story clearly was not written in a spirit of "hate," still less of advocating that others should abandon homosexual lifestyles by becoming Christian. She was only pursuing a story about a minority within a minority—gays who abandoned the lifestyle after a religious conversion—to provide a little balance and wider context for what is going on in current Maltese society. For her pains, she, too, was the subject of a lawsuit.

It's clear from the many instances documented earlier in the present volume that Muslim countries often use highly prejudicial notions of "blasphemy" to attack Christians. But it's coming to be true in Western societies that there is a kind of "blasphemy" system now developing in many places that demonizes certain Christian moral statements—not attacks or attempts to target actual individuals but simply moral statements that don't accord with the current orthodoxy, usually about sexuality.

[236] Anugrah Kumar, "Christian Man Facing Prison for Sharing Ex-Gay Testimony in First-of-Its-Kind 'Conversion Therapy' Case," *Christian Post*, January 22, 2023, https://www.christianpost.com /news/malta-prosecutes-christian-man-for-sharing-ex-gay-testimony .html.

The Martyrs of the New Millennium

In Grech's case, lurking in the background is the absolute ban on "conversion" therapy for homosexuals in many Western countries, a ban that prohibits psychologists and psychiatrists from treating people with same-sex attraction, even if the individuals themselves desire to change their "sexual orientation." It's true that some Christians have crudely, even insensitively advocated "praying away the gay." But their simplistic approach to a complex problem does not invalidate the right of people to seek "conversion therapy," and it certainly shouldn't penalize anyone who, after undergoing a religious conversion, comes to practice a different kind of life. That much is evident under the most basic rules of free, democratic societies.

It's important to recognize that this is not just one bizarre, random occurrence. There have been principles planted in Malta's legal systems (and not only there) — principles similar in their vagueness and infinite elasticity to what has been used in blasphemy cases in several Muslim countries — that give police and prosecutors wide powers and discretion in pursuing what, by any sane reckoning, are not "hate crimes." I mentioned in the introduction, for instance how the Finnish Lutheran bishop Juhana Pohjola and Päivi Räsänen — onetime chair of the Finnish Christian Democrats, and a physician, a former member of the Finnish parliament, and a former minister of the interior — were prosecuted for "hate speech," Räsänen for merely tweeting the passage in Genesis "male and female he created them" (1:27). They were exonerated, but that such a charge could even be brought in a highly secular country such as Finland is significant. Postmodern secularism, however, has its own orthodoxy. And it is, unfortunately, not hard to imagine similar cases being brought in Europe or North America.

In the Grech case, how is it "hate," for instance, for a formerly active homosexual to describe to a journalist how his life has changed since becoming a Christian? And how is it "hate" for the reporter to report on the story, not least when there are scores of people "coming out" in public as belonging to sexual identity groups of all kinds, often based on identities that they have merely chosen. The double standard here reflects a single standard: people may choose to belong, or discover that they belong, to some formerly marginalized sexual minority. They may never, whether via religious conversion, psychological counseling, or mere changes in their life circumstances, go back to what is being challenged as "normal."

Clearly, this is a problem not only in Malta but for many of the developed, formerly majority Christian nations.

And there are other legal problems of an anti-Christian character emerging. In 2023, for example, Isabel Vaughan-Spruce was arrested for merely *praying* silently outside an abortion clinic in Birmingham, England. In the past, it would have been unthinkable that someone could be arrested for "thought crimes" in a Western nation, given that, among the primary foundations of modern free societies, are religious liberty and pluralism: people have a right to follow what they believe to be true in matters of faith and morals without interference from governments, as long as they conduct themselves lawfully and peacefully as citizens. Is it now possible that merely *thinking* in certain ways related to gender ideology and abortion trump the most basic guarantees of freedom in Western cultures?

Vaughan-Spruce was not the only one so charged in the United Kingdom. In 2024, in a criminal trial under the 2014 Anti-Social Behaviour, Crime, and Policing Act, Adam Smith-Connor was convicted of praying near an abortion clinic. (He was there because he regretted having had his own child aborted twenty-four years earlier.) That law doubtless has many valid uses in protecting social spaces, to be sure. But it is indicative of a worrisome development of what constitutes a serious offense in public spaces that a man praying silently and, as came out at the trial, out of sight of the abortion clinic, could be fined almost twelve thousand dollars and released on conditional probation—presumably meaning that he and anyone else planning to pray near an abortion clinic have been warned.

The main question, of course, is what he actually *did*—since standing quietly away from an abortion facility, however much it may upset people to notice his presence, is not on its face dangerous antisocial behavior. In a pluralistic society, everyone has to tolerate behavior by others that they deem objectionable, as long as there is no infringement on their freedom and safety. The judge disagreed: "He was capable of being seen, he was engaged in prayer, and it would have been perceptible to an observer. He said he would not be looking at anyone so he could not breach their privacy, but I find his presence and the circumstances could cause detrimental impact." Smith-Connor argued that there was indeed detrimental impact—an Orwellian offense against the British principle of freedom of thought—and, as a British army veteran, he continued: "How can we ask British troops to put their lives at risk defending freedom abroad while fining, arresting and imprisoning people back home for the thought crime of praying? This court has decided even a silent prayer is now a criminal act."[237]

In the United Kingdom, there have even been more worrisome parallels with the types of "blasphemy" cases I have documented

---

[237] Charles Hymas, "Army Veteran Convicted over Silent Prayer for Aborted Son Outside Clinic," *Telegraph*, October 16, 2024, https://www.telegraph.co.uk/news/2024/10/16/army-veteran-convicted-over-prayer-at-abortion-clinic/?msockid=07a969226c3d68b40af2795b6dc06944.

in various majority-Muslim countries. In 2023, for instance, a scuffle occurred in Yorkshire over the alleged desecration of a copy of the Quran—something that might lead to a charge of blasphemy in places such as Pakistan but hardly something to be expected to cause social outrage in the British Midlands. Four non-Muslim boys, students in the Kettlethorpe High School in Wakefield, were threatened after one of them, who had bought a paperback edition of the Quran to read about Islam, dropped it, causing minor damage to the book.[238] There was no disrespect to a sacred text, though the right to do precisely that—say, ripping up the Old or New Testament in public—is protected under British law. It's wrong, socially, to show contempt for anyone's faith, of course, but that was not even what happened here. According to the head teacher at the school, there was "no malicious intent by those involved."

Instead, an all-too-familiar scenario took place. As we have seen has often happened in Muslim-dominated nations, according to a journalist who examined the case:

> Somehow, rumours spread. Activists came to believe that the Quran had been kicked or spat on, which inflamed a "huge uproar" in the Muslim community. Some even suggested that the Quran had been torn up in front of Muslim students. Had *that* taken place it would have been deplorable. (Just as if a Bible had been torn up in front of Christian students, or a Torah in front of Jewish students.) As far as I can tell, though, there is no evidence that it did.[239]

---

[238] Ben Sixsmith, "Britain's Blasphemy Laws," *Critic*, February 26, 2023, https://thecritic.co.uk/britains-blasphemy-laws/.
[239] Sixsmith, "Britain's Blasphemy Laws."

The four boys were subjected to death threats, however, and suspended from school. At least one leader from the local Muslim community sought to tamp down violence, but the journalist further observed:

> He is asking local Muslims to be *magnanimous enough* to tolerate an outrageous provocation—when in reality it was a non-event that should not have caused a scandal to begin with.... That Muslims view the Quran with great reverence is entirely their right. But in a secular society they cannot expect everyone else to do the same.... Somehow, Britain has adopted *de facto* blasphemy laws.... This cannot be allowed to continue.[240]

It would be comforting to think that this is an isolated case that does not suggest anything more than the mishandling of a single set of unfortunate circumstances. But anyone aware of the religious dynamics of Europe or North America in the twenty-first century can easily imagine similar events—many going unreported for the usual reasons—in almost every Western nation.

North America

North America is not immune to the several problems for Christians that occur in Europe. There are similar cases in the United States of praying near abortion clinics, offenses against "woke" pieties, and even church burnings, to say nothing of constant pressures on Christian institutions—churches, schools, even religious orders—to accept contraception, abortion, homosexual employees, and much more in hiring and insurance programs. A Catholic U.S.

---

[240] Sixsmith, "Britain's Blasphemy Laws."

president, Joseph Biden, stated boldly that "transgender equality is the civil rights issue of our time."[241] And his administration pursued that and other legal impositions on religious institutions despite the consequences for his Church and for constitutional protections. Kamala Harris, as a U.S. Senator before she ran for president, questioned a nominee for a federal judgeship because he was a member of the—presumably notorious because it was pro-life—Knights of Columbus. All these matters may appear to be merely political differences over the many thorny questions that exist in postmodern, twenty-first-century societies. But it is precisely that belief that obscures the fact that they impinge on religious liberty and are being used in ways incompatible even with America's own constitutional order.

For instance, during America's 2024 elections for president, the Democratic candidate was asked in an interview whether she would be willing to allow religious "concessions" on abortion. She said no. No concessions on "a woman's right to control her own body." The substance of the abortion question aside, the very use of the term "concessions" by both the interviewer and Kamala Harris is an assumption that has done great damage—and not only to the unborn. The American Constitution does not speak of religious liberty as a concession by the government to citizens to do what the government would otherwise control. The First Amendment's protection of religion, speech, assembly, and so on is simply a recognition of natural rights, rights given us by the Creator—as America's Declaration of Independence states

---

[241] Sarah Parshall Perry, "Biden's Executive Order on Gender Discrimination Has Muddied Waters on Title IX. Challenges Could Clear That Up," Heritage Foundation, February 19, 2021, https://www.heritage.org/gender/commentary/bidens-executive-order-gender-discrimination-has-muddied-waters-title-ix.

explicitly—that precede and exceed the authority of every government. In the past, most Western states would have agreed.

This whole question of whether the U.S. government can issue concessions for religious belief and conscience—or not—was already settled when George Washington wrote a letter to the Newport, Rhode Island, Touro Synagogue, which he visited in 1790. Moses Seixas, the warden of the synagogue, later wrote to Washington asking for assurances of religious freedom for Jews. Washington could have granted the request—if he believed the federal government had such authority. He did not. Instead, he wrote back invoking principles, American principles, that deny the very idea of government granting "concessions" to religious liberty:

> All [American citizens] possess alike liberty of conscience and immunities of citizenship. It is now no more that toleration is spoken of, as if it were the indulgence of one class of people, that another enjoyed the exercise of their inherent natural rights, for, happily, the Government of the United States, which gives to bigotry no sanction, to persecution no assistance requires only that they who live under its protection should demean themselves as good citizens, in giving it on all occasions their effectual support.[242]

That was a principle long respected. But in recent decades, there has begun what can only be called a kind of soft, and sometimes not so soft, encroachment on the rights of religious individuals and groups—Catholics, in particular, as the largest and strongest body resisting the new sexual ethos. Inoffensive and compassionate groups

---

[242] George Washington to the Hebrew Congregation in Newport, Rhode Island, August 18, 1790, Founders Online, https://founders.archives.gov/documents/Washington/05-06-02-0135.

such as the Little Sisters of the Poor found that government support for their work among the elderly and the destitute was threatened because they did not offer contraceptive and other sexual coverage in insurance plans for employees. The courts, for the most part, adhering to the rights of religious institutions to set their own mission and follow it—a key feature of American liberty enshrined in the First Amendment to the Constitution—have so far protected such groups from legal pressures. But the new ethos has spilled over into something more than soft persecution in ways that the legal system is slow to act on, and often does not act at all. Unless this tendency is recognized for what it is—creeping coercion bordering on persecution—and halted, it bodes ill for religious liberty.

Church Burnings in North America

There are even more pressing threats. For example, in 2022, Maeve Nota, a thirty-one-year-old transgender "woman," vandalized a Catholic church in Bellevue, Washington, spray-painted obscenities inside and outside the church, resisted when the police came to arrest him (or her), and was taken into custody. The motive was allegedly the Catholic Church's influence a few months earlier in the *Dobbs* decision, by which the Supreme Court reversed the infamous 1973 *Doe v. Bolton* ruling that had legalized abortion in all fifty states, even though a majority of states, as was their constitutional right, had laws prohibiting or limiting what had always been regarded as an immoral practice.

The Nota case was an interesting example of what radical social activists have come to call "intersectionality." Maeve Nota, born a male, had no possibility of becoming pregnant. As a transgender "woman," even allowing that designation to be taken fully seriously, it would be impossible for Nota to father children either. But in the dark, twisted conflation of all the sexually radical causes with one another—and with opposition to the Catholic Church's morals on various matters—Nota's anger over the Supreme Court decision and against the Church makes a kind of sense, at least in some quarters.

When Nota's legal case came before a federal court—the severity of the offense and the amount of damages qualified to make it a federal "hate crime"—the Department of Justice only recommended no jail time and three years' probation. Critics were quick to point out that around the same time, the Department of Justice had conducted an early-morning raid on the home of pro-life leader, Mark Houck, who had gotten into a minor scuffle outside an abortion clinic in Philadelphia with a pro-abortion activist who had shoved Houck's son. The Justice Department sought a sentence of *eleven years* for this minor disturbance. A Philadelphia court had dismissed the case—the murky details and brief mutual shoving didn't amount to much for the local jurisdiction. But federal prosecutors invoked the Freedom of Access to Clinic Entrances Act (FACE) as if Houck's behavior had shown him to be a dangerous felon.

Even to describe such cases is to see how petty the back-and-forth has become on sex-related matters and also how disproportionately they are handled by police and legal officials—and how great a presumption of what can only be called criminal bigotry traditional believers face. Such cases have become increasingly more common. Meanwhile, the far more serious offenses—by any sane standard—of burning or defacing houses of worship, real *hate crimes*, continue to grow.

In 2024, the U.S. Conference of Catholic Bishops issued a report detailing how:

> At least 360 incidents have occurred across 44 states and the District of Columbia since May 2020. Incidents include

arson, statues beheaded, limbs cut, smashed, and painted, gravestones defaced with swastikas and anti-Catholic language and American flags next to them burned, and other destruction and vandalism. This list shows incidents of vandalism, arson, or other destruction at Catholic sites that have been publicly reported in news media. It excludes incidents where circumstances suggest a motive other than hostility toward the Church.[243]

The bishops' report detailed the offenses, case by case, which amount to a staggering record of anti-Christian acts almost entirely ignored by the American media—and therefore invisible to the American public.

It's sickening to read the bishops' long list of anti-Catholic attacks, sometimes even involving Satanic rituals or symbols, or sexual images; Communion Hosts scattered in parking lots; reliquaries stolen, tabernacles defaced, holy oils poured out, crosses set on fire (reminiscent of traditional Ku Klux Klan burnings); political messages or violent threats or swastikas spray-painted; multiple attacks on the same church while police seem uninterested in stopping them. Some of the cases would be comic if they weren't so tragic: in Orlando, Florida, a fire set on the altar spread to the entire building—a building being used as a temporary church because the actual Incarnation Catholic Church had been previously destroyed—also by arson.[244] A similar study in 2023 found that church burnings had doubled since the previous year. And

---

[243] "Arson, Vandalism, and Other Destruction at Catholic Churches in the United States," United States Conference of Catholic Bishops, October 25, 2024, https://www.usccb.org/resources/Attacks_on_Catholic_Churches_in_the_US-10-25-24.pdf.

[244] "Arson, Vandalism, and Other Destruction," 2.

The Martyrs of the New Millennium

2024 was also on the way to being another record year, portending even worse in the near future.

It would be too easy to attribute all this to the generalized violence and disrespect that has overtaken public spaces—and not just churches—in America. That's a partial explanation, to be sure, but it's no excuse. Such events display an anti-Christian element in the culture *in addition to* the usual criminality and political passions.

And this is not a problem only in the United States. In 2021, a report was published that "mass graves" had been found at schools for First Nations, schools created by the Canadian government but often run by the Catholic Church and other religious bodies. Several years later, although ground-penetrating radar suggested the existence of such graveyards, no bodies have been found. There has been speculation that the initial reports were mistaken—and that even if children had died in such schools, it was not evidence of gross mistreatment but of the pandemics that periodically strike. But all that didn't matter. The Canadian government documented twenty-four church burnings, mostly related to the charges, from May 2021 to December 2023. One does not need to be convinced that the churches, or at least specific individuals in the churches, were wholly without blame in the ways they ran those schools—which were created by the Canadian government to help with assimilation—to believe that the proper response is not to burn down places of worship.

Canada's prime minister, Justin Trudeau, offered a mixed message in response: "I can't help but think that burning down churches is actually depriving people who are in need of grieving and healing and mourning from places where they can grieve and reflect and look for support." That was all to the good. Unfortunately, he added, "It's real and it is *fully understandable* given the shameful history we are all become more aware of" (emphasis added).[245] No, church burnings are not understandable, at least not in a country that respects the rule of law and protection of religion. It's only "understandable" when the principle of group identity replaces the clear legal principle that people today who belong to an organization are not guilty or responsible for what people of previous generations in that organization may have done. That approach to public matters only perpetuates grievances and divisions—and will inevitably lead to violence between "groups"—including religious groups.

All this is an indication that North America cannot consider itself immune from pressures on Christian churches, let alone superior to other places in the West where social forces exert such pressure. The threat may not be as acute as it is in certain parts of Latin America, the Middle East, Africa, or Asia, but prejudice leading to violence against Christianity is a global phenomenon. And it needs to be recognized and resisted—as early as possible and before it becomes an established phenomenon—wherever it shows itself. It's a global cancer. And it can happen anywhere.

[245] Jim Morris, "Trudeau Denounces Church Burnings, Vandalism in Canada," PBS News, July 2, 2021, https://www.pbs.org/newshour /world/trudeau-denounces-church-burnings-vandalism-in-canada.

About the Author

Robert Royal is the founder and president of the Faith & Reason Institute in Washington, D.C., and editor-in-chief of *The Catholic Thing* (www.thecatholicthing.org), an online publication that appears daily and is translated into five foreign languages. He writes and speak on questions of ethics, culture, religion, and politics; has appeared frequently on EWTN as a special commentator on Church matters, and on various television and radio stations around the United States; and has lectured in fifteen foreign countries. His most recent book is *A Deeper Vision: The Catholic Intellectual Tradition in the 20th Century*. Other books include *Dante Alighieri, Columbus and the Crisis of the West, The Catholic Martyrs of the Twentieth Century: A Comprehensive World History, The Pope's Army,* and *The God That Did Not Fail*. Royal holds a B.A. and an M.A. from Brown University and a Ph.D. in comparative literature from the Catholic University of America and received fellowships to study in Italy from the Renaissance Society of America and as a Fulbright scholar.

Sophia Institute

Sophia Institute is a nonprofit institution that seeks to nurture the spiritual, moral, and cultural life of souls and to spread the gospel of Christ in conformity with the authentic teachings of the Roman Catholic Church.

Sophia Institute Press fulfills this mission by offering translations, reprints, and new publications that afford readers a rich source of the enduring wisdom of mankind.

Sophia Institute also operates the popular online resource CatholicExchange.com. *Catholic Exchange* provides world news from a Catholic perspective as well as daily devotionals and articles that will help readers to grow in holiness and live a life consistent with the teachings of the Church.

In 2013, Sophia Institute launched Sophia Teachers to renew and rebuild Catholic culture through service to Catholic education. With the goal of nurturing the spiritual, moral, and cultural life of souls, and an abiding respect for the role and work of teachers, we strive to provide materials and programs that are at once enlightening to the mind and ennobling to the heart; faithful and complete, as well as useful and practical.

Sophia Institute gratefully recognizes the Solidarity Association for preserving and encouraging the growth of our apostolate over the course of many years. Without their generous and timely support, this book would not be in your hands.

www.SophiaInstitute.com
www.CatholicExchange.com
www.SophiaTeachers.org

Sophia Institute Press is a registered trademark of Sophia Institute.
Sophia Institute is a tax-exempt institution as defined by the
Internal Revenue Code, Section 501(c)(3). Tax ID 22-2548708.